Simple, Safe & Secret

The 1981 Murder of Joan L. Webster

Eve Carson

Genius
Book Publishing

Milwaukee Wisconsin USA

Published by:
Genius Book Publishing
PO Box 250380
Milwaukee, Wisconsin 53225
GeniusBookPublishing.com

ISBN: 978-1-947521-85-8

220627 Digest

Contents

This book is dedicated to my beautiful daughters
and in loving memory of their Aunt Joan.
The truth allows genuine healing.

"There is no crueler tyranny than that which is perpetuated under the shield of law and in the name of justice."

—Charles-Louis de Secondat, Baron de Montesquieu

Preface

The nightmare of a missing and murdered loved one is impossible to describe. Fear and sorrow test the very core of your being. You're left in a suspended state of grief. Coping with tragedy requires truthful answers, even when the responses are bleak. Trust is an immeasurable component of healing and safety, but trust can be betrayed. In the end, I had to trust my instincts to find answers for myself.

When Joan disappeared, I was pregnant. My miscarriage, on the same night Joan disappeared, was a bond that connected me to her beyond the loving familial ties of a sister-in-law. As I learned more about what really happened during my investigation into her death, my love and respect for Joan grew infinitely. Joan was always there to help others; I witnessed and experienced her kindness for myself. Bringing new life into the family made me the logical audience for Joan to share family confidences. If Joan died trying to forewarn me, a real possibility based on what I learned later, I owe Joan immeasurable gratitude and the resolve to share her story. The prospect of her sacrifice humbles me. Recalling the nightmare in excruciating detail shed light on other Webster mysteries I endured. Joan wasn't the only untimely and unjust loss I suffered as part of the Webster family.

Two events spurred my deep dive into Joan's case: the discovery of a horrifying letter alleging a felony by a member of the Webster family and the family's support of a fallacious book by former prosecutor Tim Burke. Motivated by Joan's courage and the discovery of other victims, my path took a challenging direction. My conscience and core won't allow me to be silent.

This book is written in the third person; the story is not about me. It was written for the other innocent victims unfairly scarred by the state's disingenuous investigation into Joan's murder, both directly and from other crimes that may have resulted. But understand, there is real and personal pain on these pages. The text reveals the actual findings from source documents relevant in Joan's case. Knowledge is empowering. The journey has taken many years to gather the pieces and put them together. Sleepless nights and flowing tears punctuated the trauma of reliving the burdensome events in my life.

The book begins in the hours before Joan disappeared. I introduce you to the Webster family and provide insight into the family dynamics. Unlike other efforts to unravel the mystery, I examine the investigation itself, and the questionable entangled matters. The highly publicized investigation involved an unusual number of departments and agencies on the local, state, and federal level. The list includes three District Attorneys' offices in Massachusetts, the Massachusetts State Police, multiple FBI jurisdictions including FBI headquarters, and numerous police departments in several states. The extraordinary number of people who touched Joan's case was one of the complexities obstructing justice. A character list is added to aid the reader.

To understand how the state's case against their suspect unfolded, I had to delve into the 1979 murder of Marie Iannuzzi. Authorities improperly entangled the two cases, further complicating the pursuit of truthful justice. This enmeshed case involved the same prosecutor, lead police officer, and suspect, but had no similarities to the circumstances in Joan's case. I pull back the curtain on the inner workings of a dysfunctional system bent on a predetermined outcome. The book carefully documents the dates, times, and discrepancies, and exposes a manipulated investigation. Dialogue and details are derived directly from source documents involving both murder cases and other allegations the state piled on their suspect.

My intention is not to exonerate anyone for crimes they may have actually committed, nor do I want to implicate someone wrongly. This book reflects where the evidence points. Joan Webster was a rose among many thorns. She deserved the best from all of us. Sadly, the dysfunctional system, hidden agendas, and secrets further devalued a wonderful human being. Authorities delegated with the responsibility of truth and justice are accountable. When evil cast a dark shadow over my life, I chose to turn the other cheek. Good triumphs evil, and the truth finds its way to the surface. The positive outcome of my extensive research gives Joan's life the meaning her sacrifice earned and the key to help others.

Every crime has a solution. Sometimes the answers are obvious, but other times, layers of deceit cover up the truth. Fortunately, as a member of Joan's family, I knew where to look. Seeking true justice requires an honest commitment, with the blinders removed and a thick skin.

Simple, Safe
& Secret

Chapter One
"Oh, Men of Dark and Dismal Fate"

The audience rose to their feet with thunderous applause as the ensemble reached the crescendo at the end of Act I. Joan tapped her gray shoes still humming "Oh, Men of Dark and Dismal Fate." She loved the theater and the exhilaration of New York City. The empty seat next to her in the heaving playhouse was the only blight on her otherwise perfect evening of Friday, November 27, 1981.

As the curtain rose for the second act of *The Pirates of Penzance*. Joan settled back into her seat next to her parents and her sister, Anne. Their older brother, Steve, was half a country away, living in Illinois with his pregnant wife, Eve. Joan smiled, not daring to show her disappointment. Family logistics nixed the planned visit of her friend over the Thanksgiving break. The Websters organized their calendars down to the smallest detail. The shift in the schedule was out of character, but the adjustment set the stage for the dramatic chain of events about to unfold.

Joan's father George nodded to the songs of Gilbert and Sullivan as the actors belted out uncanny premonitions in Act II. The comedic constables on the stage voiced a logical notion. When criminals were not engaged in their enterprise, they did normal things anyone might do. The players' lyrics warned of impending despair, keeping the audience on the edge of their seats. Joan's mother Eleanor thumbed the pages of her Playbill. Subliminal messages, delivered in an entertaining performance, reassured her everything was prepared. A swashbuckling troupe challenged the young actor on stage with a paradox when he left the fold. The verses held more meaning than

Joan could have foreseen. The librettos projected a dismal fate for the lamb straying from the flock and the contradictions of her guardian.

When the curtain came down on the musical comedy, George, Eleanor, Anne, and Joan walked out of the Minskoff Theatre on W. 45th Street in New York City's theater district. George played the soundtrack cassette in the car as he drove to a favorite watering hole for a nightcap. Cosmos knew George by name and gladly entertained his requests on the piano. Joan's father gulped down his Scotch and placed a folded bill in Cosmos' gratuity snifter. The patriarch subtly signaled to his brood; it was time to leave. Docilely, his entourage took their positions in the blue Buick station wagon. George turned into the Lincoln Tunnel headed for home turf in New Jersey.

The family entered the house through the garage door by the pantry. The girls headed upstairs for the night, and Eleanor settled in the den to watch the late news. George opened the liquor cabinet and poured another two fingers of Scotch. He carried the bottle to the den and placed it on the mirrored table beside him. His body gradually slid to an uncomfortable, half-reclined posture on the loveseat: his head tilted back, bobbing unsupported, and his spectacles askew. The guttural tone of George's voice resonated as he mumbled and snored in a semi-conscious stupor. The pattern was familiar. Eventually, Eleanor nudged and coaxed her husband to bed.

The girls were already in place at the small kitchen table the next morning. George walked through the front hall and tapped the turtle's tail announcing his presence. The turtle was a whimsical dinner bell, a symbol of the privilege of George's upbringing. Eleanor busied herself dutifully in the kitchen. She moved to the table with George's first course and a hot cup of coffee. As she sashayed through the kitchen, the itinerary tacked on the refrigerator rustled and reminded George to coordinate the day with his fledglings.

His upcoming trip was uncharacteristic. As a senior executive with International Telephone & Telegraph (ITT) in Nutley, New Jersey, George would normally delegate rather than interrupt his holiday. The impending agenda demanded his personal attention. None but the person in charge could know the full purpose of his mission.

George went to the cupboard to add some libation to his second course. The Bloody Mary began the daily ritual of numbing his senses. He pushed up his wire-rimmed glasses to peruse the news of the day in the paper. Only an occasional grunt suggested a story caught his attention. He pushed away from the table and headed back upstairs while Eleanor played the scullery maid, clearing the dishes. Dark, sullen eyes stared back at George from the bathroom mirror. He ran his fingers through his thick, wavy mane before splashing on the hair tonic to slick back the curves.

Joan retreated to her room to pack her belongings. She folded the essentials she had brought home for the long weekend and tucked them neatly in her Lark suitcase. She tossed a single green sock in her bag hoping its partner was back at the dorm. She carefully wrapped the folded clothes around a stack of photographs, memories from the family's summer vacation in Nantucket. When Joan opened her bedroom door, she heard the door across the hall shut tightly. Her bedroom sat across the hallway from George's upstairs small study. She could hear her father's low guttural tones talking on his private line as she pulled bed linens out of the closet to take back to school. That second line into the house sat on George's desk and was off limits. It was the rule of the house not to disturb George in his office.

The baby of the family, with two older siblings, Joan was a 25-year-old student at the Harvard Graduate School of Design. Before returning to school, she lived in Manhattan for two years, working for Skidmore, Owings & Merrill. The independent student had even traveled alone through Europe. During her time in New

York City, the petite young woman was the victim of a street crime when an assailant snatched her purse. She learned to be aware of her surroundings. As the dorm proctor at Perkins Hall, she passed along safety tips to the coeds she mentored. In her second year of graduate school, she was an excellent, award-winning student with a promising future.

On the Monday before the Thanksgiving break, Joan had presented an 11-week auditorium project to rave reviews before riding to New Jersey with her sister. It was disappointing her friend couldn't come to visit as planned, but George's trip over the weekend took precedence for the family. Rather than wait to ride back to Boston with Anne on Sunday, George made arrangements and scheduled a flight for Joan on Saturday night.

Eleanor announced that lunch was ready. George made his way back to the kitchen table, poured a glass of beef broth, and diluted the consommé with a shot of vodka. He confirmed that everyone knew the drill. The foursome would grab an early bite at the club before making the rounds and then drive Joan to Newark Airport. Everything was planned down to the minutest detail as if they had synchronized watches.

Joan collected a few last-minute items and stuck them in her leather carry-on tote bag. She added a few vinyl records from the musicals she enjoyed on Broadway, the Playbill from the night before, rolled up sketches and architectural pamphlets, and her pair of gray shoes.

The upper-middle-class family fit a finely tuned image. In public, the Websters embodied all the social graces to be on every guest list. Their credentials boasted all of the best schools and social connections. The charismatic men in the Webster family were engaging pied pipers. George and his son Steve often played the piano and entertained listeners with humorous tales. Irish wit and charm centered them in any gathering, and they relished the adulation. To the outside observer, they were a perfect family in complete harmony. Any hint of discord evaporated when the Websters opened the door from their inner sanctum.

Glen Ridge, New Jersey was a small hamlet near Manhattan. Families were close knit, and the children all grew up together. Vacations and holidays became community affairs. The Websters' Georgian home was tastefully decorated, but a bit out of date. However, any connoisseur noticed the expensive paintings on the wall and the gold and silver trophies of prestigious regattas and thoroughbred victories at the track. A very large, round diamond on Eleanor's finger fractured the light into a rainbow of color, brightening her otherwise bland attire. Wealth and status were an important part of the image but carefully displayed without being garish. George and his offspring all wore gold signet rings as if the circles identified exclusive membership in the clan.

George was the first to come down the curved staircase prepared for his upcoming trip. He double-checked his travel itinerary taped to the refrigerator. After loading the wagon, he headed straight back to the house to pour a distilled beverage over the cubes in his glass. He tapped his fingers to the beat of Gilbert and Sullivan tunes as he waited for his entourage to assemble. A sport coat, flannel trousers, and a Brooks Brothers tie completed the uniform George always wore to neighborhood fetes. The standard garb was a multipurpose wardrobe suitable for the theater, parties, or travel. Any acquaintance could anticipate the patriarch's attire with certainty. George and Eleanor had developed their predictable patterns when they met working for the Central Intelligence Agency (CIA) in the early 1950s. Attention to detail, subdued outward behavior and dress to avoid drawing unwanted attention, planning to the point of obsession, contingencies, and secrecy were all part of the intelligence mindset. The ladies were ready to go. George slipped on his dark overcoat and loaded Joan's suitcase and tote bag into the back end of the wagon.

"Fundador," George announced with a single clap and then rubbed his hands. The buzzword was a call to attention.

Two family friends hosted small holiday gatherings that Saturday evening. The Joys and the Wittpenns warmly welcomed the Websters into their homes. By the time he hung his coat, the bartender had George's beverage ready and handed him the tumbler. The scene repeated itself when the family moved on to the next party. These social gatherings were regular affairs, a chance to catch up with everyone before going off in their own directions. The younger generation clustered and exchanged their latest endeavors. Joan's friends fully expected to hear good reports about her accomplishments at Harvard; things were going very well at school. Joan was upbeat and her normal, bubbly self. Her giggle was infectious, and her smile lit up the room. Anne was the quieter of the two sisters, but Joan's enthusiasm buoyed them both. Joan held a warm cup of grog, a traditional holiday punch served by the Wittpenns.

Eleanor was in another gaggle of guests boasting about her offspring and dropping names to amplify the importance of her children's successes. She was insecure. She had very humble beginnings; she was conceived out of wedlock. Her parents married, but the calendar was too short to disguise her inception. In her generation, the branding of illegitimate unfairly inflicted shame on a child, which Eleanor carried deeply within her soul. Her parents divorced when she was a young girl. The estrangement from her birth father lasted for the rest of her life. Her mother remarried, and the new husband adopted 14-year-old Eleanor and her younger sister as his own.

After graduating from Mount Holyoke College in 1948, Eleanor married Thomas Hardaway, a West Point Lieutenant. Thomas called his wife Terry, a nickname Eleanor embraced to distance herself from her shame. Her happiness didn't last long. Thomas was killed in Korea in 1950. Loss became part of Eleanor's existence. Soon after Thomas died, John Selsam, her stepfather, passed away.

Eleanor moved to Washington, D.C. to work for the CIA. She met George in the agency, a charismatic man raised in the circles Eleanor envied. He had attended Taft Boarding School, Yale, and had a brief stint at Harvard before joining the Merchant Marines during the war. George's father was a wealthy, prominent businessman who raced thoroughbreds and wintered with the elite in Palm Beach, Florida. The young widow grasped her brass ring tightly. George and Eleanor married on May 16, 1952. Two lives, poles apart, merged into one and formed their foundation on intelligence training. Doors finally opened for Eleanor; she guarded her station.

George swallowed one final gulp of his cocktail and announced the family's departure. He slipped on his coat and kept his flock on schedule. In the car, George strangely broke with his normal routine. It was customary for George to make airport runs himself, solo, but this journey was different. Their house was only minutes away, an easy stop to drop off Eleanor and Anne before driving Joan to Newark Airport. After all, Anne had a long drive back to Boston the next day. Instead, Eleanor and Anne rode along to bid farewell to Joan. On the cold November night, the heater fan circulated a strong whiff of alcohol through the car, but George didn't relinquish the wheel. Eleanor didn't drive after dark, but Anne could have obliged if that was the reason to bring them along. The Websters never did anything without planning or purpose. The most logical explanation for Eleanor and Anne to ride along to the airport was for the drive home if George was not in the car.

George tapped his fingers on the wheel replaying the performance the family had enjoyed last night. He pulled up to the curb for departures at the Eastern Airlines Terminal still humming "Oh, Men of Dark and Dismal Fate." He unloaded Joan's bags, placed them on the curb, handed her money for a cab, and kissed her on the forehead. Joan turned to her family with a broad smile and waved goodbye before clutching her assorted belongings. Unsuspecting, she turned and walked toward the gate.

In a dark mind, the task at hand was *simple*.

Chapter Two
The Blue Car

Joan boarded Eastern flight number 960 from Newark to Logan Airport on Saturday, November 28, 1981. She settled in for the hour-long flight seated near a priest and a couple bound for Boston, Massachusetts. The petite passenger stored her brown leather tote bag and brown Chesterfield coat during the flight and rested her red leather purse in her lap. The buoyant young woman introduced herself with light, friendly banter. Fellow passengers attentively listened to the enthusiastic and confident grad student talk about her studies at school and attending *The Pirates of Penzance* on Broadway.

As the plane started to descend, passengers stared out the windows at the orange-red glow lighting up the night sky. On the ground, first responders battled a 12-alarm fire in Lynn, Massachusetts, ten miles north of Boston. The fire had started in a shoe factory at 2:35 a.m. that Saturday morning. The spark soon mushroomed into an inferno enlisting assistance and services from 94 communities. The Great Lynn Fire of 1981 raged for two weeks before firefighters finally extinguished all of the smoldering embers. The governor called in the National Guard to secure the area from vandalism and looting. Joan could breathe a sigh of relief that her intended destination was in a different direction.

Joan waited her turn to deplane and joined the collected assortment of passengers walking through the terminals to the baggage claim. The Troop F Station, situated below the control tower, between Terminals B and C, reassured weary travelers of safe journeys. The Massachusetts State Police Barracks was next to the medical station and the Logan Airport Chapel, tending the fatigued and feeble or those lifting a prayer.

Joan's plane landed at about 10:30 p.m. on Saturday night. On this night, the airport was not heavily congested. Airport personnel expected heavier traffic on Sunday, the customary travel day after Thanksgiving. Five airliners taxied to their gates within a short span of time, including Eastern flight number 960. Mechanical malfunctions shut down multiple conveyors in the claim area, and airport personnel funneled all of the arrivals to a single operating carousel. Joan patiently waited alone for her suitcase to move around the trolley. Joan smiled and waved to a friend she recognized stationed along the slow moving trail of suitcases. When her checked bag made it around, she lifted her Lark suitcase off of the belt and checked the tag. The suitcase was dark navy blue nylon with brown vinyl trim and red, green, and tan striping on both sides. A gold horseshoe, embossed on one side of the blue plastic tag, identified the owner with her parents' New Jersey address.

Another classmate returning early saw Joan, laden with her belongings, talking to a man seated behind a counter in the claim area. Strangely, Joan paused to talk to someone before walking outside to the cab line. Still dressed for the get-togethers in New Jersey, she wore a black worsted skirt and jacket with a red printed blouse. The petite student also dressed for the typical inclement weather in Boston in late November. She wore a long, heavy, brown Chesterfield coat, knee-high, brown leather boots, and wrapped a black and red paisley ascot neatly around her neck. Joan accessorized her attire with two black onyx and gold rings, her gold signet ring with the initials JLW, a gold neck chain, and gold scalloped-shell earrings. Joan removed the distinctive gold charm bracelet she wore to the parties and secured the treasured talismans in her carry-on items. It took all of her diminutive five foot four and 115 pound frame to manage her suitcase and tote bag and to keep her purse strap from sliding off her shoulder. At the curb, Joan set down her luggage and tapped on the window of Town Taxi number 1229. Her next destination was her dorm room, at least that was her intention.

"Cambridge?" Joan smiled as she politely asked the cabbie.

"Sure," the driver replied before opening his trunk and loading Joan's suitcase inside.

"Wait a minute, there is another person with me," she announced and nodded to the man beside her.

Somewhere between the man behind the desk in the terminal and the Town Taxi Joan engaged in the cab line, a man had caught up with Joan. Cab driver Fenton Moore turned to see a bearded man standing next to his fare. The new arrival seemed to be familiar to Joan. Moore reached for the man's luggage to store it with Joan's in the trunk of his cab. Moore handled a lot of bags in his line of work, but either the heavy suitcase or the demanding man made an impression. The second passenger had a large blue bag with a streak of lime running through it. The cabbie was struggling to load the noticeably weighty suitcase when the bearded man stopped him.

"I don't appreciate how you're putting my bag in the trunk," the bearded man argued.

Joan quietly watched the bearded man exchange words with the cabbie. She had secured the Town Taxi before she announced the man's presence; Moore had been ready to drive her to Cambridge. The elevated volume of the two men caught the attention of the cabbie's dispatcher. Joan's upbringing kicked in, and she receded from any display of disagreement with a person of authority.

The bearded man turned to Joan and directed, "I don't think *we* want this cab."

The Town Taxi driver removed Joan's luggage from his trunk. The bearded man guided Joan to another vehicle, a blue car in the cab line, with no identified markings of any known livery service. Joan trusted her companion. She was a seasoned traveler mindful of her surroundings. The man insisted on changing vehicles, and she respectfully complied. With bags loaded, the driver of the blue car pulled away from the curb with Joan and the bearded man committed for the ride.

A woman's voice came over Moore's radio after the commotion. The dispatcher checked, "Is there anything wrong?"

"No, they just wanted another cab," Moore replied as he watched the taillights of the blue car disappear into the night.

Meanwhile, Eleanor soaked in a hot bath at their home in Glen Ridge. Anne packed her assorted belongings for the five-hour drive back to Boston the next day. The phone never rang.

Chapter Three
"Lenny the Quahog"

The gavel came down, bringing the courtroom to order. Leonard Paradiso appeared uncomfortable in his snug-fitting black jacket. The suit coat was the only proper attire Lenny had in his closet for his appearance in court on Monday, November 30, 1981. Lenny had gone through some setbacks earlier in the summer. After serving time in jail for an assault conviction, he had tried to establish himself selling the seafood catch along the coast. A few connections added inventory Lenny then sold to local restaurants and bars. For a while, his life seemed to be moving forward. Now, back in court, the paroled petitioner had again fallen on hard times.

Lenny grew up in an Italian community in the North End of Boston. Each summer, the North End honored their patron saints with festivals and parades. The locals celebrated a different saint each week and swelled the neighborhood with revelers through a summer of feasts. Lenny earned a reputation pushing his cart through the narrow streets. Crowds clustered around Lenny's pushcart, watching his big hands artfully shuck the clams. He awarded the delicacy inside to paying customers and earned the nickname "Lenny the Quahog." Carmen Tammaro was a competing vendor Lenny grew up with in the North End. To take advantage of Lenny's popularity, Carmen positioned his cart on the opposite corner selling fruits and vegetables to passersby.

The annual feasts of patron saints weren't the only notable activities in the North End. Boston was notorious for the wise guys and Mafia who settled in the Italian community. Even small disagreements festered into full-blown vendettas between the clashing Italian personalities. Rackets, revenge, and murder plots hatched from the North End terrorized the public for years. The bosses greased the palms of corrupt public servants willing to turn a blind eye. The bad apples enabled ruthless actors that disrupted the good. The system in Boston was dysfunctional at best.

The man standing before the court had an eighth grade education. He earned his living with sweat and toil, counting on the generosity of the sea. Cruising the waters of the Atlantic paid his bills, but also offered recreation. The ocean gifted Lenny with his happiest memories. Friends enjoyed Lenny's harbor tours on the various boats the skipper proudly navigated over the years. His knowledge of the sea supported him and compensated for what he lacked in degrees. Lenny took his boats out of the water by early November and stored them at the Beachmont Yacht Club. Harsh New England winters damaged small vessels still bobbing and banging against a mooring in the water.

His most recent vessel was a 26-foot Chris Craft Cruiser that he christened the *Malafemmena* after a popular Italian song from the 1950s. The captain steered from the cockpit elevated above the blue hull. Lenny had equipped the boat with a Ray Jefferson depth finder, model 5300, and a Ray Jefferson radio, model 1400. The small cabin below deck provided a cramped area for minimal entertainment or maybe a nap. Lenny stood six foot two and weighed over 200 pounds, leaving him no headroom in the cabin, much less comfortable space for anyone else.

Lenny's girlfriend Candy Weyant had purchased the preowned boat on May 3, 1980, and insured the boat and equipment in her name with Liberty Mutual Insurance. In a title state, Candy actually owned the boat, but Lenny used it. If their relationship soured, Lenny was out of luck. The couple moored the boat by the Erie Barge at Pier 7 in Boston. The barge sat much higher than the boat.

Jumping down was okay to board for any able-bodied person, but debarking required considerably more effort and probably a ladder.

Lenny and Candy went to the pier in July 1981 to strip the *Malafemmena*. The boat was already a bit leaky, but Lenny had discovered a broken rudder. He didn't have the money to fix it, and the boat wasn't navigable in that condition. The couple removed anything of value including the navigational equipment and the liquor bottles from a shelf in the cabin. Lenny stayed behind at the pier. He ripped up the toilet, pulled out the bilge plug, and disconnected the seawater intake hose to the engine. The boat sank at Pier 7 by the Erie Barge mooring and settled about 35 feet under the murky waters.

Candy filed an insurance claim the next day on July 26, 1981, indicating the boat was missing. Before recovering any damages for the sunken Chris-Craft, the shellfish peddler's business prospects dwindled. He was broke. On August 26, 1981, Leonard Paradiso filed for bankruptcy. His lawyer helped draw up the papers that excluded the *Malafemmena* as an asset. The boat legally belonged to Candy, but all she had now was her insurance claim. Once paid out, any recovered property belonged to the insurance company. After conducting their own investigation, Liberty Mutual paid the claim on September 29, 1981 to Lenny's girlfriend, the titled and insured owner of the boat.

On Saturday, November 28, 1981, Lenny woke up to the news of the blazing fire burning in Lynn, Massachusetts. He lived in Lynn in an apartment along the shore. Navigating all the chaos going anywhere was a headache and slow. Roadblocks detoured traffic, and emergency vehicles jammed any open arteries to a crawl. The glimmer of sunshine was the hearing on Monday to discharge his debt in the bankruptcy case. He prayed for the court's favor.

Lenny wolfed down turkey leftovers at the Weyant's kitchen table. Lenny lived with Candy and her parents in Revere, Massachusetts.

After gulping one last bite of stuffing, Lenny pushed away from the table and retreated to the workshop in the basement. He'd found a treasure combing the beaches, an artillery shell he wanted to polish. Shined up, the shell would make a great conversation piece along with his prized shark's tooth. He slowly pressed the explosive against the grind wheel. Sparks started to fly, and the munition sounded like fireworks going off on the Fourth of July. Lenny grabbed his left index finger to assess the damage. It could have been worse. Like many big, brawny guys, he ignored the pain, at least for the time.

The court expected punctuality for any petitioner, fire or not. On Monday, November 30, 1981, Lenny stood up in front of the judge and tugged on his tight jacket to feign a comfortable fit. The judge granted his petition and struck the gavel to end the hearing. Relieved and grateful for the court's dispensation, Lenny refocused on his throbbing digit. The pointer on his left hand had gotten worse and needed attention. A friend recommended a visit to the emergency room to get the finger checked. Lenny dreaded heading back into the fire zone, but Lynn Hospital was the destination. The hospital was busy with the fire intensifying each day. Lenny finally got in to let the doctor take a look. The attending physician ordered X-rays, and Lenny waited for the results. The radiologist could see what appeared to be three microscopic metal splinters, embedded in the tissue of Lenny's left index finger. Sometimes, a splinter works its way out on its own. Lenny scheduled a follow-up and hoped for the best.

While Lenny made his appearance in court and waited in a hospital emergency room for treatment in a burning part of town, classes resumed at the Harvard Graduate School of Design. Joan's seat was empty.

Leonard Paradiso

Chapter Four
Every Parent's Worst Nightmare

Eleanor busied herself on Tuesday morning with routine domestic tasks. As she put away the groceries, she checked the itinerary tacked to the refrigerator to estimate George's return. Her husband would get dinner on his flight, but he might want a sandwich by the time he got back to the house. The phone rang, breaking her silent calculations.

"Yes, hello," Eleanor answered.

"My name is David Duncan," Joan's concerned classmate began. "Is Joan sick? Is she still at home?"

"No, Joan flew back to Boston on Saturday night. Why do you ask?" her mother replied.

"She hasn't returned to classes," David explained. "Notes are tacked on her door at Perkins Hall. No one has seen her."

Eleanor interrupted the long, silent pause. "Thank you for calling. I'll do some checking to see where she is, but call me if Joan shows up."

The news was every parent's worst nightmare: Your child is missing. But Joan's mother remained calm, drawing on the discipline of her intelligence training. She carried the phone over to the kitchen table and started to look up numbers. Eleanor was not sure where to start; three days had passed since Joan had flown back to school.

Anne was at work when her mother called. "Anne, one of Joan's friends called and said Joan wasn't back in class. Can you go by the dorm and check her room?"

"Okay, it will be a while," Joan's sister said. "Is there anyone you want me to call?"

"If you get a chance, when you go to the dorm, talk to her friends at school," Eleanor instructed. "Check the hospitals."

Joan was not the type to take off on a whim and not tell anyone. Anne checked emergency rooms and Eleanor called the morgues. No one fit Joan's description. While Anne made Boston area calls, Eleanor notified the New Jersey State Police. Eleanor quietly pondered her daughter's disappointment when George's schedule canceled the planned visit of Joan's friend over the Thanksgiving break.

"Judy, do you know what time George's flight is landing?" Eleanor asked George's assistant.

The call was redundant. George's secretary at ITT recited the same schedule Eleanor had posted in the kitchen. The classmate had rung hours ago asking about Joan. As the gaslights illuminated the tree-lined sidewalks in Glen Ridge, Eleanor finally notified other family members that Joan was missing.

"Steve, Joan didn't return back to school. No one has seen her," Eleanor informed her son. "Does Eve know Keith's number?"

Joan's brother bounded up the stairs and breathlessly told his wife Eve that Joan was missing. Emotions were already fragile for Eleanor's daughter-in-law. She'd suffered a miscarriage on Saturday night, the same night Joan flew back to Boston. The number Eleanor wanted was for the young man planning to visit Joan and meet her parents over Thanksgiving break. He had been a fraternity brother with Eve's younger sibling during his undergrad years at Purdue. He'd met Joan when he attended the Harvard Business School in Cambridge, Massachusetts. After graduating, Keith moved to Detroit for the first step on his career ladder.

Eve looked at her husband in shock and disbelief. After a few moments of silence, the enormity of the words sank in: Joan was missing. Tears streamed down her cheeks.

"You have no right to cry," Steve angrily insisted, echoing the family legacy. "She's my sister."

Hours had passed since Joan's classmate had alerted Eleanor of her daughter's absence from school. Finally, at 11:12 p.m. on Tuesday, December 1, 1981, Eleanor called the Glen Ridge Police to file a missing person report. The duty officer dispatched a patrolman to the Websters' home. George eyed the patrol car while he peeled off some bills to pay his driver. George walked in the side door at midnight and dropped his bags by the pantry. Eleanor took George's overcoat while he poured a drink. Officer Thomas Guthrie briefly stood in respect then sat back down at the kitchen table. Eleanor brought George up to speed before calling the Harvard Campus Police at 12:34 a.m. Wednesday morning. This call set up tandem interviews; officers took down vital information in two locations at the same time.

Watches seemed to be synchronized. As George and Eleanor gave Joan's description to the New Jersey officer sitting at their kitchen table, three Harvard Campus Police officers arrived at Perkins Hall, room 316. They found Anne sitting in her sister's room, talking to her mother on the phone. Anne informed her mother no one had been in the room for a week or more. She found unopened mail and notes tacked on Joan's door. None of the items Joan packed for her return flight to Boston or the clothes she had been wearing were in the room.

Eleanor sat back silently, exhaling a sigh of relief. George was *safe*. The verdict was still out on Joan's well-being.

℃

Anthony Belmonte had found something important to Joan's disappearance. He placed a call to George's office Wednesday morning. George's secretary redirected the call. Belmonte spoke to Jack McEwan, ITT Head of Security in Nutley, New Jersey. The ink was barely dry on the missing person report, not nearly enough time for police blotters to pick up the story. It seemed peculiar that the honest man didn't try to contact the owner of the clutch first. The next logical step would be the police. Instead, this first lead went directly to George Webster. Belmonte informed McEwan that he'd found Joan's wallet while he was digging for clams in the marsh area on the southbound side of route 107, a known dumping ground. McEwan informed the good citizen that the young lady was missing and asked him to report his discovery to the local police. Belmonte agreed he would file a report and contacted the Saugus Police Department.

Detective Joe Marshall returned to the marsh with Belmonte, about seven miles north of Logan, and recovered Joan's purse. Sergeant Neil Meehan in Saugus filed the report. The area wasn't far from the flames still raging in Lynn, but the location was in the opposite direction from Cambridge, Joan's intended destination. Around lunchtime, the Saugus Police conducted an air search of the area but had no new developments to report. Two clues, or maybe three, but no Joan.

While the Saugus Police scoured for evidence along Route 107, Lynn Marsh Road, Sergeant Carmen Tammaro of the Massachusetts State Police received the initial reports of the missing grad student. Within hours, George and Eleanor landed in Boston. The pair walked through the concourse to the F Barracks at Logan. Technically, Joan wasn't missing from the airport because no one actually lived there, but Logan was the last place she had been seen alive. Tammaro was the duty sergeant in charge and patiently listened to Joan's parents. Until Saturday night, none of the 40 million travelers passing through Logan had ever been lost, at least not completely. The officer comforted Joan's parents, saying that sooner or later people turned up. Tammaro encouraged the remarkably composed couple that things would work out all right.

George and Eleanor felt reassured. They were confident Tammaro had their best interest in mind. The sergeant at F Barracks coordinated with other departments to help in the arduous task of finding Joan Webster. The Saugus Police continued search efforts in the marshy area for a second day, enlisting helicopters, scuba divers, the Harbor Police, and a backhoe. A search party of about 25 men with tracking dogs walked the area but found nothing. Saugus Police received a call from the Boston Federal Bureau of Investigation (FBI) after Glen Ridge officers alerted the agency. Police verified Joan had disembarked Eastern flight number 960 in Boston. There was not much more anyone could do as the day waned with no more clues to solve the mystery. Reinforcements were on the way the next day to swell the ranks and cover more ground. Exhausted, the Websters gratefully accepted a ride to the Sheraton in Cambridge. Once up in the room, Eleanor drew a hot bath. George tossed his overcoat on the chair and poured a stiff drink. For the next few days, the Sheraton was their home base.

Jack McEwan arrived from ITT to cover George's flank. The Glen Ridge Police dispatched two of its detectives, Tom Dugan and Ken Swain, to assist local law enforcement in Boston. When they arrived, they spoke to the Websters first and then received a briefing on the status of the search. The collective authorities broke into teams to conduct extensive interviews at the airport of flight attendants, passengers, airport workers, and transportation personnel. Officers dialed from flight manifests, contacting hundreds of passengers who had arrived in Boston on Saturday night. McEwan worked with the team at the cab pool.

Cabbie number two, Fenton Moore, reported that he had almost picked up a fare matching Joan's description on that fateful Saturday night. He lined up in the cab line outside the Eastern Terminal around 10:45 p.m., and soon had a young lady requesting transportation to Cambridge. The Town Taxi driver described Joan in precise detail, including her nice teeth. The detective arranged to question Moore further at the precinct.

On Saturday, low, dark clouds carried a blizzard into Boston. The Glen Ridge detectives departed for Glen Ridge, New Jersey with George and Eleanor in the backseat of their squad car. Ordinarily, that image would mortify Eleanor, but under the circumstances she sat back for the ride. As they drove, 16 inches of heavy snow blanketed the ground and covered any tracks leading to Joan. Back home, the couple discreetly slipped out of the backseat. The gaslights lining the streets in Glen Ridge cast a ghostly glow on the Websters' silhouettes before they retreated behind their closed doors.

The next day, an officer showed the Websters how to operate the answering machine and tape recorder for the trap installed on their home line. The detectives returning from Boston answered a stack of media inquiries on the status of the investigation. The officers responded to CBS, NBC, and the New York Daily News with information released by the Websters back in Boston. Joan had arrived in Boston on Saturday, November 28, 1981. She was last seen at the luggage carousel. After leaving the claim area, she vanished. A clam digger found her purse and wallet in a marsh area north of the airport and reported his discovery to the police. Joan's parents drew on their early training, using the media to their advantage. CBS TV and NBC TV interviewed the parents at their home on Sunday afternoon with Detective Swain, one of the officers who drove them back from Boston. The update deviated in one particular detail reported in the *Newark Star Ledger*.

"Officer, this is Jack McEwan, ITT Security," the caller announced. "I'm concerned about the article that appeared in the *Star Ledger* last Saturday. They reported information the police don't know about."

The news item McEwan questioned ran on December 5, 1981, at the same time McEwan interviewed cabbies at Logan with the police. The police knew Joan had been seen. According to the article, a classmate saw Joan talking to a man behind a counter in the claim area at Logan. The classmate had a family connection with the reporter for the *Star Ledger*. Detective Dugan checked the details and relayed them back to McEwan. The possible lead evaporated, and the narrative continued that Joan disappeared from the baggage area without a trace.

About an hour after the officer updated McEwan about the article, McEwan called back, apparently taking an alternate approach to Joan's investigation. He requested information from the hospital in Dayton, Ohio, where Joan was born. The Head of ITT Security had turned to mysticism and contacted a psychic who needed the time of Joan's birth.

Back in Boston, Sergeant Meehan probed Fenton Moore for any additional details he could remember. Moore described a man with Joan who argued over handling his heavy suitcase. The man with Joan was a middle-aged, white male, under six feet, and approximately 160 pounds. He had dark, curly hair, wire-rimmed glasses, a beard, and wore a dark overcoat. Moore described the man's suitcase and his difficulty getting it loaded into the cab. The young lady willingly changed cars with the man after he exchanged words with him over the suitcase. They left the airport in a blue car, but Moore did not mention the driver. By omission, the cabbie snuck in another subtle clue, the possible involvement of a second person. Moore assisted the officer in building a composite using IDenta Kit templates, and mentioned that his dispatcher had also heard the commotion.

D ' ✔

INCIDENT NO. 81-17884

HARVARD UNIVERSITY POLICE DEPARTMENT

NARRATIVE SUPPLEMENT

INCIDENT REPORT ☐ ARREST REPORT ☐ INVESTIGATION REPORT ☐

00:34 Hrs. Missing Person, Perkins Hall

Received information from base that a female grad student was reported missing by the students Mother who resides at 588 Ridgewood Ave. Glenridge, N.J., tel. # 1-201-744-0322. This officer, along with unit #235, and #264, went to Perkins hall, room #316, where the young girl resides to see if she had returned, and when we arrived we found the sister of the missing student in the room talking on the phone with her Mother.

The sister of Joan L. Webster, (missing student) Ms. Ann Webster, who resides in Acton, Ma. home tel. #1-263-7344, and who works at Poloroids, tel. #577-4040, stated to this officer that she and her sister went to the airport, (Eastern Airlines) on 11/28/81, in N.J. at 9:35 P.M. and that was the last time Ann had seen her sister as she was walking down the ramp to board the plane for the flight to Logan airport.

Ms. Ann Webster also stated that her Mother had contacted the State police there in N.J. and Ann herself had contacted the local hospitals, a couple of morgue's, the Camb. Boston, and State police depts. here in Boston with negative results. This officer contacted the State police at Logan to see if a list is kept of passengers boarding or departing the airports, and they stated that the list is held for one day and then sent to the main office in Miami, Fla. State police will contact that office in the morning.

A photo was obtained by this officer of the missing student and will foward same to C.I.D. for composites.

(Descriptions as Follows)

Joan L. Webster, W/FM, D.O.B. 8-19-56, age 25, Dark brown hair, Brown eyes, Ht. 5'3", Wt.115lb.

Att; Lt. L. Murphy C.I.D.

REPORTING OFFICER	DATE	APPROVED BY	DATE
Sgt. Peter O'Hare	12/2/81		

Harvard Missing Person Report

OFFENSE REPORT

NO __26-81-12__   Missing Person   NO __28900__
Classification

1 COMPLAINANT'S NAME (Firm name if business)		2 AGE	DESCENT	SEX	DOB	3 PHONE (Business)
Joan L. Webster		24	W	F	8-29-56	
4 COMPLAINANT'S ADDRESS		5 CITY				6 PHONE (Residence)
528 Ridgewood Ave.		Glen Ridge NJ				744-0322
7 COMPLAINANT'S BUSINESS, EMPLOYMENT OR SCHOOL		8 OBJECT OF ATTACK (Burglary, theft, assault, etc.)				

9 PLACE WHERE OFFENSE OCCURRED	10 TYPE OF BUILDING (Residence, store, bank, etc.)
Newark Airport	

11 REPORTED BY	PHONE	12 REPORTED TO
Mrs. George Webster (Mother)	744-0322	Dispatcher Burns

13 DAY, DATE AND TIME OF OFFENSE	14 DAY, DATE AND TIME OF REPORT
November 28, 1981 at 2045	December 1, 1981 at 2312

15 BODILY INJURIES TO	HOSPITAL?	16 HOW REPORTED (In person, phone, on view, other)
		Phone

17 M/O (How done · force used · at what point · with what tool or weapon · other acts or trade marks)

17A EXACT WORDS USED BY OFFENDER

18 VEHICLE INVOLVED IN OFFENSE (Year · color · make · model · auto license no. · year · state)   Complainant's ☐ Suspect's ☐

19 DIRECTION OF FLIGHT STREET OR ROAD	☐ N ☐ E ☐ S ☐ W ☐ AUTO ☐ FOOT ☐ UNK. ☐ OTHER	20 WILL COMPLAINANT PROSECUTE?

21 NAME AND ADDRESS OF SUSPECT(S) · OR AGE, DESCENT SEX DESCRIPTION

1. Complainant - W/F Dark Brown Hair - Brown Eyes - 5'2"   long

22 CIRCLE IF SUSPECT IS
Employee · Relative · Acquaintance   suede

2. LSW Brown boots, tan coat, red print blouse, black skirt and brown luggage bag

23 WITNESSES NAME	BEST CONTACT ADDRESS	AGE	BEST PHONE	OTHER PHONE	PARENT OR GUARDIAN
1.					
2.					

24 NARRATIVE (Write in any available details not covered above)

Complainants mother called H.Q. and reported that her daughter was missing She was last seen at approx. 2045 on Saturday November 28, 1981 when she was dropped off at Newark Airport to take a flight back to Boston. Complainant is a student at Harvard University in Cambridge, Mass. Her classes were scheduled to begin on November 30, 1981 and she never show up for them. Mrs. Webster stated that her daughter is a good student and dedicated to her work at school. Car 30 Ptl. Guthrie dispatched for further information. Mrs. Webster reported that her daughter is approx. 5'2" with long dark brown hair, brown eyes and 125 lbs. She was last seen wearing a black skirt, red print blouse, brown boots and a navy blue neck scarf. Parents last saw their daughter at Newark Airport were she was to board an Eastern Airlines Flight to Logan Airport in Boston, Mass. This flight departed Newark at 2135 on

25 INVESTIGATING OFFICER(S) Ptl. Thomas Guthrie	26 REPORT MADE BY twd	DATE 12-2-81
27 CASE FILED Yes ☐ No ☐	28 THIS CASE IS Cleared by arrest ☐ Unfounded ☐ Inactive ☐ Other ☐	29 APPROVED BY

FORM OB-3   Use supplementary report for additional information not covered above.

Glen Ridge PD Missing Person Report (pg. 1)

SUPPLEMENTARY REPORT

NO. 26-81-12

Missing Person
Classification

NO. 28900

Name of Complainant	Address	Phone No.
Joan L. Webster	528 Ridgewood Ave. Glen Ridge	744-0322

Offense

Missing Person

DETAILS OF OFFENSE, PROGRESS OF INVESTIGATION, ETC.:
(Investigating Officer must sign)

Page No. 2   Date Dec. 1 1981

November 28, 1981. The daughet was to have returned to her college dorm
but never arrived.

2328 - This officer phoned Eastern Airlines to check the passenger list on
the above flight. I spoke to a Mrs. Vee who will contact this department
when she has some information.

ATTACHED TO THE DETECTIVE BUREAU COPY OF THIS REPORT IS A RECENT PHOTO OF
COMPLAINANT.

Glen Ridge PD Missing Person Report (pg. 2)

28

On the morning of Dec. 2nd at approx. 9:45 I Anthony
Belmonte, while on the embankment of the Pines River I
found a wallet belonging to Jean L. Webster In the wallet
I found a card from I.T.T. of Mr. Webster On it was
written, If found to call that # I called asking for
Mr. Webster. I spoke to his secretary and she connected
me with Security I spoke with Mr. McKuen and he
informed me of the situation, that the young lady was missing.
I was then contacted by Mr. Marshall of the Revere P.D. who
then accompanied me to the river where we later found
the Red Leather pocketbook of Miss Webster It was hers
because a checkbook inside the Pocketbook was hers,

Work - ▉▉▉▉▉▉

Home ▉▉ ▉▉▉

Saugus Police Interview Anthony Belmonte

Cab Driver #2 ✓ D?

POLICE OFFICER'S REPORT SUPPLEMENT		RECORD # — —	INC. CODE — —	GEOCODE
1 of 2		ARREST # A — —	☐ -SUPPLEMENTAL REPORT ☐ FOLLOW UP REPORT	

INCIDENT		LOCATION		DATE OF THIS REPORT
PRINCIPAL PARTY'S (OR FIRM'S) NAME - LAST, FIRST, INITIAL MORE ALLAN FENTON		ADDRESS ███ ██ █		PHONE ███

PROPERTY-TYPE	MFG. OR TRADE NAME	MATERIAL	SIZE	I.D. OR SERIAL NO.	PRES. VALUE $	HOW ESTABLISHED
TYPE	MFG. OR TRADE NAME	MATERIAL	SIZE	I.D. OR SERIAL NO.	PRES. VALUE $	HOW ESTABLISHED

REPORT:

REC. INFO. FROM FENTON MORE WHO STATED THAT HE WAS OPER A TOWN TAXI ON

NOV. 28, 1981 AT APPROX 10:45 PM - 11:30 PM TAXI # 1229 . AT THIS TIME

A W/F WHO HE DESC AS BEING APPROX 25 YOA wearing a Blk SKIRT, LONG DRK

HAIR APPROX. 5/4" HGT NICE TEETH AND CARRYING A BLK PLASTIC TYPE CASE

AND ANOTHER BAG WHICH HE DOES NOT RECALL KNOCKED ON THE PASSENGER WINDOW

AND ASKED "CAMBRIDGE " WHILE HE WAS PARKED AT THE EASTERN AREA TERMINAL.

HE STATED "SURE" AND THEN PROCEEDED TO OPEN THE M/Vs TRUNK AND TO PUT IN HER

BAG. AT THIS TIME SHE STATED WAIT A MINUTE THERE IS ANOTHER PERSON WITH ME.

MOORE DESC THIS PERSON AS BEING A W/M APPROX. 40 Y.O.A. 160 Lbs 5/6 to 5/7
DRK HAIR
HAVING A BEARD , GLASSES, WEARING DRK OVERCOAT AND HAD A SUIT CASE WHICH

HE DESC AS BEING LARGE BLUE WITH LIME COLORED THROUGH IT. WHEN MOORE

PUT THE CASE INTO THE TRUNK HE OBSERVED HOW HEAVY IT WAS. BECAUSE IT WAS

HEAVY MOORE HAD A DIFFICULT TIME WITH IT AND THE MALE STATED HE DID NOT

APPRECIATE WAY CABBIE WAS PUTTING BAG IN TRUNK AND WORDS WERE EXCHANGED.

(AM STATED) I DON'T THINK WE WANT THIS CAB AND HAD LUGGAGE REMOVED. MOORE

STATES THEY THEN ENTERED THE CAB BEHIND HIM WHICH HE STATES WAS A BLUE COLORED

CAB BUT DOES NOT KNOW THE CO. HE STATES THAT THE FEMALE DISPATCHER CAME OVER

TO HIM AND ASKED IF THERE WAS ANYTHING WRONG AND HE REPLIED

☐ CONTINUED OVER
☐ SUPPLEMENT

STATUS	I HEREBY CERTIFY THAT THE CONTENTS OF THIS REPORT ARE TRUE AND CORRECT TO THE BEST OF MY KNOWLEDGE AND BELIEF.		COMPLAINANT'S SIGNATURE
ACTIVE INACTIVE UNFOUNDED CLEARED	REPORTING OFFICER	SECOND OFFICER	FURTHER ACTION (PURGE INFO)
	SHIFT COMMANDER	REVIEWER	COPIES TO

Saugus Police Interview Fenton Moore (pg. 1)

CE OFFICER'S REPORT SUPPLEMENT			RECORD # __ — __	INC. CODE	GEOCODE
__ of 2			ARREST # A __ — __	☐ SUPPLEMENTAL REPORT ☐ FOLLOW UP REPORT	
CIDENT		LOCATION			DATE OF THIS REPORT
PRINCIPAL PARTY'S (OR FIRM'S) NAME - LAST, FIRST, INITIAL MOORE ALLAN FENTON		ADDRESS			PHONE
PROPERTY-TYPE	MFG. OR TRADE NAME	MATERIAL	SIZE	I.D. OR SERIAL NO.	PRES. VALUE $	HOW ESTABLISHED

REPORT:

NO THEY JUST WANTED ANOTHER CAB. THE NAME OF THIS FEMALE DISPATCHER IS LAURIE RICCO BENE OF ▓▓▓▓. SHE WAS CONTACTED VIA PHONE BUT COULD NOT RECALL INCIDENT BUT WILL MEET WITH CABBIE IN PERSON WHICH MAY HELP HER TO REMEMBER. SHE WILL CONTACT THIS DEPT AT LATER DATE.

LAURIE RICCOBENE CALLED AND STATED SHE MET WITH FENTON MOORE AND AFTER MEETING WITH HIM SHE DOES RECALL THE HE DID HAVE SOME TYPE OF INCIDENT SHE DOES NOT REMEMBER ON WHAT DATE OR IF IT WAS WITH TWO SUBJECT THAT HE DESCRIBES BUT SHE DID GO TO HIM AND SHE RECALLS ASKING HIM IF HE WAS HAVING ANY PROBLEM AND HE STATED NOTHING HE COULDN'T HANDLE HIMSELF THAT THEY WANTED TO TAKE ANOTHER CAB. OF JAMES STODDARD HAD COMPOSITE MADE BY FENTON MOORE.

att to Conroy Subj to Hypnosis unit. Subj exited Cruiser in Somerville & stated we were hit men out to get him.

Saugus Police Interview Fenton Moore (pg. 2)

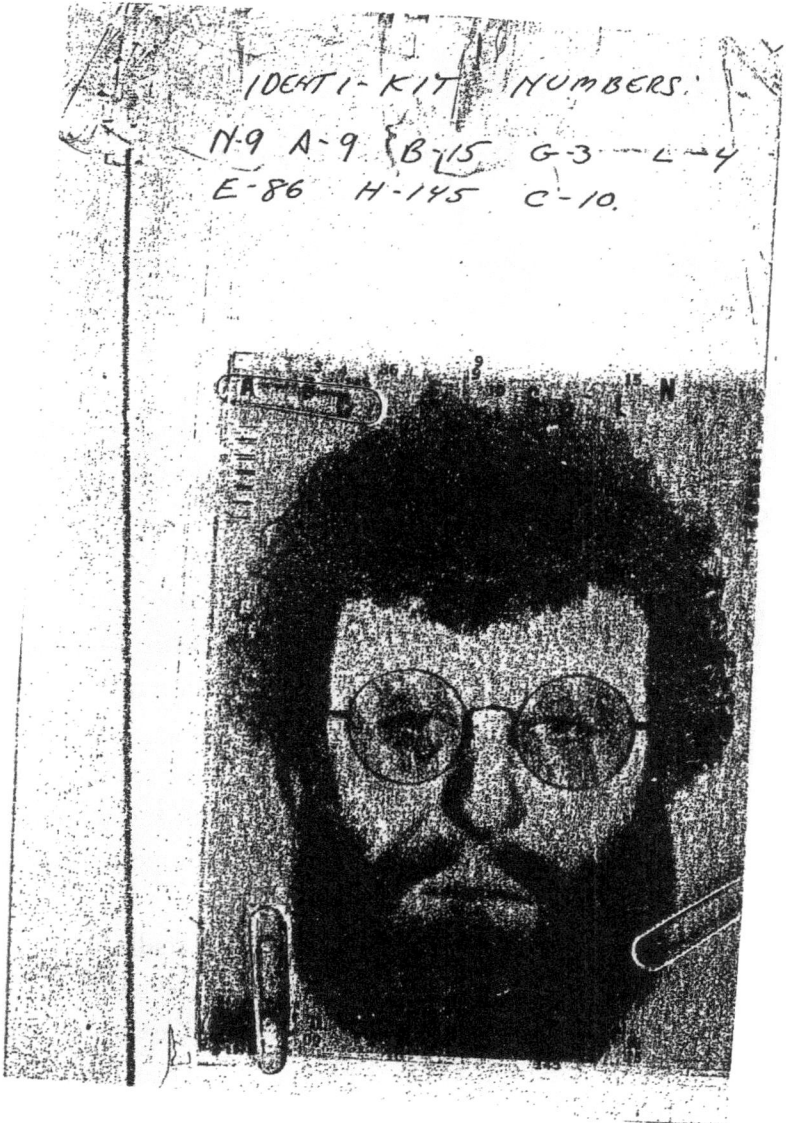

Saugus Police Interview Fenton Moore (pg. 3)

Chapter Five
Extortion

Dramatic headlines of missing persons stir the seedy elements in society to prey on a sad situation. The Websters' phone rang at 9:48 p.m. on Wednesday, December 9, 1981.

"We have your daughter," the caller said. "All we want is money."

The caller quickly hung up. The call was too short to capture the whole number, but the trap traced the exchange "284." The digits the phone company snagged were the same exchange numbers for the ITT offices in Nutley, New Jersey. Two more calls came during the wee hours on Friday, December 18, 1981, the voice on the other end of the line demanding money for Joan's safe return. George answered the next call at 1:23 a.m.

"I want $20,000 in small bills; five, ten, and twenties," the coercer demanded. "Wear a blue hat and blue coat, and deliver the money to Columbus Circle. No, make it the European Bank on 58th. Don't contact the police."

George barely had the receiver back in the cradle when the phone rang again at 1:44 a.m.

The extortion caller repeated his demands. "Fives, tens, and twenties, used bills. Be smart. Don't play games or be stupid if you want to see your daughter. You're being watched."

The caller knew Joan's name and knew about the case, but he had the wrong house number for the Websters' residence. The phone trap pinpointed the time of the calls, but failed to capture the number because of a glitch in the computer system. Police arranged for the phone company to install another phone at the Websters home right away, unaware George had a separate line in his study upstairs. The home phone rang again at 6:40 p.m.

"You'll hear your daughter's voice in two hours," the caller said and hung up.

The maze of intersecting phone networks complicated tracing the call. This call came through Newark's hub and could have come from anywhere. However, the caller planned the drop-off in New York City. The locations were closer to their home than Joan's disappearance in Boston. Everyone was on alert, and the Glen Ridge detectives instructed George and Eleanor what to do if the man called back. The Websters carefully managed what the press reported, and none of the attempted extortion incidents ever leaked.

એ

The Saugus Police shared with the Harvard Campus Police the lead and description of the bearded man seen with Joan at Logan. Lieutenant Murphy did not have any directive what to do with the lead. Notifying the family seemed like the responsible next step, but first he placed a call to Detective Dugan at 10:10 a.m. on Monday, December 21, 1981. He left a message. Before Dugan could return Lieutenant Murphy's call, he took an incoming call from Jack McEwan at 11:00 a.m.

"This is Jack," McEwan began. "ITT may be offering a very substantial reward for information, possibly in the next week or so, in the Boston area."

"Keep me informed," Detective Dugan replied.

"Oh, and I'm going to try to put together a drawing of a suspect based on a description from the psychic," McEwan added.

The officer noted the conversation, then picked up the receiver to return the call to the Harvard Campus Police at 11:20 a.m.

"I have a composite of a suspect in the Joan Webster case," the campus officer said. "A cabbie provided a description of a man he saw leaving Logan with Joan on November 28, 1981. I have the IDenta Kit template numbers for you. Make a note, the hair was less kinky than the overlay."

The New Jersey detective took down the specifics. He passed the information to a colleague who went to the neighboring town of Bloomfield, New Jersey to borrow their IDenta Kit and reconstruct the composite from the template numbers. By 2:00 p.m. on Monday afternoon, December 21, 1981, Detective Richard Corcoran hand-delivered the image. Eleanor held the chilling likeness of the bearded man in her hands, perhaps the last person seen with her daughter alive.

The New Jersey department had documented an odd coincidence. Within one hour of each other, two callers talked to a Glen Ridge detective about composites of possible suspects. The Harvard officer conveyed specific details taken from an eyewitness at Logan. McEwan suggested a drawing based on a psychic's vision. Coincidence or not, competing composites complicated the evidence. It was now the second time George's intermediary, McEwan, muddied the waters over a lead.

❧

George and Eleanor selected their wardrobe carefully to record an appeal to the public for information to help them find their missing daughter. The networks planned to air the segment on Christmas Day. People would be home and gathered with family, assuring a broad audience. The taped message tugged at heartstrings. Families gratefully reflected and embraced their own children who were safely in the nest while feeling sorrow for the Websters. The parents never shared either composite, and the open plea for help ignored the information they had from a cabbie that might jog other recollections. This paradox was invisible.

With the statement already in the can, attention turned to the rest of the family coming in for Christmas. Anne drove in from Boston and George hired a car to drive Eleanor's mother from her retirement village in Pennsylvania, while he made the airport run to pick up his son and daughter-in-law. Waiting at home, Eleanor tied on an apron and busied herself in the kitchen. On Christmas morning, George tapped the turtle's tale and walked into the living room to pass out the presents piled under the tree.

"She's gone," George stoically pronounced. "We have to move on."

Eve gently untied the ribbon on the small box Eleanor placed in her hands. Opening the lid, she found a pair of scrimshaw earrings Joan had bought for her last summer in Nantucket. Joan's sister-in-law closed her eyes, remembering the excitement in Joan's voice when she learned Eve was pregnant. In spirit, the two young women shared a strange sort of sad bond: the loss of life on the same night Joan disappeared. The family fixed their gaze on the tears streaming down Eve's face. The Websters were very passive; they offered no comfort. Even alone with family, in the inner sanctum, behind closed doors, Joan's parents and siblings never shed a tear.

Moving to the dining room, Eve's eyes welled up again. Six places for the six people sitting down for dinner. Eleanor sat near the kitchen at one end of the table, Steve sat on her right side and Grammy on the left. George motioned for his daughter-in-law to sit next to him, and Anne sat across the table on her father's right side. The patriarch stood at the head of the table offering a toast. Eleanor could have set a place for Joan in a gesture of hope, but she didn't. Instead, the setting was surreal. The past weeks seemed like an eternity, but in fact the calendar was just approaching one month since the youngest Webster had disappeared. The conversation did turn to the current status of the investigation.

"Joan's purse and wallet turned up north of the airport," Eleanor said. "It doesn't make much sense. She had money for a cab and was going in a different direction."

"After she picked up her suitcase, she vanished without a trace," George added. "We don't have much to go on. No real leads."

The promising lead and composite, locked in the filing cabinet upstairs, never crossed George and Eleanor's stiff upper lips. The bearded man with Joan in the cab line at Logan was a *secret*.

SUPPLEMENTARY REPORT

<u>MISSING PERSON</u>
Classification

NO _____   NO _28900_____

Name of Complainant	Address	Phone No.

_Joan L. Webster_____528 Ridgewood Ave., Glen Ridge, NJ___744-0322_____
Offense
Missing Person_____

DETAILS OF OFFENSE, PROGRESS OF INVESTIGATION, ETC.:
(Investigating Officer must sign)

Page No. _____R-10_____   Date_Dec. 1_____ 19_81_

Monday 12/21/81

1400 Hrs. Sgt. Dugan gave this officer the IdentiKitnumber used to make a
   composit of the individual that may have left Logan Airport with
   Joan Webster. The numbers were from the Identi-Kit II, NN09, AA09,
   BB15, GG03, LL04, EE86, HH145, CC10. Sgt. Dugan also said the
   person was around 42 years old, full beard, hair was less kinky than
   the overlay.
   This officer went to Bloomfield Detective Bureau to use their
   Identi-Kit Composites made at Bloomfield Police Dept.
   This officer then went to the Webster House and left a copy of the
   composite with Mrs. Webster. I also picked up the tape of the
   last extortion call made on 12/18/81 around 1840 hrs. This tape was
   then turned over to Sgt. Dugan at Police Headquarters.

25 INVESTIG.	ORT MADE BY Det. R. Corcoran	DATE 1/14/82
27 CASE FILED	29 APPROVED BY	
Yes ☐		

FORM L86-3R

Glen Ridge Police Composite Report
and Composite Drawing of Man with Joan Webster
at Logan Airport

Chapter Six
Messaging

The New Year started with bone-chilling winter winds typical in New England. A young woman missed her bus on Saturday, January 9, 1982 at the Park Square Greyhound Bus Station in Boston. The distraught traveler approached the ticket counter for assistance. The clerk calmed the woman and then waved a casually dressed man over to help. He was a large white male, over six feet, with curly brown hair and a long face. He introduced himself as an undercover cop before offering the woman a ride to the Trailways Terminal. She accepted the ride from the stranger because everyone working at the station seemed to know him. The pair moved to a large, unmarked sedan parked by the buses, a reserved area. The woman didn't notice a radio in the car. The man didn't try anything or hurt her; he dropped her off safely to catch another bus. The woman getting a ride from the undercover cop did not *seem* to be a piece of the Joan Webster puzzle, at least not at the time.

Investigators in multiple states tracked down futile leads to find Joan Webster. In the early days of the investigation, George confirmed his daughter was very upbeat before she disappeared. She had earned high marks on the semester's architectural project she presented *before* departing for New Jersey for the long Thanksgiving weekend. Her father never disclosed the planned visit of Joan's friend. George reasoned that this information intruded on Joan's privacy. But his daughter was still missing, and the questions persisted. *Why did Joan go back to Boston early?* The messaging subtly shifted.

"Joan went back early to work on a class project," George said. "She planned to meet with a couple of classmates on Sunday."

The lack of good leads bogged down the investigation, and the Websters didn't want the story to fade from the headlines. George and Eleanor packed their bags for another trip to Boston. The couple scheduled a news conference the morning of January 19, 1982, and announced a $10,000 reward for information. Before the Websters' appeal went to print, the *Boston Globe* interviewed Saugus Detective Meehan on the status of the Joan Webster investigation. That story ran first.

"The only potential clues to Miss Webster's disappearance were found four days after her flight," Sergeant Meehan reported. "Her purse and wallet were in the Lynn marshes that border Route 107. Since the items were on the southbound side of the highway, the thinking is they were tossed from a car heading toward the airport, not away. Someone might have spotted her getting into a taxi or a private car. She [was] scheduled to meet classmates Sunday afternoon to work on a project."

The messaging about Joan's early return to school matched the Websters' explanation but offered no witnesses to support it. The classmates never materialized. Sgt. Meehan was the same officer that had interviewed the Town Taxi cabbie. He *knew* Joan had been seen leaving the airport. Two sentences at the end of the article escaped scrutiny, but the guarded evidence leaked:

"A taxi driver gave us a description of a bearded man he saw with Joan at Logan," Meehan said. "A composite circulated without success."

What the detective considered circulation wasn't clear. Sergeant Carmen Tammaro coordinated efforts from the different departments. Massachusetts State Police files contained the eyewitness description and composite. Saugus forwarded the information to the Harvard Campus Police. Lieutenant Murphy called the Glen Ridge, New Jersey department. They reconstructed the composite from template numbers and handed it to Eleanor Webster on December 21, 1981.

The likeness never made the papers or evening news. Authorities and the Websters kept the lead close to the vest and buried the clue. The paradox was invisible at the Webster press conference. Parents pleading for information and offering a reward had a *secret* lead tucked away in a filing cabinet. Their appeal reinforced the story that Joan left the terminal and vanished without a trace. According to public reports, no one saw Joan leaving the airport.

An anonymous call came into the Saugus Police the next day. The woman told the Saugus Police Chief, Donald Peters, that Leonard Paradiso was involved in the Webster disappearance and the 1979 murder of an East Boston woman named Marie Iannuzzi. The woman offered no details of either matter and refused to identify herself. Unknown to the department, the anonymous caller grew up in the North End, the Italian neighborhood rife with vendettas, with Sergeant Tammaro and Leonard Paradiso. Paradiso was one of two suspects considered in the unresolved Iannuzzi murder, but police had insufficient evidence to arrest and charge him with the crime. The other suspect was Marie's boyfriend, David Doyle. The couple had a known abusive relationship. Despite overwhelming circumstantial evidence against the boyfriend, Essex County prosecutors failed to try him. Of note, Marie Iannuzzi, David Doyle, Leonard Paradiso, and his girlfriend Candy Weyant all attended the same wedding on August 11, 1979.

ക

On January 29, 1982, the Massachusetts State Police received a radio call to proceed to the Park Square Greyhound Bus Station, the same terminal where that undercover cop had given a stranded traveler a ride. The station had lockers with a 30-day limit. If contents went unclaimed, employees removed items from the locker to a caged storage area for another 30 days. Someone had left a

Lark suitcase in locker number 1434 sometime before 9:30 a.m. on November 29, 1981, the morning after Joan landed at Logan. Key number 3711 for that locker was still outstanding. No one claimed the luggage. Ordinarily, the station shipped abandoned items to headquarters after 60 days for further disposition, but an observant employee noticed the tag. The story of the missing grad student had plastered the papers for two months. Park Square Greyhound Bus Station had one of Joan Webster's suitcases; the carry-on tote wasn't there. The recovery added another baffling piece of evidence. The bus terminal, located west of the airport, was nowhere near the Saugus marsh where Joan's purse and wallet had turned up. The protocol for the lockers assured the depositor ample time before anyone found Joan's belongings.

Next, the Websters requested a meeting with all of the official parties involved in their daughter's investigation. George's clout and influence assembled a large group of representatives for a strategy session held on the Harvard campus in late February 1982. The packed room included counsels and state troopers from three county district attorney's offices. Middlesex County, covering Harvard, had handled the early stages of Joan's investigation. Logan Airport was in the boundaries of Suffolk County, the last place Joan was seen alive. Essex County was handling the cold Marie Iannuzzi case. Sergeant Carmen Tammaro represented the Logan Detective Unit along with his subordinate, Trooper Andrew Palombo. The chief over all of the state police detectives also attended as well as officers from the Saugus Police Department, where the purse was found, and the Harvard Campus Police.

When the door finally opened after the conclave regarding Joan, authorities initiated a confusing scheme to go after a suspect for her disappearance. Trooper Palombo, an undercover cop assigned to the F Barracks at Logan Airport, teamed with a young prosecutor in the Suffolk County District Attorney's Office. Palombo was the lead officer who had handled the Marie Iannuzzi case since February 1981. The authorities had shifted the Iannuzzi case from Essex to Suffolk County using an obscure Massachusetts law. Because Marie's body was within a certain number of rods, an archaic method of measuring distance, from the county line, either county could prosecute the case. George Webster's summit set the stage for Trooper Palombo and prosecutor Tim Burke to go after Leonard Paradiso for the cold-case murder of Marie Iannuzzi.

Palombo was six foot four and weighed approximately 230 pounds. The former defensive lineman was an imposing presence. Undercover, his appearance ranged widely to suit the assignment. His looks stretched anywhere from a clean-cut man in a tailored suit to a long-haired Hell's Angel riding his Harley, or anything in between. He lived in a small house just west of Lynn, Massachusetts with his wife and four young girls, the youngest one barely walking. His tastes were expensive on a trooper's salary with a growing young family. He liked fast cars, motorcycles, and sailing.

Palombo's new partner was a novice prosecutor on murder cases. Tim Burke had received one cold case, a triple homicide, in September 1981. He didn't seem to have the experience in four or five months to handle a high-profile case like Joan Webster, but he got the assignment anyway. It seemed odd that George settled for anyone less than the best lawyer in the District Attorney's stable, but he never did anything without a final objective in mind.

Like George, Burke understood the power of the media. A reporter for the *Boston Globe* composed an exposé about a triple homicide Burke had on his desk. He hoped the piece would renew interest in the case and generate some new leads. The article appeared on Saturday, February 27, 1982, on the front page of the Metro section.

Burke had no time to bask in any media attention Monday morning. He prepared grand jury subpoenas, orders compelling witnesses to appear in court, for a hearing at the end of the week. He summoned the family, friends, the boyfriend of Marie Iannuzzi, and Leonard Paradiso on Tuesday, March 2, 1982. On Friday, witnesses lined the hall outside the courtroom waiting their turn to take the stand. The grand jury is a secret hearing for the prosecutor to present his case, one-sided, without any rebuttal—and jurors are allowed to ask clarifying questions. The judge gaveled cause number 038655, the *Commonwealth v. Leonard Paradiso,* into session. The bankrupt shellfish peddler was the target.

Authorities kept a tight lid on the allegations against Paradiso in the Webster case. No one knew about the anonymous caller who dropped the dime or the Websters' undisclosed meeting. Paradiso had been targeted for Joan's disappearance beginning in January 1982, but they kept the suspect a *secret.* Rather than tell the truth why he took over the Iannuzzi case, Burke concocted a story that no one checked. He claimed Marie Iannuzzi's sister had read the article about the triple homicide and called Burke for help with Marie's cold case.

To swallow Burke's explanation meant Marie's sister, Kathy Leonti, had called Burke's office on Sunday or Monday, after the article appeared, and asked him to handle a case maintained in another county. By Tuesday, Burke delivered subpoenas. He falsely portrayed the hearing as a "John Doe" grand jury on March 5, 1982, to determine who committed the crime, Lenny Paradiso or David Doyle. On Friday, less than a week after the supposed call from Marie's sister, the jurors heard testimony in a hearing that named Paradiso as the suspect, not John Doe. Even though the prosecutor's timeline didn't work, the manufactured excuse covered Burke's rear end and disguised the real objective of the hearing.

The first witness Burke called was Kathy Leonti, the sibling he had just entangled in his web.

First Reward Poster for Joan Webster

Park Square Greyhound Bus Station
10 St. James Avenue, Boston MA

D³

POLICE OFFICER'S REPORT SUPPLEMENT

| RECORD # | — — | INC. CODE 39 | GEOCODE 19 |
| ARREST # | A — — | ☐ SUPPLEMENTAL REPORT ☐ FOLLOW UP REPORT | |

1 of 1

INCIDENT	LOCATION	DATE OF THIS REPORT
suitcase found	Greyhound Terminal Bost.	
PRINCIPAL PARTY'S (OR FIRM'S) NAME - LAST, FIRST, INITIAL	ADDRESS	PHONE
Webster Joan	520 Ridgewood Av.Glen Ri	

PROPERTY-TYPE	MFG. OR TRADE NAME	MATERIAL	SIZE	I.D. OR SERIAL NO.	PRES. VALUE	HOW ESTABLISHED
suitcase	Lark	nylon/l.a			$	
TYPE	MFG. OR TRADE NAME	MATERIAL	SIZE	I.D. OR SERIAL NO.	PRES. VALUE	HOW ESTABLISHED
					$	

REPORT: aprox 9:30am 1-29-82 recvd radio call to meet Lt. O'Connor ...
re: suitcase believed property of Joan Webster
      suitcase as described above and had been stored sometime since ...
29,81 in Locker # 1434 left unopened 30 days case removed to Greyhound pro.
room for 30 more days when reviewing for disposition Greyhound em.loy
Collopy noticed name tag on case and contacted his superiors. Prior to not. .
tag case had been opened for review as is normal procedure.
      Lt. O'Connor handled investigation,Cpl.William anderson of Mass. State ..
photo & print unit removed same for processing at lab,telephone contact a...
 als to no avail.Case contained clothing,hairdryer
      ~~Key#xforxlockerxx~~ 3711 key # for locker #1434 still outstanding, as ...
was never claimed,search of property room for second case to no avail r....
be secured and all property in room to be searched by state police for ...
of second bag.
      Bag found was a Lark nylon/leather trim blue/brown with 3 zippers   spec.
~~locking with small padlocks on zippers~~ visual observation show. all ....
appear intact but not used to lock 2 zipperheads together as would be r...
to secure case
      suitcase personal tag bears name and address of Joan Webster
      full inventory of property in case to follow from gate State ...

| | CONTINUED ☐ OVER ☐ SUPPLEMENT |

CASE STATUS	I HEREBY CERTIFY THAT THE CONTENTS OF THIS REPORT ARE TRUE AND CORRECT TO THE BEST OF MY KNOWLEDGE AND BELIEF.	COMPLAINANT'S SIGNATURE
☐ ACTIVE	REPORTING OFFICER	SECOND OFFICER	FURTHER ACTION (PURGE INFO)
☐ INACTIVE			
☐ UNFOUNDED			COPIES TO
☐ CLEARED	SHIFT COMMANDER	REVIEWER	

Boston Police Report for Suitcase Recovery

Trooper Andrew Palombo

Chapter Seven
Bait and Switch

Burke previewed the obstacles to his final objective. One by one, witnesses took the stand and pointed the finger at one of the two suspects.

"David and Marie had an argument at the wedding reception," Kathy said. "My mother heard the news on the radio Monday morning, coming home from her shift. She knew what Marie wore to the wedding; she knew it was Marie."

"Did you observe anything about David?" Burke asked.

"He came to my parents' house Monday morning," Marie's sister answered. "He just sat on a kitchen chair glazing, looking around. He said nothing; he just sat on the chair on his hands."

Burke mentally catalogued the answers and continued, "Did you see him at the funeral?"

"He never showed up," Kathy replied.

"At some point, did people go to David and Marie's apartment to get her things?" Burke asked.

"Yes," she continued. "I went Monday morning to get her a dress to wear for the wake. One of my sisters went with me. Everything was all packed up in boxes."

"What day was this?" a juror asked.

"Monday morning we started getting Marie's belongings together," she repeated.

"Did Marie have a cat?" Burke asked, taking back the reins of interrogation.

"Not at this time, she did not," Kathy declared. "Marie told us a month ago the cat ran away."

"Did you notice a scratch on David's hands and face?" the prosecutor probed.

Marie's sister answered, "I did not. Everyone pointed it out, but I did not look myself."

A juror circled back, "Everything was packed. Sunday night he packed. Did he know Sunday she was dead?"

"Monday morning it was all packed," Kathy Leonti repeatedly answered without hesitation.

Burke called his next witness, Marie's brother-in-law, Tony Leonti. The prosecutor established that the whole family learned about Marie's death early Monday morning and gathered at her parents' home. An officer came to the house. Marie's father, David, and Tony Leonti went with the officer to the morgue to identify the body. David stood next to the gurney and pulled back the sheet. It was her.

"David threw the sheet over her head in disgust," Tony said. "He was mad."

"Did he cry?" Burke asked.

"No," he answered. "None whatsoever."

Burke continued, "Did you go back to their apartment at some time?"

Marie and David lived together on the third floor of his parents' home. David's mother and father lived on the first two floors. David had Marie's belongings already packed in boxes, but didn't offer to help Marie's family move them.

"On the way up the stairs we saw blood," Marie's brother-in-law recalled. "It was on the second or third step from the bottom."

"How did you know it was blood?" Burke probed.

"You know blood when you see it," he insisted.

The brother-in-law next recalled his observations of Marie's boyfriend at the wake. He told the jurors David Doyle moped around and appeared to be on something. Doyle's mother kept her son on a short leash during the wake, *never* letting him out of her sight.

"He was always on Valium or Angel Dust," Tony recalled. "His mother chauffeured him around. He came in with her and left with her."

Testimony from the third witness almost assured Burke an indictment for Marie's murder but only if he tagged the right suspect. Benjamin Puzzo took the stand next. The aggrieved man remembered attending the wake for his niece. Visitation spanned over two days, Wednesday and Thursday, with the funeral planned for early Friday morning, August 17, 1979. He noticed David's glassy eyes and concurred with previous testimony; David was high on something. On the second night of the wake, Marie's boyfriend was so bad off, his mother had to take him out of the visitation room. A juror wanted to know about Marie's fingernails, and the witness said she kept them long and manicured.

"Where did you first see David?" Burke asked. "What did you observe about his person?"

"He came to shake hands with me on the *first* day of the wake," Benjamin recalled. "I would not shake hands; his hands were full of scratches."

"You could see them?" Burke pressed.

"Yes, they were terrible," the witness answered. "It was like raw beef, wide-type scratches. They were scabbed up oozy type things. You don't put your hands on something like that."

"You indicated he folded his arms," the prosecutor continued. "When did you see him do that?"

"On the first and second day of the wake," Puzzo confirmed.

"Would a dog cause scratches like that?" a juror asked.

"They were too wide," Marie's uncle answered. "I have been clawed by cats. It's thin, same with a dog. The scratches were deep. These looked like they were dug into and pulled."

Marie's uncle showed the jury how the wide scratches on Doyle's hands went from his wrists to his fingers. Burke put the demonstration into words for the jury, from his wrists to his fingers. The jurors asked the witness a few more questions. They wanted to know if David offered to help with the funeral. He didn't; he didn't even show up.

Marie's mother was listening to the news Monday morning driving home from an overnight shift. As she drove through the tunnel, she heard the description of the dead woman found in Saugus. Her heart palpitated. David's mother, Rosemarie Doyle, heard the same news when her brother, Vincent Milano, called early that morning. The groom's father recalled how intoxicated his nephew's girlfriend was at the house party on Saturday night. Marie's mother picked up Jean Day, Marie's stepsister, at 6:45 a.m., and the two of them knocked on the Doyles' front door. Mrs. Doyle reflexively cupped her hands to her face before a single word was spoken.

"Oh my God," David's mother exclaimed.

The three women went to the third floor to get David out of bed. He ignored them and wouldn't answer their questions. Marie's stepsister noticed the packed boxes in the apartment prior to 7:00 a.m. Monday morning *before* anyone identified the body. Doyle went with Marie's mother and Jean back to the Iannuzzis' house where other family members had gathered. The pained witness described David's demeanor for the jury.

"He stared off into space the whole time. He never answered any of us," Jean said. "His hands were under his legs. He was sitting on his hands."

"What did you see?" Burke asked.

"I noticed the scratches when he got off the chair," she vividly remembered. "Pretty good gouges across the top of his hands."

"Were the scratches on his hands fresh?" a juror asked.

"They were fresh. They were done within a couple of days," Jean replied. "He had scratches on both hands."

Marie's stepsister recalled the drop of blood on the wood stairs to the couple's apartment. Her recollection was that she had told the police about the blood. She informed the jury David was known to have a violent temper, and Jean described an argument the couple had had earlier in the summer. Marie's attire at the wedding was an important aspect of Marie's case. Marie had dressed in a red bodysuit, with no snaps in the crotch, and a matching wraparound skirt. She wore black pantyhose underneath the leotard with seams that went up the back of the legs. She accessorized the ensemble with black shoes and a black scarf around her neck. Marie's stepsister told the jurors what was missing when they found Marie's body.

"She was dressed in the body shirt and skirt," Jean said. "She was found without the nylons that go under the body shirt and without shoes and her pocketbook."

Burke called a Saugus Police officer to the stand. Inspector Arthur Cook had interviewed Doyle after identification of Marie's body. He noticed some scratches around David's eye. Marie's boyfriend said their cat caused the scratches. The Iannuzzi family told him about the scratches on David's hands when the officer interviewed them after the wake. When the officer asked David's mother about the scratches, she told him David got the scratches in a motor vehicle accident back in June, but the officer said the scratches were much fresher when he saw them.

After the wake that Thursday night, Doyle took flight. He was arrested at Newark Airport stealing suitcases. He had a brown paper bag with ladies' panties and a stolen airline ticket from LaGuardia to Boston in his possession. Doyle gave the arresting officers a fake name. Cook traveled to New Jersey to positively identify Doyle and observed the scratches on the runaway's hands.

The Saugus detective had interviewed Paradiso and his girlfriend after Marie's murder. The accounts were consistent. Candy drove

Marie to the Cardinales Nest Bar at the host's request. Candy left with Marie buckled in the passenger seat between 9:30 and 10 p.m., and Lenny stayed at the house party. Candy got back to the Milanos' house by 11 p.m., a half hour trip each way. Candy and Lenny left the Milanos' party together around midnight. When they got in Candy's car, they found items belonging to Marie. They detoured to the Cardinales Nest Bar to return the belongings. Back at Lenny's apartment, they found Marie's keys stuck between the seats and made a second trip to the bar. Candy waited outside while Lenny went in and talked to Marie. Marie was intoxicated. Lenny offered her a ride, but she said she had to meet someone and declined. Lenny held the door for Marie sometime between 12:30 and 1:00 a.m. Sunday morning as they both exited the bar. Candy and Lenny watched Marie turn the corner and walk out of sight. That was the last time they saw her.

Two of Marie's close friends swore to tell the truth. Christine DeLisi was at the Cardinales Nest Bar and saw Marie. She witnessed Paradiso holding the door for her friend as she walked out. That was the last time she saw the victim alive. Christine and a mutual friend, Ann Marie Kenney, described a frightening incident that happened in May or June 1979, a couple of months before the offender strangled Marie. Each young woman independently recalled Marie's terror after a fight with her boyfriend. Marie arrived on Christine's doorstep clutching a trash bag full of clothes. Her distraught friend needed a place to stay until things cooled down. Christine and Ann Marie both described the strangulation marks wrapped around Marie's throat: long, red impressions on both sides of her neck. Doyle had a history of abusive behavior, and Marie's friends corroborated a recent bad act. Marie spoke from the grave through her friends.

"She was screaming and crying David beat her up," Christine sobbed. "She had strangulation marks on her neck, fairly red marks, and handprints around her neck."

" 'David almost killed me,' " Ann Marie shivered, repeating Marie's haunting words. " 'He strangled me; he scared me.' "

Burke read David Doyle his Miranda rights before he started to speak. The prosecutor established Doyle's substance abuse and drug dealing. The victim's boyfriend confessed the couple had fights, sometimes physical. He excused taking off to New Jersey as an effort to get away; the stress was just too much for him to handle. Doyle wasn't clearing his head; he admitted to drinking and taking barbiturates. After two witnesses told the jury they saw boxes packed early Monday morning, before anyone identified the body, Doyle claimed he had packed Marie's belongings Monday night when he couldn't sleep. After glossing over some serious discrepancies, Burke boldly tackled a new line of questioning.

"Was Marie going out with anybody else?" Burke asked.

"I believe so, somebody named Fisher," Marie's boyfriend admitted.

"Eddie Fisher?" the prosecutor asked.

"I just know Fisher," Doyle responded. "Sometimes I would see her and question her about it. I did not ask any more."

When Burke asked Doyle about the scratches on his hands, he said he had told the police his cat scratched him; it was all he could think of. For good measure, Doyle had another explanation ready. Between David and his mother, this was now the third explanation for the scratches the grand jury heard that day.

"I got in a fight at one of the wakes in a bar across the street from the funeral home," David explained. "I was with Fisher and a couple of other guys."

The new explanation defied common sense. Doyle just admitted he barely knew the name of his live-in girlfriend's paramour. Previous testimony enlightened the jury to the fact that Doyle's mother had her son on a short leash during the wake. Rosemarie Doyle tailed him coming and going. But now, Doyle wanted the jury to believe the jealous boyfriend shook the supervision and commiserated with his live-in girlfriend's other lover in a bar across the street.

Burke never called Paradiso to the stand, but he created the perception that Lenny had taken the fifth and refused to testify. If Burke's objective was to get an indictment for Marie's murder, he blew it. The target of the inquiry was the *Commonwealth v. Leonard Paradiso*. Any reasoning person would have indicted David Doyle after hearing the testimony on March 5, 1982. Either Burke was completely inept, or an indictment against Doyle wasn't part of the plan coming out of the February meeting with the Websters.

☙

The anonymous caller in January had implicated Paradiso in the Joan Webster disappearance. The Websters convened a meeting in late February. The prosecutor seated a grand jury targeting Paradiso for the 1979 Iannuzzi murder the first week of March, but the testimony implicated Marie's boyfriend. On March 11, 1982, six days after the compelling testimony of grieving family and friends, the closest people to the victim, a Massachusetts State Police trooper familiar with Marie's case repeated an unsubstantiated tip from an unidentified source, discreetly planting more seeds of suspicion about Paradiso.

Doyle and Paradiso both had rap sheets, and the latter reported to a parole officer after serving time for a 1973 assault. Trooper Carl Sjoberg had handled Marie's case before Palombo took over in February 1981. In his new assignment, the trooper called Paradiso's parole officer to point the finger at Paradiso. "The subject may be a suspect in a new case in the Boston area," the trooper alleged to Paradiso's parole officer, who then turned around and told his superior. Sjoberg discreetly confirmed Burke's mandate to go after Paradiso.

Burke seated a second grand jury on April 5, 1982. He revised the case for cause number 038655. This new case was different. Now it was a *John Doe Investigation* for the murder of Marie Iannuzzi, disguising the target of Burke's inquest. The next tack for Burke was to call witnesses who connected Paradiso to the Atlantic Lobster Company, a business located on the northbound side of Route 107. Boaters passing by had spotted Marie's body on the rocky banks of the Pine River behind Conley & Daggett, a shuttered lobster company, late in the afternoon of August 12, 1979, the same day she died. Lenny sold his sea harvest to restaurants and businesses throughout the area, including the Atlantic Lobster Company previously known as Conley & Daggett. Lenny never did business with Conley & Daggett until new owners reopened the business and changed the name.

The current lead on Marie's case, Trooper Andrew Palombo, added the final nail. Palombo took the stand for the second grand jury proceeding for cause number 038655, the *Commonwealth v. John Doe*. He described how officers found Marie. The bodysuit and wrap-around skirt were intact. Her black scarf was double-knotted tightly around her neck. The stockings she had worn earlier in the evening would have had to go on *under* the leotard, but her pantyhose and shoes were not on the body. They were never found. The lead officer peppered the allegations against Paradiso by telling the jurors the suspect reported his car missing three weeks after the murder. Palombo named Marie's friend, Christine DeLisi, as the last person to see Marie alive. Marie had asked her friend to wait; she would be back in about 15 or 20 minutes. As she testified in the previous Grand Jury hearing, Christine watched Marie walk out while Lenny held the door at the Cardinales Nest Bar in East Boston.

Knowing Palombo's badge instilled trust, Burke turned to his witness and added a caveat to his next question. "Do you know who the person was that was last seen with Miss Iannuzzi alive, according to witnesses we have available at this time?" Burke asked.

"Yes, I do," the trooper answered. "Leonard Paradiso."

Palombo had the police reports from the Iannuzzi files. The Saugus Police identified four witnesses who saw Marie back in the bar about an hour later, at closing time. Marie had returned to the bar after her friend saw Lenny hold the door, but Christine hadn't waited. Closing time was 2:00 a.m. The bartender asked Marie to turn off the air conditioner. Marie asked a bar patron for a ride to Eddie Mack's, another drinking establishment, but the woman didn't have a car. The bar's owner, a waitress, the bartender, and the bar patron were all present at the bar the night Marie was last seen but not available for the Grand Jury, because Burke never called them for any of the hearings. The grand jury handed down a true bill on June 28, 1982 indicting Leonard Paradiso for the murder of Marie Iannuzzi. Burke wasn't finished yet. He wanted rape charges added to the indictment, so there were more *secret* sessions to come.

The strategy to substitute John Doe for the intended target in the second grand jury was brilliant, a bait and switch scheme that put a vulnerable man in the crosshairs of the authorities. However, the tactic seemed too advanced for the novice prosecutor to think of himself. Burke probably did as he was told when he named Paradiso as the target of the grand jury investigation in March. Witnesses forewarned Burke of the hurdles he faced with the other suspect and with prosecuting Paradiso for Marie's murder instead of the boyfriend. Naming Paradiso on cause number 038655 on March 5, 1982 guaranteed the grand jury would *not* hand down a true bill against David Doyle for his unfaithful girlfriend's murder since he wasn't the suspect named. An indictment of the boyfriend might have served justice for Marie, but a Doyle indictment would have cut the alleged ties to Joan Webster that were otherwise based merely on that anonymous and unverified call. Any charges against Doyle would have the connection authorities sought by entangling Marie's murder with Joan's disappearance. When Burke changed the case to a John Doe investigation and put Palombo on the stand, Burke snagged the target the unidentified female caller had accused, and the dynamic tilted in favor of the Websters' cause. The ruse was a classic bait and switch, and the diabolical scheme worked.

038655   Grand Jury, March 5, 1982   ADA TIMOTHY BURKE

COMM. VS. LEONARD J. PARADISO

Murder - 1st

WITNESS SWORN

q identify yourself.

a Katherine Leonti.

q where do you live?

a 365 Meridian St. East Boston.

q are you married?

a yes.

q what is your husband's name?

a Anthony Leonti.

q did you know Marie Iannuzzi?

a my sister.

q how old was Marie at the time of her death?

a 20.

q she died on August 12, 1979.

a yes.

q did you know who she was living with at the time of her death?

a David Doyle.

Marie Iannuzzi Grand Jury Testimony
Katherine Leonti

NAME	NUMBER	OFFENSE	SENTENCE
...SO, Leonard	1-35074	Att. Rape	6-15 yrs.
...ob 12/8/42		Unlaw carry D. W.	2½-3 yrs. cc.
		Unlaw carry D. W.	2½-3 yrs. cc.
		Poss. D. W. w/o serial	2½-3 yrs. cc.

CD	RELEASED	PAROLE DISCHARGE DATE	FULL MAXIMUM	PAROLE OFFICER
...-75	5-10-78	6-23-90		O'Neill

DATE 19 82	TYPE OF REPORT	*Moderate*	-5-	HOME: 262 Crescent Ave. Revere, Mass. 289-0568
				WORK:

DATE	TYPE	
1-20-82	V	P.O. met with subject at his Revere home. Reports that work is slow. Will be doing Independent Fish Brokerage, needs travel permit for West and So.West. Spoke of possibility of going into business by opening up his own fish market, in Revere. No other changes. JON/ml
1-28-82	M	Travel permit issued to subject for business travel for various Southern and Western States, for the reason of wholesale fish business. JON/ml
3-11-82	TC	Call from Trooper Sojoberg, Mass. State Police, 727-5105. Discussion as to subject's address and work. Informed P.O. that subject had been subpoenaed to the Grand Jury in regards to Saugus murder. See R.R. entry dated 11/19/80. Trooper Sojoberg also discussed with P.O. that subject may be suspect in new case in Boston area. (case discussed with Sojoberg). P.O. discussed case with Sup. Murphy in detail. Sojoberg stated that Paradiso did not testify. He brought his attorney. Said he would plead the 5th. JON/ml
3-11-82	C	P.O. at subject's home 6 p.m. Spoke with his girlfriends mother. She informed P.O. that he had left on a business trip on 3/8/82. Message left for subject's girlfriend to contact P.O. JON/ml
3-16-82	TC	Call from subject's girlfriend Cindy Weyant. States she spoke with subj. on 3/9/82 day after he left, was going to Alabama then to Texas on business. Told to have subject contact P.O. as to his travel schedule. JON/ml
3-16-82	TC	P.O. spoke with Trooper Sojoberg as to subject's status and whereabouts. P.O. discussed case with Sup. Murphy. JON/ml
3-16-82	TC	Call from subject's girlfriend. Message left for P.O. Subject had called from Alabama. Scheduled to go to Texas. Informed to have subject contact as to schedule. JON/ml
3-16-82	TC	Spoke with Trooper Sjoberg State Police. No further information on subj. JON/ml
3-16-82	TC	Call from subject's Girlfriend. Reports subject left Mass. 3/8/82 - Alabama to Texas. No further message. JON/ml
3-22-82	M	Post card received from subject. Post mark: Tombstone Arizona, 3/24/82. JON/ml

over

Leonard Paradiso Parole Officer Entry for 3-11-1982

-1-

038655   Grand Jury   April 5, 1982   ADA TIMOTHY BURKE
                                            STENO. ROBERT BARRY

JOHN DOE INVESTIGATION

Re: Death of Marie Iannuzzi

WITNESS, SWORN

Q   Sir, tell us your name?

A   Charles George.

Q   Would you spell your last name for the court reporter, here.

A   G-E-O-R-G-E.

Q   Mr. George, are you employed?

A   Yes, I am.

Q   Where are you employed?

A   Atlantic Lobster Company.

Q   Where is the Atlantic Lobster Company located?

A   Saugus, Mass.

Marie Iannuzzi Grand Jury Testimony
Charles George

Chapter Eight
Rollercoaster

Joan's case took a bizarre twist in April 1982. A California man contacted the Websters suggesting an incredulous assertion. Gareth Penn had studied the Zodiac murders, a spree of unresolved homicides in California in the late 1960s and early 1970s. Penn claimed he deciphered some of the Zodiac killer's cryptic codes and named his suspect, a Massachusetts Institute of Technology (MIT) professor in Boston. The theorist calculated Joan was a victim of the notorious crime spree. The intelligence-trained parents communicated with the man for close to a year. Never explaining how she got it, Eleanor even provided a credit card voucher of the suspected professor to Penn. The Zodiac hunter attempted to entrap his suspect by mailing him an anonymous package purchased with the credit card number on the voucher. George notified the FBI of the development and forwarded a 119-page manifesto Penn had mailed to him. In his cover letter, George outlined his directives to Middlesex County to check the lead. The FBI determined many of Penn's conclusions were forced and unreliable, but not before police harassed the professor to the point that he gave up his position at MIT and moved to Berkeley, California. This pursuit compounded the chaos in an already confusing investigation.

&

David Doyle and his friend David Dellaria were drinking and getting high the summer 1981. Doyle was angry because Marie was cheating on him with another guy. During the unguarded conversation, Doyle supposedly confessed to Dellaria, which was then reported to Inspector Howard Long when he interviewed Dellaria on July 16, 1981.

"She got what she deserved," Doyle allegedly admitted.

Dellaria didn't show up for a second scheduled interview with the detective. Doyle had gone after Dellaria for betraying him. The first time, Doyle locked Dellaria in the trunk of a car, but a motorcycle gang member pulled Doyle away from any further aggression, and let Dellaria out of the trunk. The second time, Doyle turned his mother's two large dogs on the snitch, wrestled Dellaria to the ground, and held a knife to his throat. The squealer rolled out from under the blade.

In the spring 1982, Doyle was drunk again at the Cardinales Nest Bar. This time he got into a fight with some girl. After she left, an East Boston resident, Michael DeLisi, recognized Doyle and sat down with him. Doyle told DeLisi he was mad at a guy who told the Saugus Police he had killed Marie.

According to DeLisi's account of what Doyle had told him, Marie called Doyle at home from the bar hours before she was murdered. He told her to come home, but she wasn't ready. He stealthily waited outside for the bar to close. Marie came out alone, and the strained couple got into another fight. They went back to their third floor apartment and continued arguing. Marie wanted to go back out, but Doyle stopped her. At first, Doyle thought she passed out, but he realized she was dead when she didn't move or breathe. Doyle panicked and decided not to call the cops. He thought about discarding the body at the dump but settled on the secluded area behind the shuttered Conley & Daggett Company. Now we had another witness implicating David Doyle as the offender.

ట

In addition to the original one consulted by Jack McEwan early in the case, other psychics offered their visions. One seer convinced the Beverly Police to search Wenham Pond in Hamilton, Massachusetts for Joan Webster's body. Joan's destination was Cambridge, but the clairvoyant envisioned a spot farther north. The location, about 25 miles north of the airport, seemed off track. Recovered items had turned up much further south and west. The clam digger had fished Joan's purse and wallet out of the Saugus marshes. A baggage handler at the bus terminal in Boston had recognized Joan's name on the tag of her unclaimed suitcase after 60 days. The fire that raged in Lynn, Massachusetts on November 28, 1981, blocked a direct path from point A at the airport to point B, the small community of Hamilton, Massachusetts. The premonition seemed like a long shot, but teams scoured the area anyway before giving up without any clues to Joan's whereabouts.

ట

The state police finally submitted Joan's suitcase and purse to the FBI for inspection the first week of July 1982. The delay contradicted the urgency authorities represented to the public. The FBI lab collected fingerprints and carefully catalogued the contents of the undisturbed suitcase. The luggage contained Joan's clothing, underwear, and accessories like scarfs, headbands, stockings, and belts. Joan had attached her sorority pin to the lining. She had also packed bed sheets, 45 photographs of the last summer vacation in Nantucket, and a single green sock to take back to school. Nothing appeared amiss or promised a possible clue. Joan had worn brown boots and tossed gray shoes in the tote bag; the FBI lab listed no footwear in Joan's recovered belongings.

The purse contained Joan's identification and makeup. Joan's family confirmed she had cash, but the offender apparently snatched the money and left her checkbook and credit cards. The lab techs skimmed over a couple of business cards tucked in Joan's wallet without recording a handwritten inscription on one of the cards. The Saugus Police recorded the clue when they interviewed the man who found the wallet in the Saugus marsh. But they overlooked the significance of the caption. A business card alone was innocuous, but the memo added an unusual element for an independent young woman to stick in her wallet.

The missing grad student's tote bag still hadn't turned up. Joan's sister Anne listed the items contained in the bag, and Burke circulated them in the press.

☙

Meanwhile, the state continued to stalk Lenny Paradiso. On July 4, 1982, Palombo watched his quarry pull up to the dock at the Beachmont Yacht Club from a distance. The shellfish peddler skippered a green motorboat, his latest vessel. Two days later, Andrew Palombo knocked on the front door of Candy Weyant's home where she lived with her parents in Revere, Massachusetts. At the time, Paradiso was still living there. The officer had directed his associates to stake out the property in case the target tried to bolt. Candy answered the door. Paradiso came downstairs and was arrested without incident for the murder of Marie Iannuzzi. The underlying motive remained a *secret*.

Police locked Paradiso up at the Charles Street Jail. In the next three weeks, authorities scoured Paradiso's parole records while Palombo searched records at the Motor Vehicle Registry and the Registry of Motor Boats.. The family dentist in New Jersey sent a copy of Joan's dental records.

Marie Iannuzzi's stepsister Jean Day had been receiving harassing phone calls warning her not to talk. That same summer 1982, an intruder broke down her door, kicked and assaulted her, and left her with a broken bone in her face. The stepsister, now a victim herself, went into hiding. Her grand jury testimony had implicated Marie's boyfriend, and any witness who threatened Burke's pursuit of Paradiso was at risk.

On August 1, 1982, Lenny Paradiso had a visitor from the old neighborhood. "Buster" was Carmen Tammaro's nickname growing up in the North End. He arrived in street clothes and took a friendly posture with his old rival. A lot of water had passed under the bridge since the two men pushed their carts during the feasts of patron saints. One was sitting in jail accused of murder, and the other was a ranking officer with the state police. Tammaro glanced around the cell and noticed pictures on the wall of Paradiso's boats. Paradiso listened with caution.

"I hear you took the Webster girl out on your boat and killed her," Tammaro said. "You threw her overboard. I hear you painted the hull white and kept the boat."

Even Paradiso, with an eighth grade education, suspected a sting. After listening to Tammaro, he realized cops had arrested him for the Iannuzzi murder only to set him up for the Webster case. Buster impugned Paradiso for his friendship with the Angiulo brothers, the sons of a Mafia boss operating out of the North End. Then Tammaro became part of the corrupt system in Boston, where there was a problem with authorities leaking information.

"The Angiulos and a lot of other guys in the North End are going to be arrested," Tammaro disclosed. "They're being watched. There's a camera in an air conditioner above the Roma Pharmacy watching the Angiulos' house. They're bugging him."

"So what?" Lenny said. "Whatever they say may be nothing at all."

"When they get through with the tapes, the Feds will make it sound different," Buster continued. "They can splice in and cut what they want."

Paradiso heeded his lawyer's advice to document everything. He was unaware of the anonymous caller from the North End who'd implicated him for Marie's murder and Joan's disappearance, but Tammaro had just accused him of murdering Joan to his face. Authorities still kept their speculations *secret* waiting for the right time to break the news to the public.

℘

On October 12, 1982, the Websters held a press conference announcing an increase in the reward for information. One reporter observed the couple's attention to detail. They handed out photos for news outlets not present for the announcement. Pictures of the couple, taken in advance, showed their somber faces holding a poster offering $25,000 for information leading to an arrest and $50,000 for information leading to a conviction. The preplanned photo showed them in the same attire they wore for the press conference. The savvy couple didn't miss a detail down to George's Brooks Brothers striped tie and the pin on Eleanor's lapel.

The appeal got results two days later. A man called the Websters and said Joan was alive. He told them he would call back later that night with instructions. George alerted the Glen Ridge Police and the Newark office of the FBI. A group gathered at the house and waited. The caller never called back that night, and the dedicated public servants went home. The phone rang again early the next morning. George kept the man on the line while Eleanor ran to the neighbor's house to call the police. For some unexplained reason, she avoided using the second line upstairs in George's study. The caller wanted the reward money, but no strings attached tying him to Joan. George agreed to a meeting in front of the State House in Concord, New Hampshire. The trap on the Websters' home phone traced the call to a payphone outside a laundromat north of the Massachusetts state line. Local agents staked out the business and identified a known felon making the calls. Back in Glen Ridge, the team put a plan in place, and the group ordered a car to take them to the airport. The New Jersey squad agreed that an agent from the Newark office would pose as George's cousin and accompany him to the rendezvous.

When they landed, the local FBI had a car ready, wired, and waiting. Next, agents put a bug on George. Special Agent Frank Barletto was the designated cousin, and he rode with George to the New Hampshire State House to meet the extortion caller. George, Barletto, and the extortion caller started driving, with federal agents listening to every word. The trio crossed state lines headed for Boston. In the end, the known felon, Harvey Martel, had nothing to do with Joan, gave a bogus address in Boston, and earned himself a free ride to the Boston office of the FBI. Martel was interrogated and fingerprinted, but strangely authorities let him walk.

This incident was another demonstration of the controlled handling of information in Joan's case. None of the extortion episodes ever made it into the papers. The Massachusetts State Police running the investigation didn't have the reports either. However, the Martel extortion incident reached the eyes on the seventh floor of FBI Headquarters in Washington, D.C. FBI Director William H. Webster initialed the report himself. Immediate family knew about the dramatic event after it was over. Ten days later, the Websters received another call claiming Joan was alive and being held in Maine. That lead didn't pan out either.

The events swung wildly between the Zodiac theory, psychic visions, and dramatic extortion attempts. The emotional rollercoaster triggered a second miscarriage for Steve's wife.

❧

The Boston office of the FBI submitted Paradiso's fingerprints to their labs for a comparison in Joan's case on November 5, 1982. The report came back on November 24, 1982: *no* match. The exculpatory evidence didn't deter Burke or Palombo from chasing the object of their obsession. A providential murder trial of Robert Bond was on the court's docket in Boston for December 9, 1982. The timing presented the inner circle on Joan's case with a golden opportunity to force their pieces to fit.

The case on the docket charged convicted killer Bond with his second murder, this time for the death of community activist Mary Foreman. Authorities transferred Bond to the Charles Street Jail for his trial. The prisoner's move set the stage and positioned a conduit to sell the state's story.

The investigative team had waited patiently for the right opportunity. A killer facing his second murder trial was a willing tool for authorities. But control of the operation originated out of state. George's liaison Jack McEwan asked Detective Tom Dugan in New Jersey to hold a date to meet with the Websters' private investigator. The date coincided with Bond's transfer to the same lock-up as Leonard Paradiso, the secretly targeted suspect for Joan's disappearance.

POLICE OFFICER'S RE.....T SUPPLEMENT

	RECORD #	INC CODE 01	LOC ODE 10
25 of 36	ARREST # A	☐ SUPPLEMENTAL REPORT ☐ FOLLOW UP REPORT	

INCIDENT Homicide (MURDER)		LOCATION Rear Conly & Daggetts		DATE 8-6-81
PRINCIPAL PARTY'S (OR FIRM S) NAME · LAST, FIRST INITIAL Ianuzzi Marie Barbara		ADDRESS 39 White St., East Boston		PHONE

PROPERTY·TYPE	M'G OR TRADE NAME	MATERIAL	SIZE	I D OR SERIAL NO	PRES VALUE $	HOW ESTABLISHE
TYPE	MFG OR TRADE NAME	MATERIAL	SIZE	I D OF SERIAL NO	PRES VALUE $	HOW ESTABLISHE

REPORT

Addendum:

On August 12,1979, information was received that a female body was at the rear of the Conly & Daggetts Lobster Co.,on Rte.#107. Myself and Insp. Arthur Cook responded and observed a young female clad in a red disco type dress over the embankment, partially in the water.(See initial reports.)

During the latter part of June 1981 and early July 1981, I started receiving information from informants in East Boston that the boyfriend of the victim Marie Ianuzzi. Information was that he was now being bothered by his conscience then drinking and doing drugs.

My informant also told me that one David A. Dellaria, of 249 Everett Street, East Boston, DOB 4-21-46, is telling several persons that David Doyle told him how and why he killed Marie Ianuzzi.

I contacted Det. Charlie Gleason of Dist. #7, and told him of my informant and asked if he would approach Dellaria and tell him that I was considering speaking to him and what info I had. Charlie did talk with David and he told Gleason that David Doyle did talk when he was drinking.

On July 16,1981, with Insp. James Stoddard, went to Dist. #7, picked up Det. Gleason and then drove to Jeffreys Point where Dellaria hung around. We picked him up, and I immediately informed him of his rights, (See Miranda Card signed by David Dellaria.) David told me that he did not want to talk at that location, and asked us to drive to the old abandoned Football Stadium, under the overpass, in East Boston. I again informed of his rights, and asked him what David Doyle had said to him relative to the Ianuzzi Homicide. He stated that Doyle told him that she deserved what she got, and Fuck Her, she did me wrong. I asked him if he knew the details, of the murder step by step, and he said that he did. He stated however that this was heavy on him and David Doyle was a good friend of his and he wanted to protect him. I reiterated to him that he could be an Accessory After the Fact to Murder, and he stated that he would give us a statement to the entire details of the murders told to him by Doyle but he wanted a chance to think about it. He then told me that he had other problems, that he was receiving death threats by a man named Forti of East Boston a member of the Trampers M.C. Club. Twice more I asked him if he knew the whole story of the murder and he said he did.

(Continued)

☐ CONTINUED ☒ OTHER ☐ SUPPLEMENT

STATUS	I HEREBY CERTIFY THAT THE CONTENTS OF THIS REPORT ARE TRUE AND CORRECT TO THE BEST OF MY KNOWLEDGE AND BELIEF Insp. Howard W. Long	COMPLAINANTS SIGNATURE
ACTIVE INACTIVE UNFOUNDED CLEARED	[signature] REPORTING OFFICER	FURTHER ACTION (PURGE INFO)
		COPIES TO

Boston Police Marie Iannuzzi Report (pg. 1)

POLICE OFFICER'S REPORT SUPPLEMENT

		RECORD #		IND CODE	GEOCODE
		—	—	01	10
		ARREST #		☐ SUPPLEMENTAL REPORT	
5 of 36		A —	—	☐ FOLLOW UP REPORT	

INCIDENT			LOCATION		DATE OF THIS REPORT
Homicide (Murder)			Rear Cooly & Daggetts		8-6-81
PRINCIPAL PARTY'S (OR FIRM'S) NAME - LAST, FIRST, INITIAL			ADDRESS		PHONE
Ianuzzi Marie Barbara			39 White Street, East Boston		

PROPERTY-TYPE	MFG OR TRADE NAME	MATERIAL	SIZE	I.D. OR SERIAL NO	PRES. VALUE	HOW ESTABLISH
					$	
TYPE	MFG OR TRADE NAME	MATERIAL	SIZE	I.D OR SERIAL NO	PRES. VALUE	HOW ESTABLISH
					$	

REPORT

Arrangments were made to meet with Dellaria and Det. Gleason at my office on July 19, 1981, and he agreed to give us an an indepth account of the murd as told to him by David Doyle. Dellaria did not show, and dropped out of si

Other Facts To Be Considered:

1. After Identification of the body, David Doyle came to my office with the victims father. He had visable scratches of his face and hands. that he stated he had received by a cat. Later his mother told invest igators he had got them when involved in a car accident.

2. Marie Ianuzzi's bags were all packed before I.D. of the body. (They were living together at his mothers.)

3. Joanne Day, sister in law to victim states now that she had observed blood on the fifth step leading to David Doyles apartment.

4. Two persons will testify that David Doyle had straggled Marie Ianuzz two months prior to her death. They saw purple straggulation marks on her throat. Christine, Girlfriend.

5. David Doyle took off for parts unknown after funeral, later arrested in New Jersey, with stolen Airline Tickets Etc.

Additional reports to follow as received.

				CONTINUED
				☐ OVER
				☐ SUPPLEMENT
STATUS	I HEREBY CERTIFY THAT THE CONTENTS OF THIS REPORT ARE TRUE AND CORRECT TO THE BEST OF MY KNOWLEDGE AND BELIEF		COMPLAINANT'S SIGNATURE	
☒ ACTIVE				
☐ INACTIVE	REPORTING OFFICER	SECOND OFFICER	FURTHER ACTION (PUBLIC INFO.)	
☐ UNFOUNDED				

Boston Police Marie Iannuzzi Report (pg. 2)

My Name is Michael Delisi I lived in Jeffries Point E.B. all my life.
In the late Part of the spring of 1982, I was down the Cordivia - next
Guy I knew Name David Doyle was there with some girl. he
got into a Beaf with her, after she left, Doyle and me sat together
Doyle was Drunk, and Started to tell me, he was mad at a guy
name Dave Dalenia, for telling the Police I told him, I killed
my girl Marie Iorizzie, Doyle told me he try to kill Delian
couple of times since then. Doyle was getting Burned out
he Started telling me how he killed his girl Marie, and why he
said Marie was fucking around on him; they went to a wedding
that day and got into a fight, later on Marie went to a house Party
later on that night she called him up at home, from the
bar, Doyle told her to Come home, she said when she was ready
apple was waiting for her. when the place close, Marie come
at alone, she was Drunk, they got into a fight outside the next
floor, that they went Back to Doyle apt, Marie wanted to change
and go out again they got into another fight again, this time he
strangel her with her scarf at first he said he though she
just Passed out. But Realize she was Dead, when she did not move or
Breath, Doyle said he was going to call the cops at first But was afaid to
he was fucked up on Dust and Us Doyle Did not want to dump her body,
S. he was going to dump her in the Pigns dump. But Something int to way
he dumped her where she was found. Doyle Said he could not Believe he
Illed her, it happen so fast, Dayl Said alot of People think I killed him. or know
no one is saying anything, What I am saying is the truth and I am willing
To take a Lie Detector test. Michael J. Delisi Jr.

Michael DeLisi Letter

Sergeant Carmen Tammaro
Photo Credit Getty Images

Page (1)   8/2/82

Hi Jimmy, I in Still Keeping Notes on what you said
Carmen (Buster) Tammaro was up to see Me yesterday
He Seemed to have Wanted to talk about Webster, Im
Starting to get the Idea, I did not get arrested for the
Ianuzzi Murder, But there trying to Set Me up, on this
Webster Case, Jimmy, I don't Know Shit about this Webster
Matter, I let Tammaro talk, he Said, he hear, I took
Webster out on My Boat Killed her and threw her over
Boord, I did not Say nothing to him, I Just listen to
Him talk, Jimmy, You Know, My Boat Was gone in July
of 81, I filed a Claim With the Insurance Company, I also
filed, a Police Report, when I found the Boat Was
issing, then Tammaro Said, I hear you Painted the
Hull White, But Kept the Boat where the fuck is
he camming up With this Shit, Jimmy When I was called
Before the Grand Jury, tim Burke wanted Me to
Testerfide aginst Doly Doyle I Refused to go Before
the Grand Jury, I did not Want to Become Involed
In this Case, So Doyle trys to Put this ane on Me
Doyle own Cousin, Said he Killed his girl, I told
his Cousin, Jimmy, I don't Want to Know Nothing
Keep me out of It anyway Tammaro Starts to come
with this off the Wall Shit, he Says I was Friendly
With Anthany Anko Anguilo I Said So What
he was My friend, Tammaro Said you like the
Anguilo Brothers, I Said ya Why, there Good

Leonard Paradiso Letter to Jimmy (pg. 1)

guys, So Buster Starts to tell Me, the Anguilos and
a lot of other guys in the North End, are going to Be
Getting arrested, there Being Watch, he even said
they had a camera in an air conditioner above
the Roma Phonoy, facing down toward Prince
Street, Watching Anguilos house, he Said to Me
there Bugging, his Store or Place, I don't Know
which Joint he Ment; Sod Said. So What, he Said
What do you Mean, Tammaro says to me, I Said
what ever they Say Maybe nothing at all, So
Tammaro Says, When they get though with
the Taps, the Feds Will Make it Sound
different, they Can Splice in and cut what they
went, So I tell Tammaro your Suppose to
Be a North End guy and your Italian Why
don't you tip them off, he Say, fuck them guys
I hate them, there Scum, So He says he was
Involved with the Investigation against thos
guys. I don't Know if I Should Believe him
or not. Maybe I Should try to get word out to
Someone in the N. End But then if I'm wrong
I'll look like a Real asshole, Why Start a
Panic, Anyway we Can get Back to that at
a nother time, he Stayed for a While, he kept
asking me a lot of Questions, he said who
Killed Webster, If I admitted I did it he

Leonard Paradiso Letter to Jimmy (pg. 2)

Page (3)

could get me a good deal, I kept telling him
I don't know anything about Webster and I didn't
Kill Mary Ianuzzi, But he kept asking me
questions, like where did I go with my Boat
why did I call it Malafemmina, things like
that, I knew he was fishing around for information.
So Between him, and what you tell me about
Webster, and the questions Burke is asking
It Points like they suspect me in her disappearance
whats the Big deal With this Webster girl, whos
to say she didn't Run off with Some guy or
maybe she was on drugs, who the fuck knows
with these Rich People, what they do. anyway I think
one of those Irish Mother fuckers down at Beachmont
yacht club, is try to Put the Punch to me. I don't
trust Tammoro. the Guys tell me if they
have to Frame Angiulo to convict him to
Put him and his Crowed away for a long time
what am I Suppose to think, he come
up in Regular cloths. the Punk Just try to
find out whats going on, I keep Writing down
what ever I can Remember, like you told me.
I Still don't know why the fuck they arrested
me for This, its Bullshit you know this
yourself, I let you know what else happens
okay, take it easy.
                                    Lenny

Leonard Paradiso Letter to Jimmy (pg. 3)

Second Reward Poster

BS0007 2921900Z

OO HQ NK

DE BS

O 191805Z OCT 82

FM BOSTON (62D-5738)

TO DIRECTOR (62-119655) IMMEDIATE

NEWARK (7A-1505) IMMEDIATE

BT

UNCLAS

UNSUB; JOAN WEBSTER - VICTIM, DOMESTIC POLICE COOPERATION,
OO:BS.

FOR THE INFORMATION OF THE BUREAU, ON OCTOBER 14, 1982,
VICTIM'S FATHER RECEIVED TELEPHONE CALL FROM AN UNKNOWN
INDIVIDUAL INDICATING HE KNEW LOCATION OF HIS DAUGHTER WHO
WAS UNDER HEAVY SEDATION AND WOULD NEED PSYCHIATRIC CARE,
HOWEVER WAS STILL ALIVE. UNKNOWN INDIVIDUAL INDICATED HE
WOULD RETURN TELEPHONE CALL AT 6 PM, OCTOBER 14, 1982 OR
EARLY AM, OCTOBER 15, 1982. AT 7:30 AM, OCTOBER 15, 1982,
UNKNOWN INDIVIDUAL RETURNED CALL TO VICTIM'S
AND INDICATED HE HAD SEEN VICTIM IN JUNE OF 1982 AND
ON TUESDAY EVENING, OCTOBER 12, 1982 WHEN FATHER APPEALED TO

FBI Extortion Incident Report (pg. 1)

b6
b7C

PAGE TWO BS 62D 5738 UNCLAS

TELEVISION AUDIENCE FOR INFORMATION LEADING TO LOCATION OF
DAUGHTER UNKNOWN INDIVIDUAL STATED HE WAS WITH THE VICTIM.
UNKNOWN STATED HE WANTED A LETTER AUTHORIZING HIS RECEIVING
$25,000 REWARD FOR HIS INFORMATION LEADING TO THE LOCATION
OF HIS DAUGHTER IN EXCHANGE FOR HER PRESENT LOCATION.

DURING ABOVE CONVERSATION, CALL TRACED TO CONCORD, N.H.
LOCAL POLICE AND FBI, CONCORD, N.H. DETERMINED LOCATION OF
TELEPHONE BOOTH WHERE CALL ORIGINATED. LOCATION WAS A
LAUNDRAMAT ON FISHERVILLE RD., CONCORD, N.H. SURVEILLANCE
INSTITUTED AT LAUNDRAMAT AND AT 10:11 AM, ON OCTOBER 15, 1982,
UNKNOWN INDIVIDUAL OBSERVED AT LAUNDRAMAT MAKING A TELEPHONE
CALL. THIS CALL TRACED FROM VICTIM'S FATHER'S RESIDENCE TO
LAUNDRAMAT AND UNKNOWN INDIVIDUAL IDENTIFIED AS A LOCAL
RESIDENT,   FBI NO. 787824B,
A KNOWN FELON.   ARRESTED 1969 FOR KIDNAPPING AND
SUBSEQUENTLY ON NUMEROUS OTHER CHARGES. DURING THE CONVERSATION,
          ARRANGED THE MEETING WITH VICTIM'S FATHER FOR 3 TO 5 PM
IN FRONT OF THE STATE HOUSE, CONCORD, N.H. VICTIM'S FATHER,
SECURITY OFFICER WITH INTERNATIONAL TELEPHONE AND TELEGRAPH, (ITT),

FBI Extortion Incident Report (pg. 2)

80

PAGE THREE BS 62D-5738 UNCLAS

THE VICTIM'S FATHER'S EMPLOYEE, TWO LOCAL POLICE OFFICERS

AND SPECIAL AGENT [   ] WITH THE FBI NEWARK, N.J.

FLEW TO CONCORD, N.H. USA W. STEPHEN THAYER ADVISED OF

ABOVE INFORMATION AND MET WITH THE VICTIM'S FATHER. USA THAYER

ADVISED NO VIOLATION OF FEDERAL LAW AT THIS TIME DUE TO THE

FACT NO DEMAND FOR MONEY HAD BEEN MADE BY [   ]

THE MEETING BETWEEN VICTIM'S FATHER ACCOMPANIED BY

SPECIAL AGENT [   ] POSING AS MR. WEBSTER'S COUSIN TOOK

PLACE AT APPROXIMATELY 4 PM, OCTOBER 15, 1982. MEETING

OBSERVED BY SPECIAL AGENTS OF THE FBI AND LOCAL AUTHORITIES.

VICTIM AND VEHICLE WIRED. VICTIM'S FATHER, S[   ] AND

[   ] PROCEEDED TO BOSTON, MASS. AFTER [   ] PROVIDED

INFORMATION STATING THE DAUGHTER WAS LOCATED IN THAT CITY.

TRAVEL TO BOSTON, MASS SURVEILLED BY SPECIAL AGENTS OF THE

FBI. [   ] PROVIDED ADDRESS WHEN ARRIVING IN BOSTON, MASS.

WHICH PROVED IRONEOUS AND [   ] INTERVIEWED AT BOSTON OFFICE

OF THE FBI.

AUSA [   ] BOSTON, MASS. AND USA W. STEPHEN THAYER

DECLINED PROSECUTION ON [   ] DUE TO THE FACT NO DEMAND MADE

FBI Extortion Incident Report (pg. 3)

PAGE FOUR BS 62D-5738 UNCLAS

AND NO OTHER FEDERAL VIOLATED BY [ ]

BT

b6
b7C

FBI Extortion Incident Report (pg. 4)

6-147 (1-14-81)   **CRIMINAL INVESTIGATIVE DIVISION**

b6
b7C

INFORMATIVE NOTE

Date ___10/20/82___

Re:
UNSUB;
JOAN WEBSTER - VICTIM;
DOMESTIC POLICE COOPERATION
OO: BOSTON

By way of background, victim disappeared on
or about 12/5/81 while enroute from her residence
in New Jersey to Smith College and Howard School
of Design, Boston, Massachusetts. Local law
enforcement has conducted investigation which
indicates victim was last seen at Logan International Airport, Boston, Massachusetts. Her
purse was found in a marsh north of Boston.
Investigation also has identified at least four
or five boyfriends of victim.

Attached teletype from Boston advises of
investigation conducted in attempts to locate
Joan Webster. Miss Webster's whereabouts
remain unknown.

On 10/14/82, [   ]
received a telephone call from an unknown male
who indicated he (unknown male) knew where Joan
Webster was located.

On 10/15/82, the unknown male again called
victim's father. This call was traced to a
laundromat in Concord, New Hampshire. Surveillance instituted at laundromat and subsequent investigation revealed the identity
of the unknown male to be [   ]
[   ] advised victim's father that he had
seen victim in June of 1982 and on 10/12/82.
[   ] wanted a reward of $25,000 for infor-
mation leading to the location of victim.
[   ] arranged a meeting with victim's
father for later that same day.

1 - [   ]   1 - Mr. Revell
1 - [   ]   1 - [   ]
1 - [   ]
PMM/RDW:mrb/jey   CONTINUED - OVER

FBI/DOJ

FBI Extortion Summary to the Director (pg. 1)

b6
b7C

On 10/15/82, the meeting between victim's father accompanied by a Special Agent of the FBI, posing as Mr. Webster's cousin, took place. ☐ provided an address in Boston where victim could be found; however, this address proved to be erroneous.

☐ was subsequently interviewed by the FBI. ☐ refused to answer any questions or make any statements about this matter during the interview.

U.S. Attorney, Boston declined prosecution on ☐ due to the fact no demand made and no other Federal laws were violated. ☐ is a known felon. ☐ was arrested in 1969 for kidnapping and subsequently on numerous other charges.

APPROVED:

Director	Adm. Servs.	Laboratory
Exec. AD-Adm.	Crim. Inv.	Legal Coun.
Exec./AD-Inv.	Ident.	Off. of Cong. & Public Affs.
Asso. AD-LES	Inspection	Rec. Mgnt.
	Intell.	Tech. Servs.
		Training

-2-

FBI Extortion Summary to the Director (pg. 2)

D-38 (Rev. 5-22-78)

FBI

TRANSMIT VIA:
☐ Teletype
☐ Facsimile
☐ Airtel

PRECEDENCE:
☐ Immediate
☐ Priority
☐ Routine

CLASSIFICATION:
☐ TOP SECRET
☐ SECRET
☐ CONFIDENTIAL
☐ UNCLAS E F T O
☐ UNCLAS

Date ___11/5/82___

TO   : DIRECTOR, FBI (62-119655)
          (ATTN: IDENTIFICATION DIVISION
          LATENT FINGERPRINT SECTION)

FROM   : SAC, BOSTON (62D-5738)(P)

SUBJECT: UNSUB;
         JOAN WEBSTER—VICTIM
         DPC
         OO: BS

Re Latent Fingerprint Case C-13738.

Identification Division, Latent Fingerprint Section is requested to compare latent fingerprint in this case with any known fingerprints for Leonard J. Paradiso, white male, date of birth December 8, 1942.

b6
b7C

62-119655—12

16 NOV 1982

2-Bureau
2-Boston

GHB/mw
(4)

62-119655

Approved: _____   Transmitted _____   Per _____
                                        (Number)   (Time)

U.S. GOVERNMENT PRINTING OFFICE : 1982 O - 385

Fingerprint Results for Leonard Paradiso (pg. 1)

(Rv. 10-06-79)

FEDERAL BUREAU OF INVESTIGATION
Washington, D. C. 20537

REPORT
of the
LATENT FINGERPRINT SECTION
IDENTIFICATION DIVISION

YOUR FILE NO.   62D-5738 (P)
FBI FILE NO.   62-119655
LATENT CASE NO.   C-13738

November 24, 1982

TO: SAC; Boston

RE: UNSUB;
JOAN WEBSTER - VICTIM
DFC

REFERENCE: Airtel 11/5/82
EXAMINATION REQUESTED BY: Boston
SPECIMENS:

     The previously reported latent fingerprint in this case is not a fingerprint of Leonard J. Paradiso, FBI #26759E.

PVM:dbw
(4)

62-119655 - 13

23 NOV 30 1982

NOV 24 1982
FBI

MAIL ROOM

Fingerprint Results for Leonard Paradiso (pg. 2)

Chapter Nine
The Snitch

The Department of Corrections transport van pulled up outside the Charles Street Jail on December 8, 1982. Officers led the shackled and cuffed prisoner inside to check in. The department transferred Robert Bond, the burly, convicted killer, from Walpole Prison for another murder trial beginning the next day. Cell door number 68 on the third tier slammed shut behind him.

Bond had a history of abusing women. Beating his wife Willie Mae didn't satiate his depravity; he prowled outside his marriage. A jury had convicted him for the 1971 stabbing death of his pregnant girlfriend Barbara Mitchell. In 1975, the imposing man lifted weights at Walpole with Paradiso while Paradiso served time for an assault conviction. The two men resided in the same block, but Paradiso never confided the reason for his confinement.

Massachusetts ran a lenient furlough program for prisoners, and Bond benefited from the experiment critics called a revolving door. During one of his state-sanctioned social outings, Bond met his next victim, a community activist with six children. Bond didn't like confinement and opted to shorten his own sentence after the approved leave. He failed to report back to prison. After his extended taste of freedom, authorities locked him back up. Despite the killer's propensity for breaking the law, the Massachusetts Parole Board granted his petition in 1981, and returned a dangerous man back out on the streets of Boston.

Bond maneuvered his victim to the basement of a drug dealer's house, a reflection of the bad company he kept. He shot the beloved woman point blank through the temple on October 23, 1981. During Mary Foreman's funeral, Bond rode around outside the service waving a gun, and threatened the rest of the family that he would kill them too. Not surprising, he lied to the police and claimed he hadn't seen his victim the day she was shot, but the evidence was strong. Police arrested Bond on November 20, 1981. He faced some serious time tacked on to his current sentence for murder.

Paradiso was not at the Charles Street Jail when Bond arrived. Overcrowding conditions had forced a temporary transfer earlier in the month. Corrections officials checked Paradiso back into the Charles Street Jail on December 8, 1982, and shut the door behind him in cell number 36. Guards locked down the facility that day because of a disturbance. All of the inmates were confined to their own cells; Bond and Paradiso were floors apart. It's doubtful the two men even knew the other was there. The keeper unlocked Bond's door and repositioned him in cell number 31, in close proximity to the state's target. Every time the cell doors opened, Bond latched on to Paradiso and the prodding began. Behind the scenes, however, wheels were in motion with a scheduled meeting in New Jersey with a Webster investigator.

That same week, on December 12, 1982, Andrew Palombo followed two young women at Logan Airport returning home from a concert. When the startled women turned to confront the stranger tailing them, the undercover cop showed them his badge. He gained their confidence and offered a ride. Andrew Palombo dropped off the first young lady in Quincy, Massachusetts. Now Paradiso's estranged daughter was alone in the car with Palombo, and the conversation made her nervous. The encounter was no coincidence. Palombo wasn't a good public servant, offering rides to save young travelers cab fare. He was an undercover cop digging up dirt and building a case against her father.

"He kills women that remind him of you," Palombo shamed Paradiso's daughter. "I'm going to put him away for a very long time."

The next day, Bond stood and faced the jury. The verdict was guilty. Bond smiled broadly and put his hands on his hips. He seemed confident his plight would improve. The customary protocol was for the court to remand a convicted felon back to prison right away. This violent offender should have gone back to Walpole, but authorities didn't follow standard procedures. Bond returned to the Charles Street Jail, close to Paradiso, for two more weeks. On December 29, 1982, the Department of Corrections finally transferred Bond to another institution in Concord, Massachusetts. On January 10, 1983, Bond faced the judge again to hear his sentence.

After the judge imposed his penalty, Bond waited in the holding cell at the courthouse. As he sat there, the twice convicted felon had a visit from the state police. He learned that a guy from New Jersey, George Webster, had sent people to see him. The conversation turned to Marie Iannuzzi, Joan Webster, and Leonard Paradiso. Carmen Tammaro dangled the Webster reward money in front of the condemned man right after the judge had just added years to his debt. Back at Concord, the menace to society put pen to paper and drafted a letter. He wrote it in two separate parts, one detailing accusations for Marie's murder, and the other alleging Joan's fate. He placed the two letters in an inner envelope addressed to prosecutor Tim Burke in Suffolk County, and then addressed the outer envelope to his wife. This level of calculation exceeded the capacity of the offender's ability to scheme, but the two-part letter was advantageous to an overzealous lawyer making a case. Bond placed the letter in the mail from Concord on January 10, 1983.

Three days later, all eyes fixed on Robert Bond in a small room at the courthouse. Sergeant Tammaro closed the door and turned on the tape recorder before questioning the informant. At times,

Tammaro struggled to keep his snitch on track discussing the two cases. Bond knew the general facts in Marie's case, information already in police files. However, he contradicted eyewitness reports and claimed Paradiso drove Marie to the Cardinales Nest Bar. In Bond's version of events, Paradiso dropped Marie at the bar and then drove his girlfriend home. According to Bond, Paradiso raced back to the bar to hustle Marie. Then Tammaro turned his attention to Joan's case. Bond had a harder time with the details.

"Like, at first, he told me he strangled her, Joan Webster," Bond struggled to remember. "The last thing he told me, he did it with a whiskey bottle. So you can pick or choose whatever fuckin' one you want."

After considerable coaching, Bond regurgitated the same boat scenario that Tammaro had suggested five months before. The snitch spewing the same story the interrogating officer suggested when he visited Paradiso was either an incredible coincidence or no coincidence at all. The same officer who planted the seeds of the boat allegation tutored a witness who had a hard time keeping his stories straight. Bond was confused about what happened, either the state police visited Paradiso three weeks after Paradiso's arrest, or Paradiso tossed Joan's belongings on the Lynn Marsh Road three weeks after he allegedly killed her. The police knew the correct answer to both.

During the interview, Tammaro even got Bond to describe pictures of the boats tacked on Paradiso's cell wall, a visual aid adding details of the alleged crime scene of Joan's presumed murder. The state's star witness struggled with the location where Paradiso had previously moored his boat, and revealed the cops as his source of information.

"I'm going to say Pier 7. That's where he kept his boat," Bond offered. "If he didn't, that's on you guys. I don't know and I don't really care where he kept his boat."

Tammaro made it clear the officers expected Bond's letter, but no letter arrived before the taped interview. The willing snitch checked with the sentry at Concord the night before the inquest. Carter, the prison guard, reminded the inmate it had only been three days since he had mailed it; he didn't think Bond had much of a gripe. Bond called his family from the small room at the courthouse and instructed them to give Tammaro and his partner the letter when it arrived.

Tammaro introduced the other interrogators in attendance for Bond's recitation, which included Trooper Andrew Palombo, Corporal Jack O'Rourke, Sergeant Robert Hudson of the Boston Police, and corrections officer John Gillen, who all heard the harrowing stories. Later, other witnesses filled in the gaps of the proposed crime, but Bond handed them the framework to build on.

Bond alleged that Paradiso picked Joan up at the airport at 10:30 p.m. driving a gypsy cab. The story contradicted the eyewitness reports secreted in the Massachusetts State Police files. Paradiso supposedly bragged to Bond about killing Joan Webster on his boat. Bond saw the pictures of Paradiso's vessels tacked on the cell wall. The pictures showed liquor bottles visible on the shelf in the cabin that suggested the weapon. According to Tammaro's conduit, Paradiso got Joan on his boat, mixed a couple of drinks, and made a pass. The accusations ignored the facts. Any boat still in the water in late November would bang against its mooring on the dark, cold, blustery night, hardly a romantic setting for Paradiso's alleged advances. The scenario exposed one of the state's problems, explaining how Paradiso got the sophisticated young lady onboard in the first place. The only thing that made any sense was Joan rejecting a proposition that would not even entice a dead fish.

"Then, what happened?" Tammaro prodded.

"That's when he hit her," Bond answered. "She had a hole right here from the whiskey bottle."

Bond gestured with his right hand and pointed to the right side of his head. He described a lot of blood all over the boat and all over

Paradiso. The questions established the alleged order of events in Bond's mind. According to Bond, Paradiso hit Joan first and then had sex with her.

"All right, he fucked her," the sergeant continued. "Then what happened?"

"He took the boat way out and dumped the body," the dimwitted witness explained. "Then he brought the boat back to Pier 7."

Bond had inserted a troubling detail. The snitch maintained that his source of information was Leonard Paradiso, confidentially confessing every sordid detail of his sins. But the state's tool relayed a fact *only* known to the police and the Websters: someone saw Joan at the airport, and that secret remained locked in the files.

Bond repeated the alleged comment from Paradiso, "They [the police] said she was seen getting in a cab at the airport."

Bond announced that Paradiso had confessed all the horrors of two murders. According to the state's snitch, the con came forward because he didn't want to see David Doyle, a man Bond didn't know, get jammed for Marie's murder. The second case was just a bonus and conveniently tied up two cases handled by Andrew Palombo. The insinuated murder of Joan Webster, still guarded by the inner circle of the grad student's investigation, was mortifying. The police detected another fly in the ointment convincing the public this was what happened to Joan. Bond didn't attest that Paradiso used anything to weigh the body down. Bodies disposed of in the water without that would rise to the surface. Yet, in more than a year, no body had surfaced. Technically, Joan was still a missing person. When asked a second time about weighting the body, Bond revealed the entrapment scheme.

"You guys haven't said anything to him since you talked to me, have you?" Bond asked.

Tammaro answered, "No."

"There's nothing that I can't get out of him," the snitch assured.

The investigative team assessed what they had and what they needed to fill in. They decided they had enough and were ready for prime time. Authorities called the FBI on January 28, 1983. The report documented that an inmate identified Leonard Paradiso as the perpetrator responsible for the murder of Marie Iannuzzi and Joan Webster, even though authorities had no evidence establishing that Joan was dead. The news broke in the tabloids on the very same day and helped move the rhetoric forward with one sensational headline after another. The papers reported that Tim Burke received an unsolicited letter from Bond on January 4, 1983. Burke massaged the date and clouded the real origin of the inmate's allegations. The disingenuous agenda to entangle the two unrelated cases had been successful. Authorities claimed they had a break in the Joan Webster case.

"Now we have something we can really investigate," Tammaro told a reporter.

Informant Robert Bond
Photo Credit *Boston Herald*

94

CONVERSATION ALREADY IN PROGRESS:

...this was...this roughly bout how he told me he
ah, murdered Marie, that he murdered her. It was, ..."Hey Bob, how
you doing", you know. "What's this   so I
told him, you know, what they had me in here for and he said "Jesus
Christ, they got me for a three year old murder," and ah, he started
telling me that he was   and that   all
reefed up and what not. But through the course of that day...that
was the 8th when I got...when we had couple of hours outside, and he
kept telling...so I said "Look man", I says, "I'm under the same thing."
I says, "Someone had to say that you with that person or they saw you
with that person or you were visiting area with that person." I
said some...I said "Yah". He said, "Bobby
He said, "I wish I had my Grand Jury minutes." He said, "I would show
you that they indicted me on that John Gilmore...", some shit he said
like that. He said like his girl had the Grand Jury minutes. He
said "They didn't even put my name on it." So I said "Lennie, they got
to have you some place with that person." You know, I said, "There's
no two ways about it. They got to...I says, "I don't see how they
got the Grand..." I said, "I'd like to see them." He said, "My girl
got them." He said "If I get them I'll let you show them...I'll show
'em to you." He never showed them to me. I never saw them Grand Jury
minutes. So,   , he kept talking, he kept talking. He
just almost told me in so many words, man, that's when I hit him with
it. I said "Lennie, don't you ever say that to anybody. I said, you
know, I said, "Because what you is saying now, you know, you're just

Interview Transcript with Robert Bond (pg. 1 of 42)
For the full transcript, visit https://justiceforjoanwebster.com

Nov 28. 1981 THANKSGIVING NIGHT"

I picked Her J.W. up at the Airport" I Ask He where She "COMING From" She Said New York" She Said She was Going to SCHOOL IN CAMBRIDGE

AND THAT I Started Feeding Her the BULLSHIT ABOUT I OWN I. I told Her I owned too FISH COMPANY'S AND A BOAT

I told Her I HAD to get some papers out of MY OFFIEE FRIST" I would take Her to CAMBRIDGE

BOBBY I went to pier 7 wHere I worked AT" MY BOAT wAS THere Bechuse THATS wHere I Kept IT.

We got ON THE BOAT to Show Her AROUND. I HAD us A Couple of drinks

BOBBY" I Always HAd Alot of Booze ON MY Box She didNT wANT ANYTHING to drink.

I MAde A pass At Her" BOBBY THIS BiTCH Said No RIGHT wAy

Wé StArTed FIGHTING" I BeAT THAT BiTCH ASS All over BoAT. SHe gAve up Becuse I HAD HiT Her wiTH A wHiSHT BoTTle" I FucK Her

BOBBY I HAD BlOOd All over Me ANd BOATC SHe HAd A 2 GHT HErC FROM THAT wHiSHY BoTTle.

I took MY BOAT "wAy" OUT ANd dumped Her BodY. Next dAy BOBBY" I took At MY BOAT THere wAS BliOd A oven iT.

BOBBY look Me iN THe eye's" I HAve Never told A ONE THIS" TOO dAys lATer I took MY BOAT OUT ANd Si iT.

MY BOAT wAS iN MY GirL NAMe.

Robert Bond Written Statement (pg. 1)

96

(2)

" WORST CIKE TO WORST I'll Tell THEM WHERE THE B.
... BUT THEY WANT FING NO BODY IN IT, THEY DON'T HA
NOTHING" BECAUSE THEY GOT TO COME UP WITH A BODY BEFOR
THEY CAN TAKE YOU TO TRIAL

THE STATE POLICE ASK ME ABOUT IT, THEY TOLD ME I PO:
HER IN MY BOAT AND BURN IT UP

BOBBY THIS BOAT WAS A FIREGLASS BOAT "NO WOOD. I TOLD
THEM I GOT RID OF MY BOAT IN JULY OF 81 I DIDNT HAVE
BOAT IN NOV OF 81

I KNOW WHO CALL THE STATE PLACE UP AND TOLD THEM THA
MY GIRL" MOTHER AND FATHER OF SAYING I WAS AT TH
HOUSE ALL DAY THAT DAY HAVING DINNER WITH THEM. I CAN
I WAS UP IN MAINE BECAUSE I WAS WORKING UP THERE DO:
... TIME.

I RENT A HOTEL ROOM BY THE MONTH UP THERE TH
RECORD WILL SHOW I WAS UP THERE THEN.

I ASK "CAN GET SOME HOSPITAL RECORDS FROM NEW HAMP
TO SHOW I WAS IN THE HOSPITAL THAT DAY. BECAUSE I HU
MY HAND DURING THAT TIME

THEY SAID SHE WAS SEEN GETTING IN A CAB AT THE
AIRPORT AT 10:00 AT NIGHT.
THEY FULL OF SHIT. WE LEFT THE AIRPORT 10:30.

IT WAS THREE WEEKS LATER WHEN I PUT SOME OF HER STU
IN SAUGUS ON THE LYNN MARSH ROAD BOBBY DO YOU KN
WHERE THAT IS.
THEY HAVE DUMPED BODYS THERE FOR YEARS

Robert Bond Written Statement (pg. 2)

③

when I heard the State Police was looking for Her Body in Pond in Sagus

I know who called them up and told them that."
My lawyer told me dont even worry about that "Because th
got to come up with a Body Before they can take any Body
to Trial.

I know who told the State Police about S.W. Peter Brander,
do you know Him" Bob," —

He's a friend of Johnny O'Masten and them." I used his Name
and address to my parole officer. He live in Lynn" He's a
fucking Asshole; He fuck up a arson Job one time for
and O'Masten

The State Police told me about 3 weeks After I was Arrest
For Marie Murder." They found some of S.W. Things on the M
Marsh Road where Marie was found.

Bobby I report my Boat Stealing way Before then; For M
insurance.

I report it to the Boston police" State Police" MDC police
and the coast Guards.

Bobby if they say to me" we know you picked S.W. up a
the Airport" Kill her in your Boat and Burn your Boat up
Bobby I'll tell them where the Boat is." Because No one
knows where that Boat is But me. That's my ace in the
Hole.

The Boat is not Burn up" the Boat is still in tact" all t
N "Ber or on it." All they will find is a lot of mug —
the Boat." the Boat is frie Glass

Bobby do you know what a Gas" Something look like on t
Boat" the Boat look like it has Been sink/tar

Robert Bond Written Statement (pg. 3)

98

(4)

N' Family" and my Girl Family or saying I was with them durin
that time "Nov 28. 1981

I hurt my hand that night in the boat." I told my Girl that a
50mm shell blew-up in my hand

My Family" and my Girl Family or saying they saw me with
bange on my hand during that time

My Girl has the 50mm shell in her house now

I have 8 people saying where I was that day.

The State Police told me some Cab Company told them I do
a Cab for him to months undercover for him.

Bobby ash. you think a Jury will Believe 8 people o
one person

can show them Hospital record about my hand. I can s.
I was staying up in Maine during that time. And I can g.
a 100 people to say I was staying at this house in
Maine.

My lawyer told me they want take a choice on bri
ng me to Court on S.W. Because if she turn up on the
west coast in some Cult Guor p." I would have the Sta
by the balls for a law suit,

Bobby let them say I burn my boat up." And put in
record." See how fast I come up with it,
My lawyer told me it take more then an om fuse pho
c is to get a indictment against you on S.W,

Robert Bond Written Statement (pg. 4)

(5)

B.3. IF A CAB COMPANY SAY I WAS DRIVING HIS CAB WITHOUT LICENCE" CANT HE GET HIMSELF IN TROUBLE AND LOSE ALL HIS BEDATS LICENCE ON HIS CAB FOR LETTING ME DRIVE WITHOUT A LICENCE.

IM SAYING I WASNT EVEN IN THE STATE IN THE MONTH OF NOV AND DEC OF 81

I WAS WORKING UP IN MAINE THEN" I CAN GET PEOPLE TO SAY, DIGGING CLAM'S.   LICENSE CAR CA

THIS GUY CAN LOOSE HIS HOLE COMPANY BY SAYING THAT BECAUSE I NEVER HAD A HAT LICENCE.

HE HAS A BLUE LOOKING BAOT IN DRY DUCKET M.S. G.L.A. (SIN

G IN LOOKING ONE IN THE WATER. M.S.G L P 23 (IAUSYERS)

HE DRINK SHER REAL AND CROWN ROYK" SOMETIME RUM - COLA.

I TALKED TO HE DEC 8" 12" 14" 15" 16" 17" 18" 19" 20" 21" 3" 24" 25" 26" 27" 2" AND THE MANNING OF THE 29.

Robert Bond Written Statement (pg. 5)

Chapter Ten
Look-Alike Photos

Journalists actually investigated the new lead about the boat. Three days after the bombshell break in Joan's case, banners in every paper cast doubt on the boat story. Dumping Joan at sea covered one base, even though there was no body, but Tim Burke had a problem with the alleged crime scene. Paradiso and his girlfriend reported the boat missing months before Joan disappeared. After Liberty Mutual conducted their investigation, they had paid the insurance claim for the missing boat two months before Joan disappeared. Multiple departments had been on the lookout for the vessel since the summer 1981. Tammaro knew that; he'd raised the question during the Bond interview. Bypassing their usual source from the authorities, inquisitive reporters dug out these same facts.

These inconvenient facts were out there, but quickly faded from the news. Three tattlers reacting to the break in Joan's case emerged in rapid succession. One young woman had hitched a ride on July 10, 1980. Janet McCarthy had escaped the clutches of an assailant and filed a police report. Now she was sure it had been Paradiso. Paradiso's picture flashed across the screen on the evening news as the anchor announced the Websters' reward. Next, Patty Bono, who had originally dropped the dime on Paradiso, now surfaced with allegations of a 1972 assault. Third, Assistant District Attorney Carol Ball in the Middlesex office handed Burke another witness, a convicted killer who once sat on death row. Ralph Anthony Pisa understood the system and made a play to get out of jail by fingering Paradiso for the Marie Iannuzzi murder and Joan

Webster's disappearance. The ground was infirm under Paradiso; he was standing in quicksand.

Laying the foundation to convict Paradiso continued behind the presumed veil of justice. Burke joined Middlesex County prosecutors interrogating Pisa, the imprisoned informant who had met Paradiso in jail in the 1970s. Ralph "Death Row Tony" Pisa had helped Paradiso with an appeal for his assault conviction. The self-styled jailhouse lawyer escaped death when Massachusetts eliminated the penalty. Pisa benefited from the outlandish furlough program and visited an attorney on Christmas Eve in 1979. Paradiso retained the same lawyer when police questioned him about Marie Iannuzzi. The lawyer arranged a polygraph for Paradiso that concluded he told the truth; he did not murder Marie. Paradiso arrived at the attorney's home with a gift, a bucket of lobsters. Pisa was there. According to Pisa, the two men stepped outside, and Paradiso confessed to killing the Iannuzzi girl. Paradiso allegedly then begged the inmate to help him engage the same lawyer Paradiso had previously retained. The dubious assertion was unverifiable.

Pisa heightened his accusations. He claimed Paradiso phoned him at the Bay State Prison on December 18, 1981. He remembered the date specifically; it was his birthday. Supposedly, Paradiso confessed to murdering the missing Harvard graduate student; he said they only found her purse. Pisa coyly referred to the 1850 John Webster case, a landmark case that convicted John Webster without a body. This hook cleverly reinforced the Webster name, a reminder Joan was still missing. Paradiso allegedly threatened Pisa's family and warned him to keep his mouth shut. If the Department of Corrections recorded calls, they missed a blockbuster confession for a highly publicized case. More than a year later, there was nothing to substantiate the veracity of this opportune con. Regardless, Pisa took a new polygraph, courtesy of the state, rewriting his involvement in the 1969 murder that sent him to death row.

Tim Burke seated another secret grand jury on February 17, 1983. In the *Commonwealth v. Leonard Paradiso*, the prosecutor endeavored to pile aggravated rape charges onto the Marie Iannuzzi murder indictment against Paradiso. Burke sought to ensnare Paradiso's girlfriend Candy Weyant coming or going, but the poor woman rejected Burke's relentless pressure by pleading the fifth. Robert Bond had polished his story by the time he took the stand. Now he knew Marie wore a bodysuit with her wrap-around skirt, a fact he'd fumbled during the police interview a month before. On both occasions, Bond alleged Paradiso strangled Marie only once, a critical detail impacting the prosecution's case. On June 6, 1983, the grand jury handed down a true bill for cause number 043033, aggravated rape, against Leonard Paradiso in the case of Marie Iannuzzi.

Meanwhile, the Websters had sent out another alarm on March 3, 1983. The Interpol Blue Notice was a logical step, especially for someone who disappeared from an international airport. The FBI collected Joan's personal data, dental records, passport number, and photos to disseminate abroad. For all appearances, the Websters were trying everything to find their daughter. The Websters' baffling timing, however, rendered the notice essentially useless. Issuing an international Blue Notice for a missing person more than a year after the woman disappeared was a waste of time and resources. Not surprising, the alert produced no results. The paradox was invisible, and the eyewitness report and composite remained *secret*.

After the Websters widened the search with the Interpol Blue Notice, Burke traveled to the FBI training center in Quantico, Virginia on March 28, 1983 to tighten the noose around Paradiso. He updated agents on the status of the investigation and strategized how to handle the obstacles he faced. The boat was a problem with existing reports out in the public. Burke knew about Paradiso's bankruptcy petition and found a vulnerability to exploit in that.

Paradiso, the hapless shellfish peddler, hadn't listed the boat as an asset when he filed for bankruptcy.

At the same time, Andrew Palombo worked the system through the Iannuzzi case. This was when he finally submitted a sworn warrant to the courts to search the Weyant home in Revere, Massachusetts where Paradiso had been living with his girlfriend and her parents. Palombo's petition declared that Tim Burke had received a letter from Robert Bond on January 5, 1983, detailing two murders, Marie Iannuzzi and Joan Webster. Based on the receipt of the letter, Palombo swore, under pain and penalty of perjury, that Burke had scheduled an interview of witness Robert Bond with the state police. Palombo attended the taped interrogation on January 14, 1983. During that meeting, Bond indicated mailing the letter to his family on January 10, 1983, with an inner envelope addressed to Tim Burke. Palombo's superior, Carmen Tammaro, arranged to pick up the letter from Bond's family during the interview because the letter had not arrived yet. Bond hadn't even mailed it on the date the officer avowed Burke received it.

The warrant under the Iannuzzi cover listed specific items: navigational aids, compasses, depth finders, and other contents of the boat. Palombo also specified one textbook of Mayan civilization, assorted photographs of boats, personal pictures of Leonard Paradiso, and Joan Webster look-alike photos. Enforcers descended on the Weyant home in full force, an invasion of troops looking for evidence to support the state's allegations in Joan's case. Not a single item Palombo wanted had anything to do with Marie's case. Sergeant Tammaro moved through the house inspecting the discoveries on each floor. They recovered boat paraphernalia including an Italian flag, a boat manual, and a flare gun. The haul confiscated navigational equipment, photo albums, a coffee table book on Mayan civilization, and a .50 caliber machine gun bullet. None of the items removed from the house furthered Marie's case.

Even though Burke and Palombo weren't collecting evidence in the Iannuzzi case, Burke offered Paradiso a lesser charge, a plea deal for the Iannuzzi case. When Paradiso declined the bargain, he understood what they wanted was Joan. Burke rescinded his offer on June 2, 1983. Although witnesses lined up for Marie's case left gaping holes for reasonable doubt, the system backed Burke. Cooperation has its rewards, and the court finally granted Pisa's motion for a new trial after seven previous attempts failed.

Burke contacted the Boston office of the FBI on May 3, 1983. Special Agent Steve Broce knocked on the door of Burke's small office a week later, and the ensuing maneuver was underway. The next tack added new case numbers under the Financial and Personal Crimes Unit at the FBI. The plan created a fork in the road to a final solution for Joan's presumed murder, and Burke directed the traffic. Burke instigated a federal investigation claiming Paradiso lied on his bankruptcy petition. The agency reported the boat was integral for resolving the Marie Iannuzzi and Joan Webster cases. Burke and Broce blurred the lines; Marie's case had nothing to do with a boat. Any boat.

In early July 1983, the federal prosecutor issued a warrant for the Haymarket Co-Operative Bank. Higher ups desired a favorable outcome in the Paradiso bankruptcy case to bolster their murder case against him. The agency had options and methods not available to state officials. Paul Leary, the number two man in charge of Burke's office, picked up the phone to speak with Robert Swan Mueller III (RSM), the number two man at the Department of Justice in Massachusetts. RSM contacted the prosecutor handling the bankruptcy case. She reached out to Burke, gathered additional information and records, and reported back to RSM. The power elites were watching.

Burke convened another grand jury, a *John Doe Investigation* into the disappearance of Joan Webster, on July 12, 1983. Burke grilled Candy Weyant about the *Malafemmena*, the boat she'd bought and Paradiso skippered. Burke had Paradiso's girlfriend in a quandary. Answering questions exposed her to incriminations in Joan's disappearance. After the judge granted Candy immunity in Joan's case, Burke re-called her to testify in front of the grand jury on July 27, 1983. The prosecutor had set a trap but Burke wasn't getting all of the cooperation he wanted. Even though the hearing pertained to Joan, some of Candy's answers applied to either case, Marie's or Joan's.

The first warrant for the Haymarket Co-Operative Bank gave FBI Special Agent Steve Broce access to records. He submitted a petition on July 27, 1983 to search the safety deposit box jointly held by Paradiso and his girlfriend, Candy, and searched it the next day. The spoils from box number 59 probably weren't what officials hoped for, but the disappointment didn't diminish Burke's speculation. A red silk jewelry pouch sheathed Lenny's prize shark's tooth. Burke and Palombo both said the pouch belonged to Joan. Burke told the Feds that a roommate of Joan's had identified the pouch from a black and white photo. Palombo had a slightly different version. He had a lineup of bags, and the unnamed witness picked out the desired pouch. Supposedly, she said it looked like the bag where Joan kept her pearls. The witnesses were a mystery since Joan lived in a single room at Perkins Hall. Troopers had missed the opportunity to positively identify the item. They didn't confiscate the box and two matching pieces of the three-piece set when they rummaged through Candy Weyant's drawers. Without the facts, Burke and Palombo added the jewelry pouch to their list of Joan's presumed belongings.

Palombo submitted the Mayan book to the FBI numerous times for a fingerprint analysis. Not surprisingly, Paradiso had left a couple of prints on the pages of his book, but the lab found none of Joan's prints. The edition found in Paradiso's bedroom had been out of print since 1975, six years before Joan took the fateful flight to Boston. His volume was about 10 inches by 13 inches in size, a coffee table book with a lot of glossy pictures, and weighed roughly eight pounds. Burke said the Massachusetts Institute of Technology canteen once stocked the book, but he never mentioned which edition or when the store sold it. Burke said Joan had a receipt from the MIT canteen, but the receipt wasn't for the purchase of any edition of this particular book. The explanation got even more absurd when Burke claimed Paradiso had wiped down every page of his edition to remove any prints. These pathetic links hardly made a case that Paradiso had Joan's textbook, but they went ahead with it anyway.

On August 12, 1983, Special Agent Broce received a 302 report, an agent's summary account of a witness interrogation. Federal marshals had interviewed the developer who had renovated Pier 7 in 1980, John O'Connell. O'Connell had defrauded the government of Housing and Urban Development grant money for the project. He was currently in the penitentiary for perjury. The FBI started surveilling the man in October 1981 and confiscated his business records from Pier 7. On November 24, 1981, the Feds secretly videotaped him at a Sheraton in Orlando, Florida, hundreds of miles from Boston Harbor. Federal prosecutors played the recording during his trial in Jacksonville, Florida. At the time O'Connell renovated Pier 7 in 1980, Paradiso moored his boat by the Erie Barge. The developer sent his divers into the water to locate dropped tools. The waters at the pier were murky, and as thick as pea soup. (His divers had found a Mercedes Benz resting on the bottom, hidden by the churning mud from the boat traffic at the pier!) Burke seized on an opportunity to use an anonymous source familiar with Pier 7, even though the informant was a convicted liar.

The day before Broce received his report, Candy Weyant stood before the court and pleaded not guilty to charges Burke had filed naming Candy as an accessory to murder in the Iannuzzi case. Then, Burke met with the federal prosecutor about bankruptcy and mail fraud charges against Paradiso and Candy. The FBI documented the strategy, a squeeze play to pressure Candy to incriminate her boyfriend. Burke met with Broce about the whereabouts of the missing boat, Burke's alleged crime scene. Candy continued to plead the fifth in the Webster grand jury. She had relief from the Webster case, but was vulnerable to charges in the Iannuzzi case. The judge found her in contempt for not answering questions, and sentenced her to three months in jail. Candy's lawyer successfully petitioned the court for a stay of the sentence.

SUFFOLK, ss. Court

(Search Warrant)

TO THE SHERIFFS OF OUR SEVERAL COUNTIES, OR THEIR DEPUTIES, ANY STATE POLICE OFFICER, OR ANY CONSTABLE OR POLICE OFFICER OF ANY CITY OR TOWN, WITHIN OUR SAID COMMONWEALTH:

Proof by affidavit having been made this day before JOSEPH R. FALETRA, CLERK/MAGISTRATE
(Name of person issuing warrant)

by ANDREW C. PALOMBO A MASSACHUSETT STATE POLICE OFFICER ASSIGNED TO LOGAN AIRPORT *that there is probable cause that certain property has been stolen, embezzled, or obtained by false pretenses — certain property used as the means of committing a crime — certain property has been concealed to prevent a crime from being discovered — certain property unlawfully possessed or kept or concealed for an unlawful purpose

WE THEREFORE COMMAND you, at any time of the day or night) to make an immediate search of 212 CRESCENT AVENUE, REVERE, MASS.
(description of house or houses)

(occupied by CANDACE WEBSTER AND OTHERS) and of the person of
(Name of occupant)

CANDACE WEBSTER , and of any person present who may
(Name of person)

be found to have such property in his possession or under his control or to whom such property may have been delivered, for the following property:
(Description of property)

NAVIGATIONAL MAPS, COMPASSES, DEPTH FINDER AND OTHER CONTENTS OF THE BOAT
1 TEXT BOOK ON CELESTIAL NAVIGATION
ASSORTED PHOTOGRAPHS OF BOATS, PERSONAL PICTURES OF LEONARD PARADISO AND JOAN WEBSTER LOOK-ALIKE PHOTOGRAPH

and if you find any such property to bring it and the persons in whose possession it is found before the CHELSEA DIVISION DISTRICT COURT DEPARTMENT
(Name of court)

at SUFFOLK COUNTY, CHELSEA, MASSACHUSETTS
(Court location)

in said County and Commonwealth. This warrant to be served and in any event not later than seven days of issuance thereof. (Officer to whom warrant is issued)

Witness, JOSEPH R. FALETRA , Justice, at BOSTON

this 25TH day of APRIL

in the year of our Lord one thousand nine hundred EIGHTY-THREE

[signature]
CLERK/MAGISTRATE
Special Clerk

Marie Iannuzzi Search Warrant Submitted by Andrew Palombo

CONFIDENTIEL
A l'usage exclusif de la police
et de l'autorité judiciaire

WEBSTER
JOAN LUCINDA

Née le 16 août 1956 à DAYTON, Ohio (États Unis d'Amérique).
Fille de WEBSTER George Armstrong et de SELSAM Eleanor Katherine. Célibataire.

IDENTITE EXACTE - NATIONALITE AMERICAINE EXACTE

PROFESSION : étudiante en architecture

SOBRIQUETS : "Joanie", "Joni", "Dib".

SIGNALEMENT : Voir photo et odontogramme. Taille 160 cm, cheveux châtains, yeux marron.

RENSEIGNEMENTS COMPLEMENTAIRES : ETATS-UNIS D'AMERIQUE, a été vue pour la dernière fois le 28 novembre 1981 alors qu'elle prenait l'avion, de l'Etat du New Jersey vers le Massachusetts, pour retourner à l'Université après avoir passé des vacances avec sa famille.

Il n'a pas été possible de découvrir son lieu de séjour et même de savoir si elle était toujours vivante.

Au moment de sa disparition était vêtue d'un long manteau "Chesterfield" marron, d'un tailleur en laine noir, un chemisier rouge imprimé et de bottes en cuir marron allant aux genoux.

Pièces d'identité : carte de sécurité sociale N° 136-36-0034, permis de conduire du New Jersey N° W 2087-40273-58562 ; passeport américain N° 2101232 délivré le 19 janvier 1974.

Sa famille offrira 50.000 dollars US de récompense à toute personne qui fournira des informations menant à l'identification, à l'arrestation et la condamnation de ou des criminels responsables de sa disparition.

MOTIF DE LA DIFFUSION : Effectuée à la demande des autorités AMERICAINES en vue de retrouver son lieu de séjour (recherches dans un intérêt des familles). En cas de découverte, demander à cette personne si elle consent à ce que son adresse soit communiquée à sa famille.

Prière d'informer : Interpol National Central Bureau, Department of Justice, 9th & Pennsylvania Avenue, N.W., (INTERPOL WASHINGTON via PARIS SG) - Réf. : 830203301/ du 7 mars 1983 ainsi que l'O.I.P.C.-INTERPOL, Secrétariat Général, BP 205, 92212 SAINT CLOUD CEDEX.

Joan Webster
NAME   ADDRESS

UPPER RIGHT   UPPER LEFT

Composite
Alloy   Alloy {Alliage}
Alloy   Alloy

Alloy   Alloy
composit   Alloy
(alliage) Alloy

LOWER LEFT

O.I.P.C. PARIS (S.G.)   du dossier : 428/83
                                                         de contrôle : D-34/5-1983

Interpol Missing Person Blue Notice

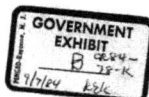

FEDERAL BUREAU OF INVESTIGATION

1.

Date of transcription ___8/12/83___

currently incarcerated in the
Massachusetts,
was interviewed by Special Agents of the Federal Bureau of Investigation. was interviewed at the office of the United
States Marshal, Boston, Massachusetts.

O'Connell Seafood
Company, Incorporated (OSC), located at 290 Northern Avenue,
Boston, Massachusetts,

Leonard Paradisso owned a boat named the Malafemme. The
boat was a twenty-three to twenty-five foot wooden cabin cruiser
pleasure boat. It was a leaky boat, always full of water and had
no lifeboat in it. Paradisso was a friend of Frank and Joe Zanti,
owners of Commercial Lobster Company.

guy who   described Paradisso as a real mousey kind of

same time that Joan Webster was reported missing.

stated that the water
between the barge Erie and General Ship, is at least thirty or forty
feet deep. The water is very murky and nothing would be seen
in it.   a diver down for tools and the diver found a
Mercedes on the bottom.

stated that   opinion Paradisso could have
let his boat fill with water, cut it loose, and it would have
easily sunk in front of the OSC facility.

Investigation on ___8/1 & 8/8/83___ at ___Boston, Massachusetts___ File #
SAS Denise Anne Shea and
Dennis R. Carney   DAS/ef
by

Date dictated ___8/11/83___

This document contains neither recommendations nor conclusions of the FBI. It is the property of the FBI and is loaned to your agency;
it and its contents are not to be distributed outside your agency.

Broce 18

FBI 302 Report Regarding John O'Connell

Chapter Eleven
Confidential Sources

The diver broke the surface holding a blue door. Treacherous conditions in the dark, cloudy water slowed the progress of the Massachusetts State Police and Boston Police dive teams. Scuba teams worked all day and into the night digging mud and silt away from the hull and laying straps underneath the sunken vessel. Burke alerted all the news outlets. By the next morning, reporters and cameramen lined the shore, the curious peered from the dock and restaurant windows, and crowded boats congested Pier 7. The media circus created its own spectacle waiting for the deep to give up its secrets. Gawkers fixed their eyes on the water to see if any bones rattled. The large crane moved into position and the gears slowly started to turn. As promised, the *Malafemmena* broke the surface on September 27, 1983, like a Phoenix rising from the ashes. Water drained from the barnacle-encrusted boat as it dangled in the air, but Joan did not fall out. The state's snitch, Robert Bond, had predicted she wasn't there.

Onlookers started to thin out when the crane lowered Paradiso's blue boat onto a flatbed and moved the alleged crime scene to Pier 1 under around-the-clock guard. FBI technicians moved in and began the laborious task of picking the boat apart. Assigned divers returned to the dangerous waters at Pier 7 over the next two months. They had a grueling task of their own turning over every grain of sand for evidence, but they had sophisticated equipment to help their endeavors. Teams recovered nuts, bolts, and fish bones from the spot where the boat rested. A campaign poster for Burke's boss,

District Attorney Newman Flanagan, was even part of the haul. Day after day, assigned divers dredged up the rubbish and grunge from the floor at the pier, but they found nothing to further a case against Paradiso.

After the boat came up, Palombo took his bows early and headed for the Lynn Hospital. The trooper reexamined the X-rays of metal splinters in Paradiso's left index finger. The speculated weapon was a whiskey bottle, but glass does not show up on X-ray films. Two of the splinters had worked their way out when Paradiso had returned for a follow up in December 1981. The officer surmised one splinter was still in the digit. A contingency plan was hatched.

Burke took his own diver to Pier 7 on October 20, 1983, while assigned divers still scoured the waters. Burke had allegedly received a tip from a confidential source. Special Agent Broce funneled the lead generated by the marshals who interviewed the imprisoned developer who had renovated the pier in 1980. Burke spun the story. According to Burke, John O'Connell sent his divers into the water at Pier 7 in April 1982, a time the witness was under FBI investigation for fraud. The way Burke told the story, divers came up with a gun, and the developer told them to throw it back in the water where they found it. At the pier, Burke pointed to a spot right where Paradiso's boat had settled on the bottom. Burke's own diver went down and soon came up with a gun that assigned divers suspiciously missed. The authorized team had already collected nuts and bolts and fish bones from the very same spot. The firearm looked realistic, but it was a fake .357 magnum with the serial number scratched off. In Burke's mind, the fake gun belonged to Paradiso despite no evidence to support his assertions. The story unfolded, and Paradiso allegedly used the weapon to force Joan on his boat.

Meanwhile, the Massachusetts State Police checked the photos from the albums confiscated during the search of the Weyant home. One picture had an inscription, "To Lenny, One in a million, Love

Charlene." Two days after the boat came up, the FBI got a tip from a confidential source. The caller alerted the Feds about a woman named Charlene.

"Paradiso dated a woman named Charlene," the tipster said. "He lavished her with gifts of jewelry… from his murder victims."

The informant provided specifics to find the woman of interest. The confidential source did not know the woman's last name, but he predicted what she would say. She would be a valuable witness if authorities could find her. The squealer had to have had access to police evidence to know about the photo. Paradiso's modus operandi now included stealing jewelry from his victims, but the only missing jewelry was in Joan's case. A day later, the informer called back.

"Charlene knows where Webster's body was dumped," the source asserted.

A week after the boat came up, Broce located Charlene Bullerwell. The woman had dated Paradiso six or eight times over a couple of years. He once gave her a gold-dipped seahorse charm, but took it back to have a link put on it, and never gave it back. The tall, slender woman with blonde hair broke the profile; the team had asserted that Paradiso trolled young women with long, dark hair. Nevertheless, Burke breathlessly welcomed the news about Charlene to add a new name to his cast of characters, and claimed she looked like Joan.

"We confiscated a photo of a woman," Burke told the FBI. "She's wearing an identical bracelet to the one missing in Joan Webster's case."

After sharing the information about the missing bracelet, Broce and another interrogator turned up on Charlene's doorstep on October 4, 1983. Palombo worked closely with Broce and confirmed that working on insurance matters was in the Feds' wheelhouse. The collaboration blurred the lines of jurisdiction. Palombo had access to the picture, and Burke's story about jewelry aligned with the confidential source. When the agents descended on Charlene, she lived down the street from Paradiso's girlfriend. Broce and his partner promised to move Charlene and her son. The two men asked Charlene for a description of the interior of the boat. She had been onboard on two occasions, one of those times with her son. She revealed Paradiso's plan to sink his boat for the insurance and offered a couple possible locations. She said that the last time she saw Paradiso was around Christmas in 1981, a brief encounter when she was out shopping. After two long hours answering questions, the woman unwillingly plugged a leak in the state's allegations.

So far, Burke and Palombo had discovered Paradiso possessed a book of Mayan civilization and a red silk jewelry pouch. The team inferred the items belonged to Joan. They raised a boat but kept the FBI findings a *secret*. The team paired at the Webster meeting had gained an indictment for the Marie Iannuzzi murder after changing the name to John Doe. Burke's own diver retrieved a fake .357 magnum and supposed Paradiso had wielded the gun to force Joan down the plank. Now they had a new witness ostensibly photographed in a bracelet identical to Joan's. The missing bracelet was a one-of-a-kind gold charm bracelet. However, this mountain of conjecture was still not enough. The tabloids helped fuse Joan's and Marie's cases, but Burke needed to drive it home.

The federal prosecutor convened a grand jury for the Paradiso bankruptcy case. Charlene Bullerwell took the stand on February 16, 1984. Her subdued testimony recalled infrequent dates with Lenny Paradiso, the subject of the grand jury. She told the jurors that Paradiso had planned to scuttle his boat for the insurance and warned her not to tell anyone. She claimed Paradiso had said he would kill her if she told anyone about sinking the boat. The prosecutor assured her the proceedings were *secret*; Paradiso wouldn't know what she divulged. She described the only jewelry he ever gave her, but the gold-dipped seahorse didn't match the illusion created by the state.

A maritime investigator testified how the boat sank. Someone pulled out the toilet, removed a bilge plug, and disconnected an intake hose to the engine. The expert witness identified Ray Jefferson fittings on the boat, the brand of navigational equipment insured with the *Malafemmena*. The fittings were not interchangeable with other manufacturers. Palombo engaged Marine Investigator David Williams to examine the boat on two occasions. The trooper had the same report. His boring testimony nearly put the jury to sleep, but essentially established that Paradiso sank his own boat.

The next day, Palombo interviewed another witness named Janet McCarthy. She had hitched a ride on July 10, 1980, in the North End. Janet had slipped into the seat of a fairly new, big, white, four-door car, and asked the driver to take her to the strip of nightclubs in Revere. The man detoured and stopped in an isolated area near the beach. The frightened young woman fought off the man's unwanted advances. Finally, she escaped the confines of the car, climbed a plain, white, concrete retaining wall, and flagged down a passing motorist. The Good Samaritan took Janet to the police station, and officers took down the details. The incident report listed the name of the decent citizen who had helped the damsel in distress. The partial plate number Janet remembered was a dealer plate. The first responding officers observed the intoxicated young woman had messed up hair and a bloody knee. In her hasty departure, she had left her purse behind and didn't have identification. The victim looked at mugshots that night, but in her fog, she couldn't identify her assailant.

Palombo usurped the original investigators and took over Janet's case when she came forward in January 1983. The detective started with the information in the initial report. He had a remarkable way of engaging a witness and helping restore their recollections. Palombo and an unnamed partner drove the witness to a spot in Winthrop, Massachusetts, not far from the Weyant home. He stopped by a retaining wall covered with graffiti. The detective had the witness look at photos of vehicles taken from Paradiso's albums, refreshing her memory. Palombo gave Burke the nod; the witness was ready.

The trooper also interviewed Patty Bono, the childhood friend of his superior, Sergeant Carmen Tammaro. She was the one who had placed the anonymous call to the Saugus Police in January 1982 and implicated Paradiso for Marie's murder and Joan's disappearance. Bono alleged Paradiso had assaulted her in the late summer 1972. In her account, Paradiso had asked her to drive him from a bar to the hospital because he was experiencing chest pains. According to Bono, Paradiso directed her to an isolated spot at the piers where he forcibly made advances. When he couldn't perform, his aggression escalated, and he reached for a gun in the glove compartment. The witness winced when she described her envisioned accoster pressing the gun so hard against her forehead that it left a lump. She said Paradiso choked her, hit her, and broke a bone in her face. Somehow, Patty talked her way out of the dire situation. Before he started the ignition and abandoned her, the demonic man in Patty's mind warned her not to tell, or he would come back, kill her, and dump her in the ocean where no one would ever find her. The chilling contentions had a familiar ring. The story sounded a lot like the presumed fate of Joan Webster.

Burke had quite a lineup ready for a pretrial hearing.

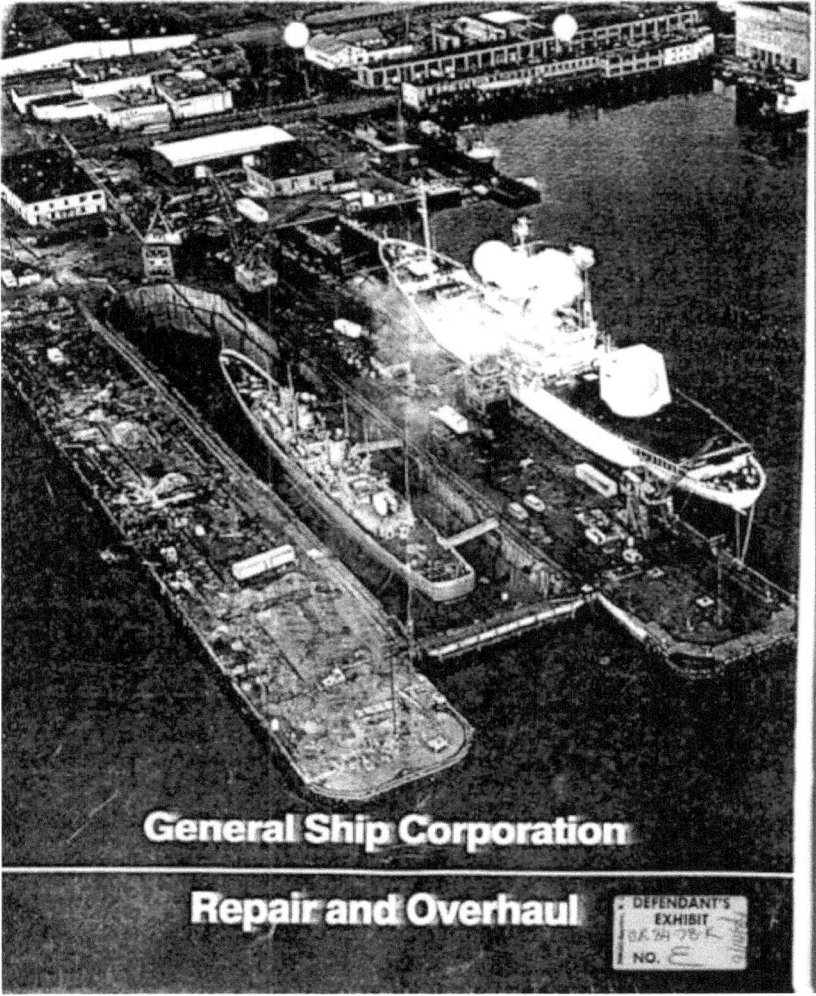

Alleged Crime Scene at Pier 7 in Boston, MA

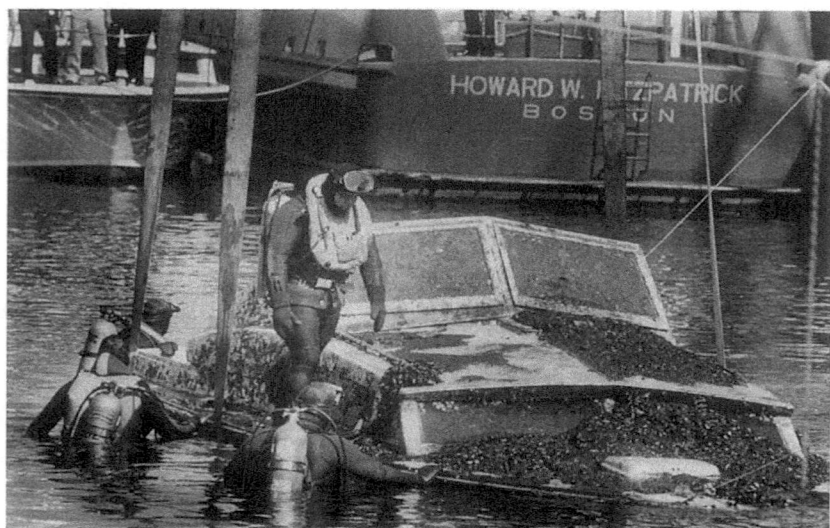

Raising the Malafemmena on 9-27-1983
at Pier 7 in Boston, MA
Photo Credit *Boston Herald*

Chapter Twelve
Terrorized Women

Leonard Paradiso was no saint. His 1973 assault conviction opened the door for Burke to make his case. George and Eleanor Webster sat near the back of the courtroom to grade how the prosecutor staged the pretrial hearing of Marie Iannuzzi's case. The lawyer's approach was sympathy and shudder on the first day, played out in front of the press. The first witness called to the stand on March 5, 1984 was Constance Porter.

All eyes watched the pregnant young woman walk to the witness stand. Porter avoided looking in the direction of the defendant. Burke knew the 1973 assault victim would evoke sympathy, and she would be the Achilles heel that left Paradiso vulnerable to other accusations. Constance had needed a ride to Amherst, Massachusetts, and stuck her thumb out for a lift, which was not uncommon then. Paradiso obliged. He turned his car off the road before arriving at her destination saying he had to pee. A police cruiser in the area stumbled across the parked car. Both occupants were out of the vehicle. Constance was on the ground, and Paradiso was zipping his pants. She told police that Paradiso tried to rape her. He claimed he had found her that way and was just trying to help. The patrol's headlights illuminated the incriminating set of circumstances that the jury believed. Burke trusted Paradiso's conviction in the Constance Porter case cast a broad net to validate any other insinuations.

Next, Patty Bono raised her right hand and swore to tell the truth. She repeated her allegations against Paradiso for an assault in the late summer 1972. She had never reported the unproven attack to the police. Even though she described a large lump on her forehead and a broken bone in her face, she never went to the emergency room or saw a doctor. Nothing corroborated her story. "She said" was all the evidence she had. Dropping the name Willie Fopiano, a notorious wise guy who operated in the North End until he moved to Las Vegas, Patty claimed he had avenged her honor beating Paradiso up to teach him a lesson. Apparently, the lesson didn't stick.

During the spring and summer 1972, Fopiano laid low in the neighborhood. He had broken his wrist beating up drug pushers who were menacing kids in the schoolyard. The fracture didn't heal, and doctors had to insert pins to stabilize his wrist. Hampered by a cast, Fopiano stayed out of sight of the clashing thugs who wanted to rub him out. As soon as he was able, the wise guy uprooted and resettled in Nevada. The absence of conflicting testimony from him favored Burke's intention to pound another nail into Paradiso's coffin.

On the second morning of the trial, Burke raised the temperature. His plan was to shock the audience and fill them with horror from terrorized victims. His next witness was the woman who Burke alleged was wearing Joan's missing bracelet in a photograph. According to a secret source, Charlene knew where the offender had dumped Joan's body. The subdued secret testimony she gave in the federal court was about to go nuclear on Burke's public stage.

Charlene described occasional dates with the defendant over maybe a year and a half. On one occasion, on Paradiso's boat, the two consenting adults were intimate. Lenny never beat her, never assaulted her, and never sexually abused her. But, according to the witness, Lenny dropped a bombshell one night after a few drinks.

"He told me he was a hit man for the mob," Charlene shuddered. "He chopped up bodies, tied cinder blocks to them, and dumped them in the ocean."

Silence fell over the courtroom to let the revelation sink in. George removed his glasses and bowed his head. All eyes in the courtroom gazed sympathetically at the Websters. Charlene told the court that Paradiso liked to do women because they were easy. The vision was not of Marie, the subject of the hearing, but the fate of the Websters' daughter. Shrewdly, the prosecutor plugged a hole in their story that Robert Bond had failed to fill in—how to keep a body down in the water: cinder blocks.

She continued, "He threatened to kill me if I told anyone what he said."

The session across town had revealed a different warning if she told anyone about sinking his boat for the insurance, but the public was not privy to that declaration. Two men had grilled Charlene for hours after the Feds identified her; one was Special Agent Steve Broce, but the other name was concealed. Charlene never told anyone about an alleged mob connection or chopped up bodies until the agents forced it out of her.

"I was pretty well pressured before I gave the information out," Charlene disclosed.

Heavy-handed tactics sweetened with promises to move her landed the witness in the hot seat in front of the cameras. The sensation outweighed the admission of federal pressure in the headlines that plastered the news. Burke understood the power of the press to sell the narrative and so did the Websters.

Janet McCarthy warmed the seat next. Palombo restored her memories of her night of terror in the summer 1980. Janet testified that Palombo drove her right to the spot; she didn't have to show him. She accused Paradiso of beating her in the face. She recalled a plain, white, cement wall, the barrier she had jumped over to escape imminent danger. She trembled, recalling the first car that stopped was the assailant, identifying the defendant. He laughed wickedly before he drove off again. According to the witness, two men picked her up, drove her to their place to freshen up, and then took her to the police station. The rewritten account contradicted the police report on the night Janet escaped the clutches of an offender, but the public only heard the new version.

"Do you remember what kind of car it was?" the defense counsel asked.

"Yes," she confidently answered. "It was a yellow car. It was a big car with dealer plates."

Burke questioned his partner, Palombo, on March 7, 1984, after the jury had a chance to sleep on the terrifying accounts of the women Burke put on the stand. Palombo recounted his trip to the wall with Janet McCarthy, but he contradicted her. In his version, Janet had a vivid recollection of events, and she directed him turn by turn to the scene of the crime. His location had a retaining wall covered with graffiti and conveniently placed the victim in close proximity to the Weyants' house. The reflection from Palombo's badge, instilling an aura of trust, obscured the discrepancies aired in the courtroom. None of the previous witnesses mentioned missing jewelry, and Palombo confirmed Marie's jewelry was intact.

Burke turned his attention to the next victim he wanted to roll into Marie's case, Joan Webster. Palombo described Pier 7 and identified photographs featuring Paradiso's boat moored at the Erie Barge. The officer detailed the discovery of the *Malafemmena* for the court but didn't try to offer any evidence to connect Joan to the boat. Earlier witnesses had brought the spectators in the courtroom to the water's edge thinking about Joan's fate. Burke showed Palombo a photograph for identification and then entered Joan's smiling face into the record. The tabloids churned out dramatic stories every night.

Another officer inserted Burke's next piece of the puzzle. Nick Saggese was a diver for the Boston Police. Under oath, Saggese described raising the *Malafemmena* at Pier 7 on September 27, 1983.

Divers carefully dug mud and silt away from the boat to prevent any pressure when the boat lifted off the floor of the pier. The witness testified the recovery didn't really cause any suction that might bury evidence under the craft. The vessel was readily identified: the hull was still blue, the registration numbers were visible on the bow, and the name was painted across the stern. The officer observed Paradiso's boat had a broken rudder. The craft was not navigable. Burke then turned his attention to Saggese's special assignment. The diver had entered the water where he was instructed on October 20, 1983. He surfaced with a firearm.

"At whose request were you there?" Burke asked.

"I was there at your request," the diver replied. "I found a gun. It was found directly below where the boat was."

The finding of the realistic-looking replica of the .357 magnum plugged another gap in the state's story, how Paradiso got a sophisticated young lady like Joan on his boat. Even though some contradictions entered the record, no one seemed to notice. Conflicting evidence, like the FBI 302 report describing a Mercedes Benz rather than a gun, remained locked in files elsewhere.

Burke had trapped Paradiso's girlfriend in a vice. In the Webster grand jury, Burke petitioned for Candy's immunity in Joan's case. However, he filed charges against Candy as an accessory in Marie's case and instigated federal charges that were still looming. Burke began his questioning, and Candy pled the fifth. The judge granted Burke's request to declare Candy a hostile witness before compelling her to answer his questions. Burke laid the groundwork. First, he showed her Palombo's pictures of retaining walls near her house. The ploy didn't work; she didn't know what was painted on the barriers. Then he handed her a picture from one of Paradiso's photo albums taken from her home. It was a picture of a yellow Cadillac his brother once owned.

"Do you recognize that car?" Burke asked. "Tell His Honor what color that car is."

"Yellow," she answered.

Burke tried to connect dots with Janet McCarthy's revised memory, but Candy didn't oblige. The determined lawyer changed subjects, and turned his attention to the boat. The fraught woman told the truth at the risk of falling deeper into Burke's trap with other charges. She had helped her boyfriend strip the *Malafemmena* before it went down.

Next, Burke asked her about the equipment confiscated from the Weyants' attic on April 25, 1983. "Did you help Mr. Paradiso strip a ship-to-shore radio, a Danforth compass, and a Danforth depth finder?" Burke asked. Burke's mistake was invisible. Secret testimony across town documented the equipment insured with the boat was Ray Jefferson. The fittings on the boat matched that equipment and were not interchangeable with Danforth models. What law enforcement recovered didn't match the equipment from Burke's envisioned crime scene. Burke didn't care because no one was the wiser.

"The boat wasn't stolen, was it?" Burke demanded.

"No," Candy admitted.

"That boat was still above water November 28, 1981, when Joan Webster disappeared!" Burke paused for effect. "Wasn't it, Ms. Weyant?"

She didn't see the boat go down, but authorities already knew Candy had filed an insurance claim the next day on July 26, 1981, four months before Joan disappeared. The theatrics in the courtroom left the desired perceptions rather than the facts. The prosecutor had whet the public's appetite and feverish chatter swirled through the weekend. On March 9, 1984, the federal prosecutor handed down indictments against Leonard Paradiso and Candy Weyant for bankruptcy and mail fraud.

Robert Bond waited downstairs while Burke tried to protect the twice-convicted killer. The prosecutor didn't want to create a media frenzy by putting Bond on the stand. The sudden concern for discretion seemed out of step with his strategy over the last few days. Burke had started with the sensation of chopped up bodies and murder at sea. He followed with a hitchhiker's night of terror. The lawyer preyed on emotions with the only legitimate witness he seated, a pregnant woman, Constance Porter. The prosecutor added an unverified, 12-year-old allegation from Patty Bono, bringing the public to a fever pitch about Joan Webster. Law enforcement spiced the stew with sinking boats and suspiciously recovered guns. Every sordid detail sold papers. Now, Burke was worrying about the privacy of a condemned felon hoping to improve his situation.

"I suppose at some time you better tell the defense who he is," the judge said.

"Judge, he's afraid," Burke replied. "He's been threatened by Paradiso. He's not going to come aboard and testify unless we can guarantee his safety."

"He can't testify out of the presence of the defendant," Judge Donahue reminded Burke.

"Unless Paradiso waives it," Burke shamelessly suggested.

The likelihood of this burly weightlifter, a killer who callously murdered two girlfriends, being afraid of Paradiso was slim to none. Paradiso's lawyer, Steve Rappaport, petitioned for discovery of Bond's allegations. Burke moved for a protective order of discovery in the next breath. He tried to slip Bond's testimony into the record without a rebuttal or letting the defendant face his accuser. The judge took it under advisement, and Bond did not take the stand on March 8, 1984.

Monday morning didn't disappoint. Ralph "Death Row Tony" Pisa was in the spotlight. The convicted killer and an accomplice had capped off a night of drinking by enjoining a security guard into their car in 1969 and killing him. On January 8, 1970, Francis Dion entered the Clam Shell Bar and commiserated with Pisa.

Dion's wife was unfaithful. Pisa offered to shoot her for him. He confided to Dion that he had killed the guard, and the more he pulled the trigger, the more he enjoyed it. Dion testified during Pisa's trial, and the judge sentenced Pisa to death row. Pisa studied in prison to learn the finer points of the law. He assisted other inmates with their appeals and funneled business to a Boston attorney. Pisa's skills as a jailhouse lawyer helped him whittle down his sentence, but he wanted out of the big house. Middlesex County opposed multiple motions Pisa filed for a new trial until he came forward against Paradiso. Pisa remembered helping the shellfish peddler with his Constance Porter appeal.

Burke produced an envelope for his witness postmarked in 1977. Paradiso had mailed the prisoner to recover his Porter files. Burke told officials about a chance encounter two years later when Paradiso brought his lawyer a bucket of lobsters for Christmas. According to Pisa, he kept his mouth shut until Paradiso's picture came across the screen connected to the Joan Webster story. It appeared that Tony had found his conscience only when it might be to his advantage. Burke told the court about the con's record but bolstered the image of a reformed man. Pisa helped establish a prison library for inmates. His work on motions and appeals for fellow criminals generated favor from an attorney who gained new clients. The witness knew about the Webster reward, but said he didn't want the money. The refusal of compensation sounded sincere, but money wasn't the reward Pisa really wanted.

"The only way I would come forward is that I do not receive the reward," Pisa said. "I prefaced this with Mr. Reilly, along with Mr. Burke, along with Mr. Webster, along with every other person I've talked to."

The altruistic assurance raised a flag no one seemed to notice. For the father of a victim to deliberate with a potential witness was not standard procedure. The defense never gleaned prosecutors collaborated with Joan's father before putting Pisa on the stand in the Iannuzzi pretrial.

Authorities had quietly shuffled Pisa into a pre-release facility at the end of February, right before the felon testified. He delivered both cases, Joan's and Marie's. Like a CIA plot, the George Webster's impact on decisions was clandestine, but the parents' presence in the courtroom clearly influenced public perceptions.

Burke and his Middlesex colleague Tom Reilly interrupted a courtroom proceeding the next day, and the two lawyers threw every ethical tenet out of the window to spring Pisa. The lawyers conveyed a sense of urgency to Judge Harry Elam that the murderer felt threatened and requested a bail hearing on the spot. The courts didn't usually grant bail to convicted felons, and a parole board determined a prisoner's release. But Pisa wasn't interested in a change of another supervised address, and Burke argued on his behalf. Authorities held open the door for Pisa to walk away from confinement.

In Suffolk County, the presiding judge, Roger Donahue, settled the motions before him that Burke had submitted during the Iannuzzi pretrial hearing. On March 13, 1984, while Burke was unlocking the doors for Pisa in Middlesex County, Donahue seized evidence in Suffolk County. The judge sealed Robert Bond's two-part written letter and the transcript of the interview with the police, and he put the con's allegations out of reach. Impounded item number 15 thwarted any penetrating review of the foundational documents for Joan's case. Burke had rescued two convicted killers in one day. Donahue denied the motion to allow testimony from Burke's alleged victims, but the intended damage had already been accomplished through the tabloids.

√

1626

REVERE POLICE DEPARTMENT

DETECTIVE BUREAU

CONFIDENTIAL

To: File
From: Det. Sgt. James Russo
Subject: Attempted Rape

July 10 1980

At approximately 1:20 AM this date this officer and Detective William Gannon were dispatched to Winthrop P.D. to investigate an attempted rape that may have occured in this city.

In Winthrop we spoke with Janet McCarthy of 49 Mount Ida Road Dorchester, age 20, d.o.b. 01-01-60, S.S. 015528704, no telephone. She stated that she had hitched a ride in the North End of Boston earlier in the evening with a white male, early thirties, chubby, dark brown hair, brown eyes operating a big white car, four door, fairly new with a dark colored interior.

This man was supposed to take Miss McCarthy to an unknown night spot on Revere Beach but instead he took her to another location near the Ocean where he parked the car and after a short conversation tried to force her into having intercourse.

The woman further stated that the man punched her several times and tried to pull her dress off. She was able to escape from the vehicle and jumped over a wall onto another roadway and flagged down another vehicle operated by one Joseph Alvoarra Jr. of 22 Beach View Ave., Saugus, tel. 233 7249 who drove the woman to the Winthrop Police station.

Mr. Alvoarra told this officer that he was operating on Winthrop Parkway near the Winthrop line when he saw the female in the roadway crying and trying to stop cars. When he stopped Miss McCarthy requested that he take her to the police.

We then left the Winthrop P.D. and on our way back to this station Miss McCarthy pointed out the spot where the attack took place. It was after the last house on the lower part of Winthrop Ave. in Revere.

At this station the woman viewed our mug files but could not identify anyone. She was then taken to the MDC Police Station on the beach for transpprtation back to Dorchester because her handbag containing a small amount of cash and personal papers had been left behind in the attacker's vehicle.

These officers observed that Miss McCarthy had been drinking and noted some inconsistencies in her statements.

Respectfully Submitted;

Det. Sgt. James Russo

Revere Police Incident Report of Janet McCarthy

Ralph "Death Row Tony" Pisa
Photo Credit *Boston Herald*

Chapter Thirteen
"It's Show Time"

The summer heat radiated off the steps into the courthouse. George and Eleanor sat near the back of the room while reporters and spectators filled every available seat. The air conditioner hummed in one corner doing little to cool the room down. The highly anticipated trial was the *Commonwealth v. Leonard Paradiso* for the murder of Marie Iannuzzi. In people's minds, the trial was a synecdoche, a part representing the whole. As if the names were interchangeable, Marie Iannuzzi symbolized justice for Joan Webster.

Jurors settled in the reserved section to judge the evidence put before them. Steven Rappaport sat with his client on one side of the aisle, and Tim Burke and his cohort Andrew Palombo sat on the other. Palombo had cleaned up his grungy undercover appearance more familiar to unsavory sorts on the streets. He had chopped off his ponytail, shaved off his beard, and exchanged his motorcycle duds for a tailored suit. Judge Roger Donahue entered the chamber and gaveled the court into session on July 9, 1984.

Burke had prepared for the case with the predetermined end and worked his way back into the crime. The defense responded with common sense. Paradiso's advocate presented reasonable doubt; there was incriminating evidence pointing to another offender. Tabloids prosecuted two cases in the public simultaneously. The papers reported the daily proceedings colored with the Websters' reactions and the imagined fate of their daughter. The jury held Paradiso's life in their hands, based on what they could see and hear.

Burke started his case with a field trip for the panel of judges. The prosecutor loaded his audience into a school bus and narrated a tour of relevant locations, effectively putting jurors physically at the scene of the crime. Back in the courtroom after the tour, he called his first witness, the priest who presided over the wedding that Paradiso and the victim both attended on August 11, 1979. This clever tactic instilled an aura of trust, but added nothing else to further the case. The choice for the opening act was inspired, a subliminal message to believe Burke's arguments.

The prosecution next called a key witness to the hot seat. Christine DeLisi had incriminated Marie's boyfriend during the grand jury on March 5, 1982. She confirmed she saw the defendant hold the door at the bar as Marie walked out. Paradiso was the last person Christine saw with her friend. As the defense took its turn, both counsels sidled up to the bench. Rappaport held the transcript of Christine's previous testimony, where she said she had seen Marie's trepidation after an argument with David Doyle, she recalled strangulation marks on Marie's neck, and that Marie said her boyfriend tried to kill her. The terrified young woman moved in with Christine for several days in 1979.

"If there is other evidence of David Doyle's involvement in the death of Marie Iannuzzi… but at this point in the case," the judge said, "I'm going to exclude the statement the victim allegedly made at the time."

Burke sat down with a smile on his face. The judge had impeded opposing counsel's defense of another culprit. The judge failed to recognize the prior act was a warning.

Rappaport handed the witness a copy of the grand jury minutes to refresh her memory. Christine's own words stared back at her. "Ma'am," Rappaport asked, "Did you ever state she had strangulation marks on her neck, very red marks, and handprints around her neck?"

"I don't remember," she replied.

Both counsels moved to the sidebar. "It's a hearsay statement," Burke argued.

Christine pleaded hardship. She told Rappaport she had suffered an asthma attack, cancer treatments, and had been hit by a truck. The extraordinary list of maladies and misfortune might blur memory, but the dramatic event with Marie took place only two months before her friend died. The jury didn't know Christine had confided being pressured to testify a certain way to a friend, Dennis Albano. She had told him that "the state police kept calling me and coming to the house until I relented. They [the police] said I would never see my child again!" Now she had a different explanation for her fogged memory.

Next, Burke painted the picture that Paradiso called his parole officer, Victor Anchukaitis, in a panic before authorities identified Marie's body. On the stand, the retired parole officer nervously wiped the perspiration from his forehead. Anchukaitis had logged his entries in a running record documenting calls, meetings, and progress for his charge. Burke handed Victor Anchukaitis the officer's own notes. According to the testimony the jury heard, Paradiso called him on Monday, August 13, 1979, about 9:30 a.m. Even though the request wasn't noted, the officer said Paradiso wanted to come in and see him right away. Burke inferred that Paradiso and his girlfriend both met with the officer at noon that Monday to discuss Paradiso's dire situation.

In reality, the first entry for August 13, 1979 only referred to a call without logging a time and only noted a scheduled change of parole officers. The next memo was August 15, 1979, recording the transfer request to the new parole officer, Jim O'Neil. Something obscured the date on the third entry, but August 13, 1979 was handwritten below it. The notation documented a meeting with Paradiso, but didn't log a time. The parolee had attended a wedding, and one of the guests was murdered. The jury couldn't see the entries were out of order, or that one appeared to have been tampered with. The defense attorney tried to bring this to everyone's attention.

"There's another notation in between the two we've been talking about, both marked August 13, 1979," the defense said. "It's a different date. It's out of sequence."

"I don't understand that one at all, sir," Anchukaitis acknowledged. "Yes sir, it's out of sequence."

Victor had actually met with Paradiso and his girlfriend outside his office on August 14, 1979. He'd bent the rules to meet his charge in a bar on the Tuesday after the victim was positively identified. The only reasonable explanation for the out-of-order notation was that his secretary made the entry the next day when Victor was back in his office and turned in his notes. Anchukaitis said he had advised Paradiso to cooperate with the police. Anchukaitis misled the court without disclosing details of the meeting that violated department policy and threatened his retirement. The way the jury heard the testimony, Paradiso had panicked and met with Anchukaitis before the victim was identified, suggesting consciousness of guilt. The fact was Paradiso met with Anchukaitis a day later after learning a guest at the wedding he had attended was dead.

Burke's next witness refused to enter the courtroom. Burke pleaded with the judge; he wanted her testimony in the record. Charlene Bullerwell had given scandalous testimony during the pretrial hearing, but her account of chopped up bodies dumped at sea didn't seem to be relevant in the present proceeding. The prosecutor argued her testimony showed a pattern.

"He doesn't bury them," Burke pleaded. "He kills them and tries to dispose of them by putting them in water."

Marie was found on the edge of the Pine River, not in the water. Her strangled body was not dismembered and not weighted down. Charlene's impact only furthered rumors about Joan as the undeclared victim in the current proceedings. Judge Donahue disallowed corroborated evidence of a prior act committed by the victim's boyfriend, but irrationally considered an unverified legend as legit. The judge was willing, but the witness was not. He summoned the witness for a lobby conference outside the earshot of the courtroom. Charlene recoiled from the media that had splashed her name in the papers a few months before. Coincidentally or not, she shared similar misfortunes with Marie's best friend, Christine DeLisi.

"I've had several seizures because of all this," Charlene lamented. "I'm on medication. I've had major brain surgery. I don't remember anything."

Burke's quest of Paradiso proved to be hazardous to the health of some of the witnesses. Misfortune wiped memories clean. Christine forgot incriminating evidence that conflicted with Burke's version of events, to Burke's satisfaction. Charlene forgot she cavorted with an alleged hit man for the mob, to Burke's dismay. She refused to take the stand during the trial. But the obstinate witness revealed a subtle clue about her forgetfulness; she remembered one thing.

"They promised me they would move me, they would pack my things," Charlene told the judge. "I got none of this. They told me my name wasn't going to get out. I got a check for two hundred dollars and moved myself."

The medical expert called to testify next revealed an inept examination at the time of the murder. The victim was still dressed in a one-piece bodysuit and wrap-around skirt. The leotard had no snaps in the crotch. The medical examiner, Doctor George Katsas, distinctly remembered removing panties from the victim, but the undergarment didn't make it to the lab. The murder weapon was a scarf double knotted tightly around her neck. Marie's hands had frozen in a clawed position; she was literally in the fight of her life. No one took scrapings from under Marie's nails, so none were tested. The pathologist determined the victim had sexual relations sometime in an eighteen-hour window before she died. No one tested the semen to identify the depositor. To Burke's dismay, the examiner found no injuries in the genital area to support rape allegations. At the time of her death, rape wasn't considered a factor.

Burke divulged that his next witness had moved to a pre-release facility at the end of February 1984, after speaking with Middlesex County prosecutor Tom Reilly about Paradiso. The disclosure did not expose other details the witness had shared during the pretrial hearing. Pisa was making assurances to Joan's father. He alleged unverifiable conversations. His assertions supplanted a subliminal reminder of Joan. Even in today's courtrooms, the John Webster case is part of a judge's instructions to the jury. Authorities greased the wheels putting Pisa on a fast track to get out of jail. The stealth maneuvers concealed Pisa's lack of credibility. Nothing confirmed Paradiso's alleged confessions to the convicted killer on the stand.

Next, Burke called Andrew Palombo to the stand. Burke had lined up his witnesses in a carefully choreographed order. The prosecutor moved to bolster trust after a convicted killer stepped down from the witness stand and before another one stepped in. Burke used the natural tendency to trust a badge to his advantage. Palombo had taken over Marie's case in February 1981, and served a warrant on the Weyants' home in April 1983. Items removed during that search had nothing to do with Marie's case, but the jury never heard what the officers were looking for or what they found.

Rappaport cross-examined the witness, and exposed a breach of ethical standards, as it was a conflict of interest for Palombo to supervise the case. The relationship between Doyle and Palombo raised suspicion about the odd couple's intentions to find Marie's killer.

"I've talked to David Doyle twenty to thirty times," Palombo said.

"Do you have any notes of those communications?" the defense asked.

"No, I don't," the witness replied.

"Do you remember the sum and substance of those conversations?" Rappaport probed. "You never kept one report?"

"No," Palombo repeated.

"Doyle was a suspect in this case also, wasn't he?" Rappaport challenged.

"Not in my mind, no," Palombo insisted. "Doyle went so far as to come to me without me asking him, to relay information or things he had heard on the street."

The undercover cop was describing the behavior of a handler in a climate where Boston's enforcers protected snitches dishing dirt. Similarly, Pisa got favored treatment from Middlesex County, getting him out of jail. Agents bribed Bullerwell with promises they didn't keep. Carmen Tammaro dangled reward money for Bond and arranged for a new lawyer to represent the convict in a new trial. Doyle was an admitted druggie who knew the pushers on the street. Drug busts added feathers to Palombo's cap.

Burke and Palombo turned to the back of the courtroom. They locked eyes with George and Eleanor Webster and waited for their colleagues to take their positions. Sergeant Carmen Tammaro, Special Agent Steve Broce, and Burke's boss, first Assistant District Attorney Paul Leary, cocooned the couple before the next witness, Robert Bond. The state's star witness confidently walked to the front of the room unchained from his shackles. The clerk administered the oath of fidelity, and the witness sat down.

"It's show time," Burke quietly whispered to himself.

Burke didn't try to hide the fact that Bond was in prison, but he softened the blow. Bond told the court his recent conviction was currently on appeal. He was sentenced on January 10, 1983, and met with state troopers later that day. Bond had to focus hard to keep events in order. He was a hearsay witness; he didn't observe anything firsthand. According to Bond, Paradiso confessed his sins to the inmate, and the defendant allegedly provided an unbelievable level of detail.

"He left the Milanos' home at 9:30 p.m. He dropped Marie off at the Cardinales Nest," Bond said. "He says he got back to the Cardinales Nest after he took his girlfriend home. He returned to the bar around eleven o'clock."

The judge had sealed Bond's letter and interview transcript during the pretrial hearing. The jury was clueless about what the witness had initially described to the police. Burke's star witness laid it on thick and added new details he supposedly heard from Paradiso. Bond said Paradiso burned his car ten days after Marie's murder to hide blood on the door. Candy reported the car stolen on September 13, 1979, a month after Marie died. But the state didn't submit any evidence of charred remains. Bond told the court that police only learned about tire tracks at the scene when he told them. First responders had actually noted the tire treads when they found Marie.

When Bond described Marie's attire, he stuttered recollecting her shoes and stockings, but zeroed in on the critical piece that apparently kept Paradiso awake at night. The jury heard this for the first time and without the benefit of Bond's previous statements. Working with the people George Webster had sent to see him, Bond added facts contained in police records.

"Paradiso mentioned a hair," Burke said. "He thinks that's the only evidence the police have about him?"

"That's what he said," Bond professed. "That's the only evidence that they had against him."

The autopsy report in Palombo's case files identified dried vegetable matter and a single dark brown hair on Marie's body shirt. Burke asserted that salt water had washed away any trace of semen, but no one tested for that. The suggestion was insane to think salt water selectively rinsed incriminating evidence but left the bodysuit dotted with other organic stains. Five years after the autopsy, the follicle still hadn't been tested prior to the start of the trial.

"They have no witnesses, no evidence whatso... other than the strand of hair," Bond insisted.

Then it was the defense's turn. "Mr. Bond, he told you on the morning of December 14, 1982 they had no evidence?" Rappaport asked.

"Yes, that was on the morning of the fourteenth," Bond confirmed.

Rappaport logically listed the evidence that pointed to Doyle and asked Bond emphatically whether Paradiso had caused or manufactured the known facts. Doyle and Marie had argued the day of the wedding. The boyfriend knew about the other man, Eddie Fisher. Witnesses noticed severe scratches on the back of the dejected lover's hands. Doyle packed up all his murdered roommate's belongings. Family members saw blood on the steps leading up to the couple's third-floor apartment just days after the crime. Doyle took flight to New Jersey the day of the funeral, and gave a false name to the arresting officers. For every incriminating point the defense questioned, Bond's answer was the same. Paradiso did not fabricate the evidence.

"He didn't put the scratches on David Doyle, did he?" Rappaport asked.

"No," Bond admitted. "I didn't say that he did, either."

"He didn't tell Doyle to run to New Jersey, did he?" the defense counsel hammered.

"I didn't say that he did," Bond acknowledged.

Rappaport had scored some points for the defense argument that there was another culprit. Bond had just confirmed the mountain of circumstantial evidence stacked against the boyfriend. Burke rushed back in to rehabilitate his witness, but ended up adding even more doubt to Bond's veracity, except the jury never discerned what details Bond added *after* the Department of Corrections moved him to Concord. Authorities had transferred Bond out of the Charles Street

Jail on December 29, 1982, cutting off dialogue between Paradiso and Bond. The only sources Bond had after the twenty-ninth were Burke, Tammaro, and Palombo. Paradiso didn't see or hear from Bond again until he faced him in court that day, July 17, 1984.

"When you said to him, Mr. Paradiso, 'Why jam him up?' meaning Doyle," Burke asked, "what did he say?"

"He just said, 'All the evidence points toward him.' " Bond said.

"Did you have any conversation with Lenny [Paradiso] when you left on the twenty-ninth?" the prosecutor asked.

"I had a conversation with Lenny," the snitch replied. "I think Lenny knew I was gonna tell on him."

"What did he say?"

" 'How do my alibi sound?' " the state's star witness answered. "I said, 'Sounds good.' I says, 'You ain't John Doe, you know.' "

Reporters didn't ask Marie's family how they felt after Bond's performance. Marie was all but forgotten in the case for her justice. Instead, they approached the Websters, the parents of the undeclared victim.

"He certainly made a good witness," George approved. "In my opinion, the man has no reason to make up a story like that."

"He has a fantastic memory," Eleanor endorsed the two-time killer.

The panel sitting in judgment had heard an unbelievable level of detail for an alleged jailhouse confession, but they didn't have the benefit of the snitch's prior versions. Bond enhanced his story after December 29, 1981, after he was transferred from the Charles Street Jail. Burke Tammaro, and Palombo had the necessary information to supplement Bond's testimony.

Burke, Tammaro, and Palombo had concluded that the skeletal story Bond had regurgitated during the police interview on January 14, 1983 was insufficient. The embellished story Bond fixed on the stand during the trial included the single, dark hair that allegedly sent Paradiso into a panic. The detail included in the autopsy report was a late entry for the prosecution; the lab tested it two days after the trial started, and the hair wasn't a match to Paradiso. Bond asserted that Paradiso feared the follicle was the only evidence the state had, and that the defendant's lawyer previously prevented a comparison.

Candy had notified the police about her stolen car on September 13, 1979, and the prosecution recovered the report. Using his extraordinary skills helping witnesses remember, Palombo elicited Bond's refreshed recollection, inserting a new alleged confession: Paradiso burned his car ten days after murdering Marie. The calendar didn't exactly align with Bond's story, but the state presented enough speculation to paint an incriminating picture.

During the January rehearsal, Bond had said Paradiso got home about 2:30 a.m. on the twelfth after killing the woman in red. According to Bond, Paradiso phoned his girlfriend, asked her to wake up her mother, grab a cab to come over, and get their stories together. At trial, Bond inflated the call list. At some point that night, Paradiso supposedly also called his boss George Murphy even though there was not a scintilla of evidence to support the claim.

According to Bond, while Paradiso waited for his girlfriend, he also received a call from an older woman wanting a little bit of action. Bond didn't know her name, but claimed the woman had had a heart attack in 1982. The older woman was currently on her deathbed at Mass General Hospital. According to Bond, Paradiso planned to use her as an alibi witness for the night Marie died. Andrew Palombo testified he checked the visitation logs and identified Elaine Covino, a friend of the hapless defendant. When police interviewed her, she scoffed at the suggested call, and affirmed Paradiso's boat was gone in July or August 1981.

"On August 12 or 13, 1979, did you call Leonard Paradiso?" state troopers had asked the older woman during an interview conducted on April 7, 1983.

"I refuse to answer that, because I smell a rat," Elaine had stated. "You know, all that publicity in the papers and news media about the Webster murder."

Dissatisfied, the officers pressed, "Do you know anything about Lenny [Paradiso] in regards to Joan Webster?"

"I was with Lenny when he noticed the boat was stolen," she responded. "It was either in July or August."

This police report was hidden in the prosecutor's files. During the trial, Burke created the illusion that Paradiso suggested he had an alibi witness to Robert Bond for the night Marie died. In fact, Elaine had contradicted Burke's theory about Joan Webster's fate, Burke's real objective, and affirmed Paradiso's boat was gone in July or August 1981. The deception was invisible to the jury who only had Bond's testimony to rely on. Elaine Covino was never called to the stand, and the police report was kept a *secret*.

Bond reciting the credentials of two attorneys who had worked on Paradiso's defense hit a ridiculous overdose of information. Bond claimed Paradiso shared the pedigrees of Judd Carhart and Walter Prince, two lawyers who had joined the defense effort for a few months. At the conclusion of his testimony, Bond had claimed that Paradiso had spilled his guts, and then some, when he told the con what he bartered to enlist legal services. This testimony that Burke had proffered was grossly overdone, to say the least.

In addition to the enlarged recitation, Burke concealed his own disturbing sleight of hand. On January 14, 1983 and February 17, 1983, Bond told authorities Paradiso strangled Marie with her scarf once. On the witness stand on July 16, 1984, Bond upped the ante. He claimed Paradiso strangled her *twice*, once to the point of unconsciousness before he allegedly raped her. Then he choked her a second time when she came to. The distinction was significant for the charges Burke wanted. In Massachusetts, it wasn't considered rape unless the victim was breathing. Neither Bond nor Paradiso likely knew that finer point of the law, but Bond had gotten these details from the people sent by George Webster.

As Burke wound down his case, he tried to tie up the loose hairs. Two days after the trial started, the prosecutor scrambled to test the single hair found on Marie's leotard. The defense had trouble finding the original examiner. Mark Grant, a new technician unfamiliar with the original findings, compared the single strand to samples Paradiso had submitted from all parts of his body. Grant took his turn on the stand, reading from his handwritten notes. The rushed analysis didn't give Burke the conclusion he hoped for, but he left a dangling follicle for the jury's imagination.

"Were there enough similarities to form an opinion as to whether or not this was consistent with Paradiso's hair?" Burke asked.

"There were enough characteristics, in my opinion, to say that it was probably not from Mr. Paradiso's head." Grant stated.

"It's probably not from his head," The prosecutor emphasized.

The emphasis Burke placed on Grant's answer left some doubt for the jury. Burke had to admit, the cut hair did not come from Paradiso's head, but he did not address the follicles tested from other parts of Paradiso's body.

Burke's skill to shape the narrative often took place at the sidebar out of the gallery's earshot. A narrow-minded judge added an advantage for the prosecution, but Burke's real secret weapon was the Websters sitting in the back of the room.

"Your Honor, at this time," Burke concluded, "the Commonwealth rests its case in chief."

Back they went to the sidebar.

"I have a motion for a required finding of not guilty," Rappaport submitted.

The request was a customary motion, but the judge elected for the jury to decide the matter based on what he chose to give them. In our system of jurisprudence, there is a presumption of innocence until a jury of peers determined guilt beyond a reasonable doubt. The defense was up against a system that had already made up their minds and held the power to direct that course.

"Mr. Rappaport, what you would ask me to do is disbelieve Bond's testimony," Donahue decided. "I don't think I can do that."

NAME	NUMBER	OFFENSE	SENTE
eonard	(U) 35074		

HOED	RELEASED	PAROLE DISCHARGE DATE	FULL MAXIMUM	PAROLE OFFICER
				P.O. AnchukAltis
				(Trans. from P.O.)

-2-   Home: 834 Summer St., Lynn
Work: Commerical Lobster Co. 295 Commercial
227-3722

DATE 1979	TYPE OF REPORT	
7-6-79 Cont.		also tells P.O. that someone stole his car and it was later recovered on the railroad tracks. P.O. told Subject that as long as his work takes him to Main and R.I. or even New York and is not over a couple of days there he has P.O.'; ok without a call. But if it goes over a couple of days then he is to get permission from the P.O. So, at this meeting, things look ok. VA:md
7-9-79	TC	Subject called, office going to be his home now. NEW ADDRESS : 134 Princeton St., East Boston, tel. 569-4112.
8-12-79.	TC	Called - waiting for new PO to check him out. This PO gave subject PO's number. Subject said he will call.
3-15-79		Request for transfer forwarded to PO Jim O'Neil.
3-79 8/19/79	CV	Subject came into the office, to see the PO. Subject tells the PO that he & his girl Candy went to a wedding last Sat. Red Milano of Saugus, a contractor married off his son. The subject works for one of the sons so he & his girl invited back to Red Milano's home in Saugus with the family. At the home a young lady started to act up. Subject & Candy did not know who she was. Appears she was the girl friend of one of the Milano cousins. The girl got so un-ruly that she was asked to leave the house. So when no one would take the girl anywhere, Candy drove the girl to East Boston & left her at a bar. Candy came back to the house. Later Subject & Candy decided to go home. When Candy & Subject got to Candy's car they found the girl's keys and papers in the car. So Candy & the subject went back to East Boston, to give the keys and papers to the girl. Candy & subject stopped at the bar where the girl was drinking. The girl came out and they gave her the keys & papers. Candy asked the girl if they could take her home, the girl told them no way, she had an appointment ; with this she walked away toward Maverick Sq. Candy & the subject them went home. Subject was concerned because he was on parole & did not want to get involved in a bum beef. PO advised the subject that if questioned he is to cooperate with the police. Subject stated he would ~~~~~ Subject stated he would be in touch with the PO.
9-21-79	77	Subject called to let P.O. know he was going to Maine to pick up a load. Subject will return on Wednesday or Thursday. Will notify P.O. when he does P.O. gave ok. VA:jcd
-23-79	N	No response. VA:jcd

(OVER)

EXHIBIT

Leonard Paradiso Parole Officer Entry

A-70

COMMONWEALTH OF MASSACHUSETTS

SUFFOLK, ss.

SUPERIOR COURT
CRIMINAL NO.S
038655
&
143033

COMMONWEALTH

v.

LEONARD PARADISO

AFFIDAVIT OF DENNIS ALBANO IN SUPPORT OF DEFENDANT'S
MOTION FOR A NEW TRIAL

I, Dennis Albano, being first duly sworn according to law, hereby say and depose the following:

1. That I make this affidavit in support of Leonard Paradiso's motion for a new trial.

2. That during or about June 1985 I had a conversation with Christine Delisi.

3. That Christine Delisi told me she had been a witness for the prosecution at the trial of Leonard Paradiso.

4. That Christine Delisi told me that she had been badgered and coerced into testifying at Paradiso's trial.

5. That Christine Delisi told me that there were criminal charges against her, or that there were going to be criminal charges brought against her.

6. That Christine Delisi did not give me specific information as to the nature of the pending, or possible to be pending in the future, criminal charges against her.

7. That Christine Delisi did tell me that the Massachusetts State Police told her that she could lose her child if the charges against her were pushed by the prosecutor's office.

8. That Christine Delisi told me that the Massachusetts State Police repeatedly called her on the telephone and visited her home until she relented and agreed to testify for the prosecution at Leonard Paradiso's trial.

Signed under the pains and penalties of perjury, this 28th day of October, 1985.

Sworn to and subscribed before me
This 28 Day of Oct , 1985

Notary Public
My Commission Expires 2/2/88

Dennis Albano

Dennis Albano Affidavit Regarding Christine DeLisi

Chapter Fourteen
Making Faces

Emotions obscured the nuggets of established facts coming out in the courtroom. The defense had a mountain to climb to overcome the boiling passions surrounding Joan Webster. Her parents sitting in the courtroom were a constant reminder of the case Burke was really after. Paradiso maintained his innocence in both the murder of Marie Iannuzzi and the presumed murder of Joan Webster, but the savvy couple from New Jersey said otherwise. Steve Rappaport took a deep breath and called Marie's boyfriend David Doyle to the stand as the first witness for the defense.

David Doyle and Marie Iannuzzi had gotten into a screaming match during the wedding reception. Doyle's mother had pulled him away from the embarrassing public display and took him home. His girlfriend went on alone to a house party. During the grand jury, Marie's boyfriend admitted to using drugs on the night of Marie's murder. At trial, his memory conveniently faded. The jury heard an overused justification to avoid answering questions.

"I don't remember," Doyle claimed a variety of times.

"Do you remember whether or not you had scratches on your hands at the wake?" Rappaport asked.

"I might have," Doyle answered.

Attention turned to Doyle's behavior of taking flight after the wake. He missed his beloved girlfriend's funeral because he was depressed, or so he said, and felt the need to get away. The first flight on the list was to Newark, New Jersey, where cops arrested the bereaved man stealing suitcases from the conveyor. Doyle gave them a false name and address. Doyle's flight from the pressure was the exact sort of guilty behavior the prosecution was trying to project on Paradiso. Doyle couldn't cope; he said so. He drowned his sorrow by washing the drugs down with booze… a concoction that helped him lift off before he even boarded a plane.

"I bought a round-trip ticket," Doyle said. "I was supposed to come back the next day for the funeral."

The police report noted that the stolen ticket in David's possession was from LaGuardia to Boston; Doyle was arrested in Newark, New Jersey. Marie's funeral began at 8:30 a.m. at the Joseph A. Langone Jr. Funeral Home in East Boston. The ticket he had in his possession wasn't going to get him there. His somber face in front of the court belied his intention. Doyle was supposed to be a pallbearer, but that obligation would have put his marred hands on full display for the mourners to see.

The defense counsel asked a question that an officer in New Jersey had asked the day of Marie's funeral, but the seated panel heard a different answer. On August 17, 1979, Doyle told the investigator in New Jersey that Marie had gotten a ride to the house party with his cousin, Freddie Milano. He couldn't remember the girl's name who drove Marie to the bar. The Saugus Police independently confirmed Marie's ride from David's mother; Marie left the reception with Doyle's cousins. Numerous undocumented meetings with Palombo had apparently refreshed Doyle's memory.

"She said she was getting a ride to the party with Lenny [Paradiso]?" Rappaport asked.

"Yes," Doyle answered, "Lenny and his girlfriend."

The cross examination handed Burke the reins. Rehabilitating the substance abuser with a rap sheet, prior bad acts of violence against his now deceased girlfriend, and a mountain of incriminating evidence was no simple task. The ends justified the means in Burke's mind, and he calculated this verdict would vindicate Joan Webster.

Burke shamelessly guided the witness through excuse number three for the scratches on Doyle's hands at the time of the murder. The jury listened as the jealous boyfriend impossibly described commiserating with his girlfriend's other lover at a bar across the street from the wake. According to Doyle, he picked up a barstool and got into a fight with a rowdy patron. He claimed Marie's brother-in-law and Eddie Fisher witnessed the fight. Scratches dug from the wrists to the fingers on both hands that witnesses saw as early as Monday morning after Marie's murder morphed into cuts and bruises.

Burke scrubbed as hard as he could. He guided the witness to explain Marie's packed belongings. Fuzzy memory miraculously became crystal clear; he packed all her things Monday night, and siblings arrived on Tuesday to pick out a dress. Then Burke whitewashed Doyle's paranoid behavior in taking flight to New Jersey. The whole room felt sorry for the miserable misfit who felt so alone at the wake. He just wanted to get out of town for a while to clear his head. The offensive counter Burke represented even whitewashed the habitual user, as if he popped pills at the wake for the first time.

"Why were you taking valiums?" Burke asked. "What's the kind of pressure you were undergoing at this time?"

When the defense got their chance to re-direct Doyle, Steve Rappaport shifted back to the troublesome scratches. Doyle had told cops at the time his cat caused them. His mother had said the scratches resulted from a car accident two months before Marie's murder. Burke tried to redefine them as cuts and bruises caused during a bar fight. The prosecution clouded the issue about just when witnesses saw the scratches, but Doyle had them, and the state had to have an answer.

"I didn't know where they came from. I don't remember," Doyle claimed. "It could have been in the fight. It could have been the cat."

David's mother swore to tell the whole truth and nothing but before taking the witness seat. She confirmed that David went home with his parents after the wedding reception at the Ship Restaurant, and Marie rode to the house party with her [Mrs. Doyle's] nephew, contradicting her son's testimony. Mrs. Doyle described her bedroom on the second floor of their house and the couple's apartment on the third floor. She always kept her door open, and would know if her son went out.

"Ma'am, has David ever left the house, oh, in the last five years, without you knowing it?" Rappaport asked skeptically.

"No," his mother replied.

Rappaport turned her attention to the damning scratches. Doyle's mother had talked to the Saugus Police soon after cops arrested her son in Newark. A Saugus inspector asked about the scratches on David's hands. It was a logical question since someone had just murdered his girlfriend, and he had flown the coop to Newark. His mother had told them that the scratches had resulted from a vehicle accident on June tenth or eleventh, two months before Marie died. Something was in the water in Boston that evidently affected people's memory; authorities claimed it was Joan Webster. On the stand, Mrs. Doyle denied giving that explanation to the police, but she added another choice for public consumption. Anyone keeping score now had four excuses for the scratches on Doyle's hands.

"I had told the officer, David fell at the MBTA (Metro Boston Transit Authority) Station," she swore.

During the grand jury, witnesses described Doyle being on something, out of it at the wake. His mother kept him on a short leash. She came in with him and left with him, never letting him out of her sight. Burke had shifted the narrative to a fight across the street that his mother didn't know about at the time, and planted two witnesses at the alleged scene, Marie's lover Eddie Fisher, and the man who observed the overly attentive Mrs. Doyle.

"Do you know if David was involved in some kind of fracas at one of the wakes?" Burke asked.

"I heard about it later on," she said.

Next, Paradiso's lawyer reinforced the another-culprit defense. Jimmy Milano, Doyle's cousin, stepped up to the plate. He had attended his brother's wedding and the house party at his parents' home in Saugus. The witness cleared up any confusion about Marie's ride after the reception. Marie and his brother Freddie both rode in the same car with him to the house party. His firsthand account was consistent with Doyle's statement to the New Jersey police at the time, but contradicted the self-serving testimony he gave in court. David Doyle had lied.

Jimmy Milano observed Marie causing a scene at the house party, and his father wanted her to leave. First, Mr. Milano called a cab, but the obstinate partier wouldn't get in. Jimmy recalled that Marie left the house with Paradiso's girlfriend, Candy Weyant.

"Do you recall how late you stayed at the house that night?" Rappaport asked.

"Until about eleven o'clock," Jimmy answered.

"Were there still some people left at the house?" the defense probed.

"Yes, there was," Doyle's cousin confirmed. "There was my parents, my sister, and Lenny and Candy."

Maybe it was the sweltering heat or empathetic jurors mesmerized in the presence of the Websters that clouded reasonable thinking. A hearsay witness convicted twice for murder told the court Leonard Paradiso was at the Cardinales Nest Bar at 11:00 p.m. on Saturday, August 11, 1979. Bond claimed Candy was tucked at home in Revere while Paradiso hustled Marie in East Boston. An eyewitness, Jimmy Milano, the other culprit's own cousin, placed Paradiso and his girlfriend a half an hour away at Milano's parents' home in Saugus at 11:00 p.m. on Saturday, August 11, 1979. The defendant could not be in two places at once, let alone three, and it shouldn't have been that difficult a choice who to believe.

Burke had tried to discredit the witness, but the fact remained in the record. Rappaport punctuated the key defense point for the jury to absorb, hoping the discrepancy didn't fall on deaf ears. When Jimmy left the party at 11:00 p.m., Marie was already gone. Candy left the celebration between 9:30 and 10 p.m. Jimmy's sister, Rosemary Sullivan, loaded the intoxicated Marie into Candy's car, and Candy drove Marie to her destination. Paradiso stayed behind at the Milanos' house. Candy returned to the party before 11 p.m.

"When you left the house party, did you see Lenny [Paradiso]?" Rappaport asked.

"He was there, yes," Jimmy confirmed.

"Was Marie still there?" the defense asked.

"No," Jimmy replied.

To watch Burke's "dance" in the courtroom, a rational observer might have gotten the impression Burke was hyped up on something. The prosecutor popped up raising objections every few minutes, as if his seat was greased. He tried to block the defense from handing the witness a copy of his own records to refresh his memory. Detective Arthur Cook had conducted many of the early interviews after Marie's death. The records contained names of four witnesses who saw Marie back in the bar around closing. Then Burke disrupted Rappaport's direct examination of the Saugus Police detective with a new tactic. The defense counsel interrupted himself and stepped up to the bench. Burke was making faces like an adolescent in junior high.

"Well, Burke hasn't objected for at least fifteen minutes," the judge said.

"I know that, but he's giving me dirty looks," Rappaport responded. "He's looking at me, you know, what are you doing?"

At the moment, the inquiry was focusing on the prosecution's witness, Christine DeLisi. The counsel needed the report to refresh Detective Cook's memory. Christine DeLisi's statements from the grand jury, documented statements in the officer's report, clearly implicated David Doyle as a suspect.

"That's certainly not upsetting to your case," the defense told the offensive counsel.

"Well, it depends," Burke objected. "If you flush something out, that's not a problem, but if you start getting down to the nitty-gritty, then that's when it becomes a problem."

Judge Donahue cloaked his bias for the moment. He set aside a request to enter the police report about the drop of blood found on the Doyle's stairs. The defense intended to call the reporting officer to the stand. Donahue reserved his ruling about evidence until a later point in time.

Jean Day came out of hiding and showed up at the courthouse on July 18, 1984. Marie's stepsister had given testimony in the grand jury that was damning to Burke's case. The defense investigator led Jean to a private room downstairs, away from the courtroom. The defense's private investigator, Dennis Slawsby, probed her memory about Marie's murder before showing her the minutes from the grand jury. Her recollection was consistent with her previous testimony, and she affirmed the accuracy of the grand jury transcript.

While the private investigator interviewed Marie's stepsister in a private room, Paradiso's lawyer, Steve Rappaport, called a bar patron to testify next. Carol Seracuse had been at the Cardinales Nest Bar shortly before the bar closed at 2:00 a.m. Paradiso had held the door for Marie sometime between 12:30 and 1:00 a.m., and Christine saw her leave. The timing was important. Marie told Christine she would be back, and Carol was one of the witnesses who said she saw the victim back in the bar. Marie had asked Carol for a ride to another drinking establishment, but she didn't have a car.

"Do you have any memory of approximately what time this conversation took place?" Rappaport asked.

"Not really," she answered.

"Ma'am, I want to show you this document," Rappaport continued.

"Yes, I know. I seen it, 1:30," the witness blurted.

"No, judge, I object to that!" Burke protested.

The time the witness told police that she saw Marie in the bar slipped in before Burke could stop it. Paradiso's team scored a point with the witness reading from the police report. Whether she still had a memory of it five years later was almost irrelevant compared to what she stated at the time of the murder. The prosecution feared that another witness had just contradicted their timeline from the witness stand.

Burke knew he had to neuter the next eyewitness. Marie's uncle had observed Doyle's severe scratches on the first night of the wake. Benjamin Puzzo's description of raw beef, oozing type gouges you don't touch wasn't in front of the jury. Burke hit a real low challenging the witness and figuratively picking scabs over the age of Doyle's scratches.

"Did you see any blood coming from them?" Burke asked.

"No, because he had a lot of mercurochrome, whatever it was, all around there," Puzzo said.

Mercurochrome is a reddish-orange, topical treatment applied to fresh, open wounds. The subtle clue about the age of Doyle's scratches slipped into the record, but sailed over the heads of jurors judging another man's fate.

Judge Donahue recessed the court. Dennis Slawsby wrapped up his interview with Marie's stepsister, Jean Day, away from the proceedings while two escorts waited outside the room. When the door opened, Tim Burke and Andrew Palombo ushered Jean to an unknown location. If the pained sibling repeated her same account in front of the gallery, all of Burke and Palombo's efforts could be lost. An hour later, after the recess, participants returned to the courtroom, and Rappaport called Jean to the stand. Her testimony conflicted with the answers she had given to Slawsby that morning. She suddenly forgot how Marie got dressed and the order she put her clothes on. Jean thought the scratches might have been done by a cat, and the drop of blood on the stairs might have been paint.

"Ma'am, when was the last time you had been at the [Marie's] apartment?" Rappaport asked.

"I think two weeks previous to her death," Jean replied.

"Ma'am, do you remember talking to me about, oh, about an hour ago?" the defense counsel queried. "That's not what you said to me outside."

While Jean was on the stand, Burke was back to complaining roughly every two minutes. However, this time the judge demurred and summoned the attorneys himself for a private session out of the gallery's hearing.

"Judge, forty-five minutes ago she tells me one thing," Rappaport argued, "I'm sure her memory must have been refreshed by Mr. Burke."

Burke was offended. The judge admonished the defense for rebutting his own witness; Rappaport couldn't be a witness and a lawyer in the same case. But the fact remained, Jean had changed her story after Burke and Palombo walked her down the hall, and the defense's private investigator, Dennis Slawsby, confirmed it. Burke made a disturbing revelation, a red flag amplifying his concern over Jean's altered testimony. He disclosed Jean had suffered injuries during an assault in July 1982, and implied Paradiso was responsible. Paradiso was in jail at the time. Burke didn't produce an incident report, but told the judge that Palombo knew when it happened and had pictures. The incident had occurred about the time Palombo arrested Paradiso for Marie's murder, and Jean negated the state's theory.

Jean was distraught over the trial and confided in her neighbor, Louis Tontodonato. After the trial was over she told him that the police wanted her to testify at the trial of her stepsister Marie's murder, but she didn't want to testify the way they wanted. When she tried to refuse, the police pressured her, took her son away, and arrested her on charges unrelated to Marie's murder. Jean feared the threats from the police and went into hiding in Somerville.

"The police told me I would be sent to prison, and that they [the police] would see I lost custody of my son," Jean cried to Louis. "I was forced to testify at the trial against Leonard Paradiso and gave false testimony."

Jean's disclosure after the trial raised the legitimate concerns of using coerced witnesses to achieve a predetermined verdict of guilt against Paradiso. Unfortunately, the revelation came after the trial proceedings.

Burke's tactics to discredit or distort witnesses during the trial went well beyond Jean Day. When David Doyle's childhood friend, David Dellaria, took the stand during the trial, Burke made a mockery of him. Doyle was angry with Dellaria for reporting him out to the police, and aggressively tried to silence his friend.

Doyle attacked his friend David Dellaria twice for ratting him out to the police. Burke exalted two convicted killers on the witness stand, but he made short order of this defense witness. The two Davids got high and chugged a few beers in the summer 1981. Doyle intimated that he killed Marie, and Dellaria told the cops. A motorcycle riding druggie pulled Doyle off Dellaria the first time. The second time, neighbors watched Doyle sic two large dogs on Dellaria and pin him to the ground. Doyle pressed a long blade to Dellaria's neck, but he rolled away from the immediate danger. The incident wasn't a recent contrivance; Dellaria had filed a report of attempted murder with the court. Burke mocked the defense witness at the same time he enabled Doyle's substance abuse. The prosecutor ignored the Doyle's aggression.

"Do you know whether or not David Doyle ever had a temper?" the defense asked.

"David Doyle is a crazy bastard!" his lifelong friend exclaimed. "Excuse my language."

The next witness the defense summoned was the second friend who corroborated the allegation that Doyle had tried to strangle Marie two months before she met her fate. Like Christine DeLisi, Ann Marie Kenney saw the strangulation marks on her friend's neck, and she heard the terror in Marie's voice when she said that David had tried to kill her. Burke appealed to keep the testimony out. Rappaport pleaded for fair due process for his client. The opposing counsels stopped for the day. The judge needed time to assess whether he would allow this evidence into the record.

The next morning, both attorneys met in the judge's lobby. Donahue went right to work castrating the defense. First, Donahue had Dellaria's statement he had made to the Saugus Police tossed. The report Inspector Howard Long compiled on August 6, 1981 detailing his conversation with Dellaria included a few other things. The disallowed record noted that Doyle had visible scratches on his face and hands in Long's office on the day examiners identified the body. Also, witnesses saw Marie Iannuzzi's bags packed before authorities confirmed the victim's name. Jean Day told police she had observed blood on the fifth step leading up to Doyle's apartment. Finally, cops arrested Doyle in New Jersey with a stolen airline ticket from LaGuardia to Boston. All this evidence was now discarded in the judge's circular file.

The next police report the judge axed was the statement given by Carol Seracuse, the witness who spoke to the victim at 1:30 a.m. just before she was murdered. Prior statements were on the block next. Burke had already sanitized Christine DeLisi's memory. The judge facilitated Burke's cause by nixing prior statements made by Ann Marie, the witness currently under oath. Next, the judge disallowed a statement in police reports from the bartender who said he had seen Marie in the bar at 1:45 a.m. and had asked her to turn off the air conditioner. Rappaport couldn't find him and wanted to enter the police report into the record. The judge said no.

The final blow the judge leveled against the defense denied their right to discovery. Burke had transcripts from the Joan Webster grand jury. He intended to use them to discredit Paradiso's girlfriend. Joan was still the unnamed victim in the present case, but nothing had been charged. Without an indictment, grand jury testimony remained secret. Innocent until proven guilty and the right to a fair trial were the cornerstones of American jurisprudence. Lady Justice was blindfolded, but the ruling robe was not. In Judge Roger Donahue's court, His Honor tipped the scales, and not for truth and justice.

Defense Attorney Steve Rappaport tried to reinforce that Doyle was a likely suspect in Marie's murder. Inspector Howard Long was on and off the seat in no time. Officers who worked the case in the early days documented their interviews and observations, and the evidence gave the Saugus Police two suspects. The deflated defense counsel asked Long whether he had questioned Dellaria, but Rappaport already knew the judge had barred the officer's August 6, 1981 report from the record. Long recalled his conversation with Doyle's friend on July 16, 1981. He remembered the patrol car idled by the curb. Detectives had picked up the known user, David Dellaria, to quiz him regarding the rumblings on the street about who murdered Marie. Dellaria squealed on a friend from the neighborhood. The seasoned investigator couldn't recall when Doyle stopped being a suspect; the officer was taken off the case. Trooper Andrew Palombo took the reins in February 1981.

Since Paradiso exercised his right not to testify, Rappaport didn't have much choice other than to put Candy in the witness chair next. While she repeated what happened on the night of August 11, 1979, the audience snickered. Tim Burke was at it again making faces. Rappaport complained about Burke's antics back at the bench, but

Donahue hadn't seen any sneering, so it didn't count. Burke wasted no time. He pulled out the secret Webster grand jury testimony to discredit the defendant's alibi witness. He asked the witness if she had ever lied for Paradiso.

"No, I haven't," Candy replied.

Burke smirked again, and handed her a document. The judge had denied the defense discovery, so Rappaport didn't know what the document said. The secret weapon came out of the Joan Webster grand jury hearings, and Burke had cleverly brought the missing grad student back into Marie's case.

"Whose signature is that right there?" the prosecutor demanded. "Real loud please."

"It's my signature," Candy said.

"I'll ask you again; did you ever lie to the police for Mr. Paradiso?" Burke accused. "Real loud."

"Yes," she admitted.

Rappaport stopped the bleeding to approach the judge once again. He couldn't hear the disturbance, but sensed something going on behind him. Vultures circled in the courtroom feeding on Burke's frenzy.

"You were shown a document," Rappaport said. "What did that document relate to?"

"An insurance claim on a boat, that the boat was stolen," Candy said.

"Was the boat stolen?" The defense counsel asked.

"No," Candy admitted. "I believe it was sunk."

Burke stepped back in and badgered the witness. He reminded the jury of another victim in the news. The boat had nothing to do with Marie's murder, but Burke had coyly fused Joan's case with Marie's. The media never reported on one case without speculating about the other.

"That boat doesn't involve simply an insurance fraud, does it?" Burke challenged.

"As far as I'm concerned, it does," Candy insisted.

"Ma'am, you're a future witness for Paradiso in another matter, aren't you?" Burke asked.

"Objection, your Honor," Rappaport demanded.

"Objection overruled," Donahue decided.

The room was restless. Whispers reached a fevered pitch, and all eyes turned to see George and Eleanor's reaction. Reporters fell over each other to get to the phones and put out the first byline of the day's news. Candy had left a door wide open that might bring unfavorable history into the record. Paradiso was vulnerable to the accusations levied against him with his prior record of assault. Paradiso understood, but still declined to take the stand in his own defense. Tim Burke had humiliated Paradiso's girlfriend, the person threatening the state's case with the truth. The image of Joan sank in as designed, and Marie took a backseat in the present case.

Joan Webster's fate was the jury's last impression as the defense rested.

160

OLICE DEPARTMENT   PREAMBLE TO SIGNED STATEM. TS   NEWARK, N.J.
(MIRANDA WARNING)
C.C. NUMBER _____

DATE August 17, 1979
TIME _____

Mr. Edward Day _____, I am Detectiv David Martinez _____ of the

Police Department of Newark, Essex County, New Jersey. I am going to ask certain questions regarding _____. However, before beginning I advise you of your rights.

1. You have the right to remain silent.
2. Anything you say can be used against you in a court of law.
3. You have the right to talk to a lawyer and have him present with you while you are being questioned.
4. If you cannot afford to hire a lawyer, one will be appointed to represent you before any questioning, if you wish one.
5. You have the right to stop answering questions or giving a statement anytime you wish and do not have to give a reason. You also have the right to demand a lawyer during the giving of a statement or the answering of questions and may stop until he arrives. If you cannot afford a lawyer, one will be appointed to represent you.

WAIVER

"I have been advised and I have read the statement of my rights shown above. I understand what my rights are, I am willing to answer questions and make a statement. I do not want a lawyer at this time but understand that I may have one at any time I so desire. I also understand that I may stop answering questions at any time. I understand and know what I am doing. No promises or threats have been made to me and no pressure of any kind has been used against me."

Signed: _____ (I do not wish to answer all questions
Time and Date: .535 8/11/79
Witness: _____
Witness: _____

Newark, NJ Police Interview of David Doyle (pg. 1)

POLICE DEPARTMENT   STATEMENT FORM   **NEWARK, N.J.**

DATE:	CENTRAL ARREST NO.:	CENTRAL COMPLAINT NO.:
8-17-1979		

VOLUNTARY STATEMENT OF:

David Thomas Doyle arrested In Newark N.J as Edward Day

OENCE:

2 Jeffries street areested address 39 Haynes street E. Boston Massachusetts

OCCUPATION:	AGE:
rubbish removal currently laid off from employment	21

STATEMENT MADE TO:

Detective David Martinez East Detective Squad started at 3:34 P:M 8-17-79

Q. David Thomas Doyle can you read and write the English language
A. Yes I can.
Q. David have you been properly advised of your rights in the Miranda warning, the form which you did read aloud, and sign.
A. Yes I have.
Q. David when you were arrested In Newark N.J, did you use the name of Edward Day, and the addre: of 39 Haynes street, East Boston Massachusetts.
A. Yes I did.
Q. avid why did you use a different name, other than your true, name.
A. Because I have five years probation facing me In Boston, for armed robbery. ←
Q. avidare you currently under the Influence of alcohol, or any narcotic substance.
A. No, I am not.
Q. David Thomas Doyle would you be willing to answer any questions, regarding an Incident that took place In Saugas Massachusetts, Involving an Individual female named Marie Iannuzzi.
A. Yes I will.
Q. Would you like an attorney present, before you answer any questions, regarding this matter.
A. No, I don't need one right now, but I would like one for the charges In Newark.
Q. When Is the last time that you saw Marie alive.
A. At a wedding reception In Winfield ass., at a place called the ship.
Q. Yes I did.
Q. Did you go to the reception with Marie.
A. Yes I did.
Q. Did you leave with arie.
A. No.
Q. Do you know who Marie left with.
A. She left with my cousins, Freddie Milano,they went to Freddies house In Saugas Mass. ⟋
Q. Did you also go to reddies house.
A. No, I did not.
Q. Why did nt you go.
A. Because I had ripped my pants.
Q. Do you know who took Marie home from your cousins house.
A. She got a ride home with a girl, who dropped her off at a bar called the Cardinals nest In East Boston.
Q. Do you know the girls name who dropped her off at this bar.
A. No, I don t.
Q. Did you ever see arie again after the reception.
A. No I did not.
Q. Do you know anything at all about her death.
A. No, only what the police have told me,and what the Massachusetts ppolice have told me, I iden- tified the body at the morgue.
Q. Has everything that you have told me been the truth, and would you be willing to take apoly- graph examination, In reference to what you have told me,
A. Yes, and I will take a polygraph test anywhere, because I did not kill her. I loved her, for two years. No further questions asked. statement read and ended at 3:53 P:M.

SWORN TO AND SUBSCRIBED BEFORE ME THIS

17 DAY OF August 19 79

SIGNATURE

DP::225A-20M 6-75

2

Newark, NJ Police Interview of David Doyle (pg. 2)

The Commonwealth of Massachusetts

Department of Public Safety

Suffolk County Narcotic Unit
450 Worcester Road
Framingham, Ma. 01701

November 25, 1983

To: D/Captain Robert J. Zullas, Investigative Services
From: Trooper William G. McGreal, Suffolk Narcotic Unit

Subject: Interview of ROSEMARY A. SULLIVAN on 11-25-83
           79-106-0900-0203

1.   On 11-25-83 at about 3:00 p.m. this officer went
to 371 Washington Street, Melrose to interview ROSEMARY
(MILANO) SULLIVAN (4-23-52) of 91 Sonstrum Rd., Bristol,
Connecticut, (203-582-9413. Mrs. Sullivan was interviewed
on one prior occasion, 8-15-79.

2.   Mrs. Sullivan recalled that on the day of her
brothers (Michael) wedding, she attended the services at the
church, then went to the reception at the Ship Restaurant then
returned to her familys home for a house party. When asked
if she knew LENNY PARADISO, she stated she had met him once
or twice before at Lee's Restaurant which her family owned,
and she further recalled he had come there on at least one
occasion with his girlfriend, Candy. At her parents home,
Mrs. Sullivanbelieves the original group might have been as
large as 100 people. She further recalls that it was a warm
evening andthat there were people inside and outside of the
house. When asked about MARIE IANUZZI, Sullivan stated she
had been drinking and was "well on her way". She described
IANNUZI as sitting in the living room and said she was "nodding",
she was sitting with her brothers-in-laws from Worcester.
DAVID DOYLE was not present but she had see IANUZZI and
DOYLE together at the Ship. At her mothers house she saw
PARADISO and WAYANT together.

3.   During the party IANUZZI became loud and didn't
want to go home, she had no way to get there. Sullivans
parents wanted IANUZZI to go in a cab. Sullivan states
that PARADISO asked WAYANT to take Ianuzzi home. Sullivan
states that she put Ianuzzi in Wayants car. Weyant then left
the area with Ianuzzi, it was between 11-12-p.m. Paradiso
remained at the party. Weyant returned at a later time to
pick Paradiso up, they stayed a short time, then left.
Sullivan later heard on the news that Iannuzi had been murdered.

MSP Interview of Rosemary Sullivan (pg. 1)

-2-

4.   Sullivan stated further that PARADISO called her about 2 years after the wedding and stated he was in jail. He asked her if she remembered pictures falling out of her pocketbook onto the seat of the car and she stated she never saw or heard of Ianuzzi showing any pictures that day.

5.   Sullivan further stated that Bob and Pat Frangelo and Eleanor and Vinny Terolino of Johnson Terrace, Saugus were also in the area that day and she does not believe they have ever been interviewed.

Respectfully submitted,

WILLIAM G. MCGREAL
Trooper
Suffolk County Narcotic Unit
Mass. State Police

WGM:j

MSP Interview of Rosemary Sullivan (pg. 2)

164

A-128

I, Dennis Slawsby, do hereby swear and aver that:

1) I am a private investigator duly licensed to operate in the Commonwealth of Massachusetts.

2) My business address is 338 Highland Street, Weston, Massachusetts, 02193.

3) During the first half of 1984 I was employed by defense counsel Stephen Rappaport in an investigative capacity relative to the case of Commonwealth vs. Leonard Paradiso, Suffolk County Indictment numbers 038655, 043033.

4) The case against Mr. Paradiso involved the murder of one Marie Ianuzzi which took place on or about August 12, 1979.

5) During the course of my investigations I had repeatedly attempted to locate one Jean Day, a sister of Marie Ianuzzi.

6) My efforts to locate Ms. Day had been to no avail until July 18, 1984 when Ms. Day appeared at Suffolk Superior Court as a result of various letters I had sent to several addresses in the belief that she might be living at one of said locations.

7) July 18, 1984 was the eighth day of trial in the case of Commonwealth vs. Leonard Paradiso.

8) I met Ms. Day at approximately 9:30 a.m. on the aforesaid July 18, 1984 and we spent the next several hours discussing what she remembered of the events surrounding her sister's death, and of Ms. Day's testimony before the Grand Jury on March 5, 1982.

1

PI Dennis Slawsby Affidavit Regarding Jean Day (pg. 1)

9) The procedure I used in interviewing Ms. Day was as follows:

A-129

a) I first asked her to recite to the best of her recollection, using only her independant memory the events in question.

b) As she recited I was comparing her recitation with her Grand Jury testimony and concluded that there was no appreciable difference between the two.

c) I then showed her the actual transcripts of her Grand Jury testimony and she orally affirmed those transcripts as being accurate representations of her testimony and memory.

10) Shortly after I concluded my interview with Ms. Day, she was escorted to another area which location was unknown to me.

11) Ms. Day was escorted to said location at or about 1:30 p.m., and in the company of State Trooper Andrew Palumbo and Assistant District Attorney Timothy Burke.

12) Ms. Day returned to the courtroom at approximately 2:15 or 2:30 and took the stand to testify.

13) Her testimony sharply contradicted what she had told me only a few hours earlier.

14) Specifically, in speaking to me, she insisted that she knew that her sister always wore her pantyhose over, not under, panties. Several hours later she testified she had no idea of whether or not her sister wore her panties over or under her pantyhose.

15) Ms. Day stated to me that Marie's belongings were packed and boxed when Ms. Day arrived at the home of Marie's boyfriend on the Monday after Marie's death.

16) Ms. Day testified at trial that she first saw Marie's packed belongings at the home of Marie's boyfriend on the Tuesday after Marie's death.

2

PI Dennis Slawsby Affidavit Regarding Jean Day (pg. 2)

A-130

17) Ms. Day stated to me that she saw deep scratches on the hands of Marie's boyfriend, David Doyle, on the Monday morning immediately following Marie's death.

18) At the trial, Ms. Day denied noticing any scratches on David Doyle's hands on the Monday morning immediately following Marie's death.

19) After becoming aware of the large discrepancies between Ms. Day's statements to me and her subsequent testimony, I informed defense counsel Mr. Rappaport of said differences.

20) I further informed Mr. Rappaport that I had taken great care not to influence Ms. Day in any way during my interview.

21) I further informed Mr. Rappaport that I was available to testify as to the events of the morning including Ms. Day's statements before her meeting with A.D.A. Timothy Burke and Trooper Palumbo and her testimony after that meeting.

22) I was not called to testify by Mr. Rappaport.

Sworn to under the pains and penalties of perjury.

DENNIS SLAWSBY

Notary Public
My Commission Expires: ~~10/17/92~~
8/14/92

3

PI Dennis Slawsby Affidavit Regarding Jean Day (pg. 3)

COMMONWEALTH OF MASSACHUSETTS   A-64

SUFFOLK, ss   SUPERIOR COURT DEPARTMENT
                               Nos. 038655 and 043033

****
                      *
COMMONWEALTH   *
                      *
-vs-   *   SWORN AFFIDAVIT OF LOUIS TONTODONATO IN SUPPORT
                      *   OF DEFENDANT'S MOTION FOR A NEW TRIAL
LEONARD PARADISO   *
                      *
****

I, Louis Tontodonato, Two Clark Street, Post Office Box 43, Norfolk, MA 02056 (formerly of Paris Street, East Boston, MA 02128), being duly sworn according to law, hereby depose and say the following:

1.   That during the Fall of 1984, one Ms. Jean Day was living in the same apartment building as myself, specifically 127 Paris Street, 2nd Floor, East Boston, MA 02128. I lived in the "Rear Apartment - 1st Floor of the same building. While living there I became good friends with Jean Day.

2.   During our many conversations Jean Day told me that he "Step-Sister" (Marie Iannuzzi) had been murdered in August of 1979, and that the police wanted her to testify at the trial of defendant, but that she did not wish to testify the way they wanted her to testify. She told me, that, as a result of her refusal to testify her son, at the instigation of the police was taken away from her. She was also arrested on charges unrelated to her step-sisters alleged murder, and she further told me, that the police had told her she would be sent to prison and that they would see that she lost custody of her son.

3.   That Jean Day told me she had taken her son out of the "Day-Ca Center", in East Boston, because she was in fear of the threats by the police, and she then went into hiding and moved to Somerville, MA so that she wouldn't be found. She told me that she lived on Flint Street in Somerville, MA. I do not know the final outcome or disposition of the unrelated charges. Further, Jean Day told me that she kept newspaper clippings of her step-sisters alleged murder and the fact that one Leonard Paradiso was being charged and tried for the murder. Further, Jean Day told me that she was subsequently arrested by the Boston Police for a drug charge, and my memory is that she mentioned other crimes as well. I do not remember if she said she took her child without permission from the "Day-Care Center", but have the recollection that she did

Louis Tontodonato Affidavit Regarding Jean Day (pg. 1)

2. A-65

and that she may have been charged with kidnapping her own son.

4.   Jean Day also told me that faced with all of these charges she was forced to testify at the trial against Leonard Paradiso, and that she gave "false testimony" at the trial because she was afraid of the charges against her and the possibility of losing her son forever. All of the above was personally told to me by Jean Day and is true and correct to the best of my knoweldge and belief. I also swear that this affidavit contains the truth as told to me by Jean Day.

This affidavit made under pains and penalties of perjury.

Dated: October 28, 1985.

By the Affiant,

Louis Tontodonato
Louis Tontodonato, Pro Se

COMMONWEALTH OF MASSACHUSETTS
NORFOLK COUNTY

SWORN TO AND SUBSCRIBED before me this 28th day of October, 1985.

My Commission Expires: *Sheila F. Stevens*
                                            NOTARY PUBLIC

Feb 25   , 1988 .

Louis Tontodonato Affidavit Regarding Jean Day (pg. 2)

Chapter Fifteen
The Other Ghost in the Courtroom

Burke had another nail to pound into Paradiso's coffin. He recalled Jean Day to the stand. What Marie wore and how she wore it on the day she died were vital to the state's case. Multiple witnesses testified in a variety of hearings that Marie wore her stockings underneath the red one-piece bodysuit. Suggesting otherwise made no sense, but Burke distorted the image. Jean succumbed to the pressure and resigned to forgetting how her stepsister got dressed.

"Underneath the skirt or underneath the body shirt," Jean said. "To me, the girl's dead. Does it matter what she was wearing?"

The prosecution needed to erase the impact of Dellaria's statement that Doyle had confessed to murdering Marie. Burke called the officer who was riding with Detective Long on July 16, 1981. Detective Charles Gleason had worked in the East Boston area for several years, and knew both David Dellaria and David Doyle very well. Burke scored a point; Dellaria's reliability was in question. Police knew Doyle's friend was a habitual drug user. Rappaport countered with a point of his own; Doyle's trustworthiness wasn't any better for the same reason.

"I want to renew my motion for a required finding of not guilty," Rappaport concluded.

The judge disclosed his bias to both counsels during a sidebar conference, outside the earshot of the audience in the courtroom. "I think on all of the testimony, there is sufficient evidence on the rape charge for the jury to find the defendant guilty beyond a point of reasonable doubt," Judge Donahue declared. "I think the same is true of the murder charge." Evidence that filtered through the bench left one impression. The critical pieces blocked at the bar and secrets tucked in other case files left quite another. For his part, Judge Donahue had already prejudged the outcome.

Next, Rappaport faced the jury. His strategy was straightforward. The defendant was innocent until proven guilty for the rape and murder of Marie Iannuzzi. He had presented reasonable doubt that his client committed these particular crimes. Evidence implicating Marie's boyfriend slipped into the record despite the opposing forces trying to squelch it. During his closing, Rappaport pointed out that Christine DeLisi's testimony had changed from the statements she made during the grand jury. Jurors saw for themselves that Jean Day changed her tune. The parole officer's notes were out of sequence. Robbery was not the motive; Marie's jewelry was still on her body.

The prosecution accused Paradiso of raping the victim. Passersby found the decedent dressed in her leotard and wrap-around skirt. Police had photographed the victim with her clothing intact. Rape was not a consideration at the time, and the lab failed to perform critical tests. Witnesses saw Marie back in the bar well after Paradiso had held the door for her. Paradiso and his girlfriend both willingly gave consistent statements to the police. Rappaport challenged the credibility of the state's unsavory witnesses.

"Ladies and gentlemen, consider their character," Rappaport implored. "Consider whether or not their stories really mesh. What type of motivation do these people have to come and say what they had to say? That's what the government's case comes down to, whether or not you're going to believe Bobby Bond and Tony Pisa."

Bond claimed the defendant panicked and burned his car a month after the murder. Police never issued a warrant to examine the vehicle even though they knew that the victim had been in the car just hours before her death. The state finally tested the single cut hair after the trial began, but there was no match to the man seated at the defense table. Mark Grant compared the single follicle with hair taken from every conceivable part of Paradiso's body; there was no match to the strand that supposedly threw Paradiso into a panic.

David Doyle's own cousin, an eyewitness, placed the defendant and his date at the house in Saugus at 11:00 p.m. Paradiso couldn't have been racing through the streets of East Boston half an hour away as Bond claimed. Marie's boyfriend was a jealous lover who behaved strangely. The couple had a history, an abusive relationship, and they argued in front of numerous witnesses that day. The other suspect packed his dead girlfriend's belongings, medicated deep gouges on the back of his hands, stepped over the suspected blood on the steps to their apartment, and took flight to New Jersey in a drugged stupor. Doyle and his mother spouted four different excuses for the ripped flesh. This was not a multiple-choice quiz. Doyle's treachery was a given; he lied and gave a false name to the New Jersey police officers who caught him stealing bags at Newark Airport.

Rappaport's arguments were logical and sincere. Certainly, there was enough reasonable doubt. Unfortunately, the defense counsel argued the present case, which was not the same justice Burke debated. To Burke, the ends justified the means. An anonymous caller had tipped off the Saugus Police that Paradiso murdered Marie Iannuzzi and Joan Webster. George and Eleanor chose to believe her, and Burke obliged. The eyewitness lead of the smaller man seen leaving Logan with Joan was still a *secret*.

Burke lowered the bar of decency in his closing. He ridiculed the appearance of Candy Weyant compared to the victim. He suggested boys will be boys, and of course, Paradiso chose an inebriated quean with a good figure. In Burke's mind, his degrading snipe cancelled Candy's credibility. Burke pronounced Candy as the one with a reason to lie. He ignored the beauty radiating from within; Candy told the truth even to her own detriment.

The insane description of Paradiso struggling to take off Marie's pantyhose defied common sense. Burke depicted the victim in Paradiso's car. When she refused his advances, he tightened the noose until she was unconscious, Burke claimed, never reminding the jury that the offender had knotted the scarf at the back of her neck. Burke demonstrated the stretchy fabric on the leotard leg and inserted a preposterous notion that Paradiso pulled out *both* legs of the pantyhose through one leg opening of the bodysuit. The leotard had no snaps in the crotch. Then, when she regained her senses, Marie resisted. According to Burke, that's when Paradiso choked her again, killed her, and threw her out on the rocks.

Burke favored convicted killers. He portrayed Tony Pisa as a model citizen without ever corroborating Pisa's assertions. The man once on death row had only agreed to come forward if he got out of jail. After Pisa made assurances to George Webster, officials handed Pisa the keys to escape his confinement. Burke then repeated Bond's accusations ad nauseam for the jury. Bond's history of lying to the police in his own murder case was out of bounds to the jury, and the prosecutor didn't tell them. No one hinted that George Webster had sent people to see Bond, or that those people enticed the snitch with reward money and a new trial with a lesser charge.

"What is true is what [Robert] Bobby Bond told you," Burke promised. "No matter what you might think about Bobby Bond, there is still some sense of decency, even among cons. He is worthy of your belief. Candy Weyant is not."

Throughout his closing arguments on July 20, 1984, Burke deployed a coy tactic. He locked eyes with the jury, and challenged any notion that he had wheeled people in to say what he wanted them to say. The preemptive denial goaded the panel to trust him.

"Do you really believe that's what we're all about?" Burke dared. "We just put people on the stand just to try to convict somebody, knowing that they're lying. You folks don't really believe that, do you?"

Judge Donahue did his part instructing the jury. Reasonable doubt was the hurdle the defense had to get over. The John Webster case of 1850 set the bar, and the direction had the added benefit of reminding the gallery of the other ghost in the courtroom with a similar name. Then the judge dismissed the jury for their deliberations.

The forelady relayed two questions to the judge. First, was it possible to rape a dead body? According to the law, it was considered rape only if the victim was still breathing. The jury then wanted clarification between first and second degree murder. The rules defined that murder in the first degree was murder committed deliberately, with premeditated malice. The jury filed back out, but didn't take long before notifying the judge that they had reached a decision. At 2:04 p.m. on July 22, 1984, they assumed their positions and responded to the questions of guilt.

"We find the defendant, Leonard Paradiso, guilty of murder in the second degree," the jury announced. "We also find the defendant, Leonard Paradiso, guilty of assault with intent to rape Marie Iannuzzi."

Paradiso bowed his head in disbelief. Officers handcuffed the condemned man and led him away. Burke and Palombo faced a gaggle of reporters on the courthouse steps. Palombo piled on more lies about Paradiso and justified spreading unverified fodder. The cop told reporters that Paradiso used to hang out at bus stations with child molesters. The innuendo drew the bus station into the team's calculations, the very location where a bag handler had found Joan's suitcase. The Websters had gone home before the verdict but word reached them, and they were pleased. The Iannuzzi decision was their decision. They insisted Leonard Paradiso had murdered Joan.

On July 25, 1984, everyone resumed their positions in Judge Donahue's courtroom for sentencing. Burke insisted on a harsh "from and after" sentence, tacking on penalties one after the other. He asserted Paradiso tried to frame an innocent man, David Doyle. He accused his quarry of dumping Marie like she was so much refuse. Burke argued that the severest penalty was appropriate for the added insult to the victim and her boyfriend.

Rappaport held up a copy of the *Boston Herald* with the statements made by the prosecution's team. There was a certain pecking order in prison, and crimes against children were on the lowest rung of the ladder. Inmates weren't concerned if the rumors were true or not. Palombo had unleashed more unseemly gossip that put another target on Paradiso's back.

Paradiso asked to address the court during the disposition of his sentence. His counsel advised him he had that right, but the judge said he did not. Predetermined guilt was evident in the judge's decisions. Judge Donahue previewed his verdict at the sidebar before the jury went out to deliberate the selective evidence he gave them. The judge granted Burke's request and heaped on "from and after" sentences to lock Paradiso away for a very long time.

Chapter Sixteen
The Only Physical Evidence

The guilty verdict in Marie Iannuzzi's case heightened emotions about Joan Webster. For many, the two young women were one and the same. The outcome for the strangled woman in red discarded on the banks of the Pine River projected the same ruling for the missing Harvard grad student. The decision emboldened Tim Burke; his quest was far from over.

The steady stream of refuse investigators collected from the bottom of the harbor clogged FBI labs for the next several months. The only exception was the fake .357 magnum that assigned divers had suspiciously missed. The item Burke's own diver recovered never went to the FBI lab for examination. The agency put every fiber and stain from the boat under the microscope. They tested each suitable grain of sand or clump of tar from the sea floor that Burke and Palombo submitted. Nothing furthered Burke's notion that Paradiso forced Joan onto his boat with a fake gun, hit her with a whiskey bottle, raped her, and dumped her at sea. No evidence connected the missing woman to Paradiso or the boat. But Burke was obsessed with proving it.

Then a partial jawbone washed ashore. Just like Tammaro predicted, a body discarded in the ocean will surface unless something weighs it down. Burke's heart palpitated. His sweaty palm clutched the phone, and he anxiously dialed the police in New Jersey. Within hours, Investigator Anthony Pascucci drove past the sign greeting passengers and pulled up to the curb at Logan Airport where Joan smiled down from a billboard as a constant reminder that no one knew where she was. The inspector for the Suffolk County District Attorney's office chauffeured the Glen Ridge, New Jersey detective to room number 603. Detective Tom Dugan hand delivered Joan's dental records on November 26, 1984, almost three years to the day after Joan disappeared. Burke's bloated expectation soon deflated; the jawbone was not Joan calling from the deep.

Burke cornered another recruit in his office to engage in his enterprise. He directed Detective Tom Dugan to collect items from the Websters' home that had Joan's fingerprints. Dugan's contact was Special Agent Steve Broce from the Personal and Financial Crimes Unit, the agent working on the bankruptcy case. Broce's task was to prove Paradiso's boat wasn't stolen. Joan's fingerprints had nothing to do with that. Burke pictured the vessel as the scene of her murder, improperly inserting Broce's hand into the state's case. Broce then called Dugan with instructions on how to submit Joan's belongings to the FBI lab.

❧

Federal prosecutors filed insurance fraud charges against Paradiso on November 28, 1984. Paradiso braced for the next wave with Burke still on his back. Burke concocted a groundbreaking motion. On December 16, 1984, he petitioned Judge James McGuire to allow the surgical removal of a presumed splinter in Paradiso's finger. The state's star witness claimed that Paradiso had injured his hand murdering Joan Webster. The emergency room at Lynn Hospital had X-rayed the left digit on November 30, 1981, and three small metal splinters showed up on the film. When doctors checked the injury again on December 22, 1981, one fragment had remained in his finger. Burke now wanted to go fishing to dig the remaining particle out.

Paradiso maintained the sliver in his finger came from a munition shell he tried to polish. Authorities found the shell in the Weyants' basement. Burke embraced Bond's version. The con claimed Paradiso had hurt his finger when he hit Joan in the head with a whiskey bottle. Burke hypothesized that the splinter was glass from a broken liquor bottle. Glass didn't show up on X-rays, so Burke claimed that the liquor bottles had a high lead content. For good measure, he threw in the option that the fragments could have rubbed off of the fake gun. Burke moved to cut Paradiso's flesh. Palombo supplemented his cohort's request to the court.

"Among the many items located in the cabin area of the *Malafemmena*, there were several shards and bits of broken glass," Palombo swore.

Inspectors had found no glass or liquor bottles on the recovered boat. Burke had submitted a single item to the lab that he called glass, but never fully identified where it was found. The FBI lab described the crud as debris unsuitable for testing. Nothing else existed on or around the *Malafemmena* to support the state's representations. The court had locked Paradiso away for a long time, but Burke wanted more. In his mind, Paradiso had murdered Joan Webster. Proving that was Burke's ultimate goal, with the Websters' support.

In late 1984, George and Eleanor welcomed a correspondent into their home. *Boston Magazine* published a lengthy exposé in December 1984 fanning passions to keep the hunt alive. The Websters were Burke's secret weapon; every parent empathized with the nightmare of losing a child. Joan's parents spoke with conviction that Paradiso had murdered their daughter. If only authorities did their jobs in other cases, Joan might still be alive. Even though the cameras captured their presence during the dramatic testimony at the Iannuzzi pretrial, George now denied that they had been there. Joan's father sadly pointed to the phone in the downstairs study, and he told the reporter that Joan had called her classmate that Saturday morning to make sure they had supplies for the class project. It was the explanation George had settled on for Joan's early return, skipping over several facts: Joan had presented her project on Monday before the break, a friend planned to visit and meet the parents, and the phone logs contradicted Joan's supposed call. The intelligence-trained parents never mentioned the eyewitness description or showed the composite of the bearded man seen with Joan at Logan.

❧

As the calendar turned to the New Year, Burke found himself in a Middlesex courtroom to pay an outstanding debt. Middlesex was outside Burke's playing field, but he had appealed to Judge Harry Elam before. With his escort from the Middlesex office, Burke joined Laurence Hardoon standing before the bar. Burke needed a counterpart from the Middlesex District Attorney's office to legitimize his presence, and Hardoon fit the bill. Harry Elam, a Middlesex County Superior Court judge, had heard the emergency bail hearing the day after Pisa testified at the Iannuzzi pretrial hearing. Burke was back in court to rewrite the murder history of the con who made assurances to George Webster.

Hardoon told the judge Middlesex County had reversed their opposition for Pisa to get a new trial in exchange for his cooperation. Pisa had helped Burke gain a conviction against Leonard Paradiso for the murder of Marie Iannuzzi. Further, he had assisted the state against the same suspect for the disappearance and presumed murder of Joan Webster. Judge Elam heard the application for a new trial and contemplated the steadfast objection from James Sahakian, a Middlesex prosecutor familiar with Pisa's history. Testimony during Pisa's murder trial had exposed the man as a cold-blooded killer with no sense of remorse. Judge Elam listened to the victim's family, but their painful protests fell on deaf ears. The judge accepted Pisa's changed plea for the 1969 murder, and his lawyer quickly withdrew the motion for a new trial. Judge Harry Elam had decided the matter right then and there; he acquiesced to the unusual maneuvers and sentenced Pisa to time served.

ຕ⟩

The Glen Ridge Police forwarded Joan's property to the FBI labs on January 8, 1985, per Special Agent Broce's instructions. The monumental efforts to blame Paradiso for her murder failed again. Joan had never touched Paradiso's stuff. If the results discouraged Burke, that didn't last for long. Proving a negative seemed to be his mission.

Burke was now back in Judge McGuire's courtroom hoping for a favorable decision to slice and dice Paradiso's finger. He had his explanation covered whether the microscopic speck was glass or metal. Burke relished the idea that force might be necessary if Paradiso failed to comply. The prosecutor channeled the public's cry for Joan's justice and implored the court's favor.

"It might be the only physical evidence connecting Paradiso to the killing of Joan Webster," Burke pleaded.

The slip went unnoticed, but Burke had just admitted his lack of evidence. Burke and Palombo both had made false representations to the courts, the Feds, and the public. The Mayan civilization book Palombo called Joan's textbook was an out-of-print coffee table book, not Joan's. Both men claimed witnesses positively identified the red silk jewelry pouch as the bag where Joan kept her pearls, but the bag was part of a set owned by Candy Weyant. Burke insisted that a photo, recovered by the police, pictured Charlene Bullerwell wearing Joan's missing bracelet. All she ever received from Paradiso was a gold-dipped seahorse without a loop, and he took it back. Burke and Palombo swore to the court that several shards and bits of broken glass littered the cabin floor of the recovered boat, and

Burke had leaked that fake news to the press. The only item Burke submitted as glass was a single piece of debris the lab couldn't even test. Just like the assertion that a single cut hair panicked Paradiso in Marie's case, the only evidence the state had against him was a splinter supposedly connecting him to Joan.

The team overlooked real clues in their possession. A business card in Joan's wallet had a handwritten note that seemed amiss for an adult woman to carry. Burke surveyed Joan's belongings in the police evidence room and described a pair of gray shoes, an item carried in Joan's still missing tote bag. The eyewitness description of the bearded man seen with Joan at Logan and the composite continued to be locked away in the files.

"The need is especially great because Paradiso efficiently disposed of the victim's body," Burke told the judge. "By taking her 'way out' and 'dumping' her in the ocean Paradiso made sure that, as he threatened Patty Bono, 'No one would ever find her.' "

While the state court considered these things in front of the press, a federal jurist discreetly filed a ruling across town. On January 21, 1985, Judge Robert Keeton, a judge in the Federal District Court of Massachusetts, changed the venue for Paradiso's bankruptcy case to the Federal District Court in Rhode Island. Media attention had persuaded the magistrate to remove the proceedings from the spectacle generated in the state courts, presumably in the interest of justice. Burke's contention that Paradiso dumped human bait in the harbor persuaded Judge McGuire to X-ray the finger. On February 13, 1985, the judge set the stage for an unprecedented surgical search warrant if a splinter showed up on the film.

"There was testimony from a named witness that Joan Webster was raped and murdered. I find that the informant is reliable and credible," Judge McGuire determined. "Should Paradiso refuse to cooperate, the Commonwealth would be warranted in using reasonable means in forcing compliance."

Burke wasted no time instructing the state police to execute the order and X-ray the inmate's finger on February 15, 1985. Paradiso objected to the invasion of his person to satisfy Burke's mania, but he was far too outnumbered to defy it. Burke summarily dismissed Paradiso's complaint of mistreatment, and no one was likely to check. To Burke's dismay, nothing appeared on the X-ray. Undeterred, he went back to the drawing board.

Meanwhile, the out-of-state ruling in Rhode Island got very little attention. Due process worked. The court acquitted Leonard Paradiso of insurance fraud for the loss of the boat. Presumably, Liberty Mutual did their due diligence to investigate the claim before they paid for the loss on September 29, 1981. Divers recovered the vessel in waters right beneath the Erie Barge mooring where Paradiso previously tethered his boat at Pier 7. The hull was still painted blue, and registration numbers were intact. The unaltered appearance made it rather hard to fathom the boat was the scene of Joan's murder on November 28, 1981, as the state alleged.

A little more than a month after the X-rays halted Burke's quest to go after the splinter, the obsessed counsel filed another motion in Judge McGuire's court. McGuire obliged Burke's contention that Paradiso somehow performed microscopic surgery on himself to remove the sliver before Burke could cut him. The court order on March 20, 1985 allowed a doctor to examine Paradiso's finger later the same day. Dr. Donald Dixon examined Paradiso's left index finger right in front of the judge and the press.

"There appears to be a puncture wound on Mr. Paradiso's finger," the doctor said.

The insinuation was ludicrous. The prisoner had been under constant surveillance. A fork from the mess hall or maybe a bent paperclip were the only conceivable surgical instruments Paradiso could have gotten his hands on. With an eighth-grade education, he lacked the medical skill for microscopic surgery, even if he had the right tools. Despite the absurdity of the story, the doctor thought Paradiso had a month-old puncture wound on his left pointer. Nothing came of the slanted opinion, but the farce served another purpose; Burke kept the story swirling in the tabloids without any facts.

Chapter Seventeen
A Case of Lying

Another jury took their seats across the state line in Rhode Island. The case on the docket was a bankruptcy fraud case, which isn't the kind of saga that typically sells papers. There were no reporters taking notes or flashbulbs blinding the panel. There were no juvenile jurists making faces to sway perceptions. Nevertheless, the mundane hearing was the next piece of the puzzle in the Joan Webster mystery. The Harvard graduate student remained a missing person. Most people presumed she was dead, but there was no body. The scant evidence of foul play had mushroomed into an alleged murder at sea. The defendant in the present case didn't list a boat in his bankruptcy filing. State officials in Massachusetts insisted the vessel was the scene of Joan Webster's murder.

Judge Bruce Selya gaveled the session to order for case CR 85-010-S on April 4, 1985. Rappaport begged off Paradiso's defense, and a court-appointed lawyer took over the monumental challenge of representing a targeted man. Owen Walker informed the court that his client needed medical attention. He was in excruciating pain and unable to sleep. The judge appropriately allowed the defendant to receive treatment. The heavy-handed use of force in Massachusetts surfaced in this out-of-state courtroom. The doctor recommended that the six-week-old broken finger needed to be reset and splinted. The age of the injury lined up with the date of the X-ray Burke had ordered.

Witnesses took the stand one by one and confirmed the facts. Candy Weyant was the titled owner of the boat in question.

Candy had insured the Chris Craft and Ray Jefferson navigational equipment. Liberty Mutual paid the claim to the defendant's girlfriend. Suggesting Paradiso was the rightful owner disregarded the titled owner in a title state. If the girlfriend made a straw purchase, the issue was moot. The government didn't levy those charges against the defendant. The indictment accused Paradiso of lying on his form by not listing an asset that was not legally his to begin with. The government never charged him with concealing assets, but that was what the prosecutor argued.

Tim Burke desired a certain outcome in this case. The boat at the center of the federal suit was Burke's alleged crime scene of Joan's murder. Burke initiated the inquest on May 3, 1983, and kept in regular contact with Marie Buckley, the federal prosecutor trying the case. Burke's boss, Paul Leary, called Robert S. Mueller at the Department of Justice to supervise the proceeding. For good measure, George Webster added his weight with a letter writing campaign.

A prepared prosecutor never asks a question without knowing the answer. Buckley flinched. Burke's office had provided his federal counterpart with two boat registrations for the *Malafemmena*. One was legitimate, but the other was not. Andrew Palombo checked boat registrations in July 1982, months before the alleged break in Joan's case. By law, the documents remained in the registrar's office, but a stealth hand had removed the records when the registrar was out sick. Both licenses had the same number. The valid identification, signed by Candy, had a machine stamped number and an official seal. The fake registration, allegedly signed by Paradiso, had the official seal but a handwritten number. The second license was invalid. The judge turned a blind eye; Buckley entered the suspicious registration into evidence.

When the court discharged Paradiso's debt in bankruptcy court on November 30, 1981, the petitioner had to be present. It was a matter of record that Paradiso also had his finger X-rayed at Lynn Hospital on that same day. Traffic jams and blockades hampered his progress because of the Great Lynn Fire of 1981. Burke alleged, through Robert Bond, that Paradiso also found time on that day to go to Pier 7, swab the deck of the *Malafemmena*, and sink the alleged crime scene to cover up Joan's murder.

Arguing over who owned the vessel was relevant in the present cause, but did not help to find out what happened to Joan. Testimony left little doubt that Paradiso sank the *Malafemmena* for the insurance money. The judge chastised Buckley for arguing crimes she never charged, but he still determined the jury should decide.

"I am very concerned about [Defense Attorney] Mr. Walker's arguments. The evidence in this case is undisputed," Judge Selya said. "Whoever owned the boat prior to the date, by August 1981, the asset was long gone."

Burke anxiously waited for the ruling. His premise of Joan's murder at sea hinged on the decision. The defense counsel tried to forewarn the court of ulterior motives. Owen Walker submitted the testimony Burke elicited from Charlene Bullerwell during the Iannuzzi pretrial. Then, the woman claimed the defendant now sitting before Selya's court was a hitman for the mob. He chopped up bodies and tied cinder blocks to them before dumping them off his boat into the ocean. The unsubstantiated fodder was a sharp contrast to the grand jury testimony she gave for the present case.

"All that the owner owned was some type of claim for insurance proceeds, rather than what this indictment charges," Judge Selya lectured. "I'm very concerned about that."

Prosecutor Buckley faced the jury and pointed the finger at Paradiso. The panel heard debate about a sunken boat, a craft long gone when Paradiso filed for bankruptcy on August 26, 1981. It didn't matter to them when the boat went down, but it did matter for Tim Burke's cause.

"Basically, this is a case about lying," Buckley concluded.

The jury found Paradiso guilty on three counts of bankruptcy fraud on April 9, 1985. Burke exhaled a sigh of relief. The guilty verdict included count C regarding the boat, but he ignored Judge Selya's finding. His Honor had debunked Burke's whole theory about what had happened to Joan Webster, the underlying cause to pile everything on Paradiso. Marie Buckley hit the nail on the head in her closing: The case was about lying. Who was lying was the real question. The *Malafemmena* rested 35 feet under water at Pier 7 on July 26, 1981, four months before Joan landed at Logan Airport.

The participants returned to Judge Selya's courtroom on May 10, 1985 for sentencing. Buckley argued Paradiso was a threat to the community. The insinuation seemed misplaced for sentencing in a bankruptcy fraud case. She pulled out three letters to the objection of the defense. Judge Selya thought the submission of George Webster's letters was a little late, but he allowed the clerk to mark them as Exhibits A, B, and C. The conviction in the Iannuzzi case weighed heavily on the sentencing decision, but the real argument during the hearing centered on the unproven speculation about Joan Webster. The judge missed the critical point that the state's allegations against Paradiso in Joan's case were untried. No charges had even been filed. Judge Selya thrust the dagger himself that discredited the suspicion that Paradiso had murdered Joan on his boat. Defense attorney Walker challenged the government's pleading for a harsh sentence. Paradiso still hoped for a successful appeal in the Iannuzzi case.

"If the prior conviction were reversed, the assumption that a defendant is a severe threat to the community would vanish," Walker challenged. "But he'd still be guilty because he's a *suspect* in another major, and probably the most notorious murder case in the state of Massachusetts in the last few years. He's guilty of that?"

Predetermined guilt for a crime that was impossible based on Judge Selya's own declaration defied common sense. Regardless,

Selya acquiesced to the prosecution's request and added a harsh "from and after" sentence to Paradiso's mounting burden. A small paragraph in the Boston papers missed the biggest bombshell out of the bankruptcy case. While the boat was long gone months before Joan disappeared, the article simply stated that Paradiso received ten more years for three counts of bankruptcy fraud.

"Suffolk County investigators are also trying to build a case against Paradiso in the suspected slaying of Harvard student Joan Webster who disappeared from Logan International Airport in 1981," the reporter added.

Burke still had the control to fill in the dates. He needed the boat floating when Joan disappeared, or his envisioned murder didn't work.

❧

Carmen Tammaro planted the seed of the boat story on August 1, 1982. George Webster had a strategy meeting in New Jersey, and then guards shifted a shady informant into close proximity to Paradiso at the Charles Street Jail. Tammaro coached the jailhouse snitch with his same allegations more than once in January 1983. The hearsay informer was the state's star witness who allegedly heard Paradiso's confessions, the tale of two murders. Robert Bond accused Paradiso of murdering Marie Iannuzzi. He said Paradiso murdered Joan on his boat, and then dumped her in Boston Harbor. Burke stuck his thumb in the dyke and fingers in his ears. There was no boat when Joan disappeared on November 28, 1981. Bond repeated what he was told, but prosecutorial tricks obscured the source of his information. Burke sealed the Bond letter and interview transcript in the Iannuzzi case. He was not about to concede his obsession. The evidence, hidden in the out-of-state court record, confirmed Bond was a false witness.

છ૭

Cloudy skies and unseasonably cool weather didn't dampen the mood on May 28, 1985. After years of gut-wrenching headlines, family and classmates gathered at Gund Hall in Cambridge, Massachusetts to celebrate Joan's life. Her class dedicated a garden in her memory. Joan's spiritual presence warmed the gathering with every caring tribute. Everyone loved Joan. The petite grad student left a lasting impression on every life she touched. The image of her unthinkable fate was still hard to digest. Guests clutched crumpled tissues to blot the occasional tears trickling down their cheeks, but the smiles returned with the next tribute to Joan's kindness. No one knew the full extent of what her parents understood, but everyone accepted their answers without question. Without a body, it was hard to go after the suspected killer.

The verdict was in: Paradiso's boat didn't exist above water when Joan disappeared. Authorities had perpetrated a hoax on the public. The finding didn't make a bit of difference to the inner circle trying to prove it. On July 24, 1985, investigators in Boston reached a consensus. They advised the FBI and Interpol that they had developed sufficient evidence to conclude that the subject, Leonard Paradiso, murdered Joan Webster in November 1981.

છ૭

As the leaves showed off the resplendent colors of autumn, Tim Burke packed up his desk at Suffolk County. Higher ups had dangled an attractive contract for the lawyer to start his own practice. Representing the Massachusetts State Police made the transition easy. Strangely, the District Attorney didn't turn over Joan's case to a new prosecutor to continue the effort but kept Burke on standby.

The state police filled at least nine banker's boxes with "evidence" in Joan's case, but the answers were not all in there. Burke walked out of the Suffolk County office with a carton of Joan's records he kept for himself. Burke had no authority to remove the files or stash them in his new office.

Palombo paid regular visits to Burke's new digs. He walked in looking like a Hell's Angel, but the cop instilled trust with a broad smile reflecting off his badge.

George and Eleanor Webster broke with the norm. The Commonwealth's obligation was to pursue justice for Joan, not Burke. When the influential couple walked into Burke's new office, he sat up straight, wiped his nose, and turned off his television set. The intelligence-trained couple drew people in with invisible tentacles. George's background and engaging wit distilled with the privilege of wealth gave him an air of authority. Mr. and Mrs. Webster were in charge of Burke on Joan's case.

&

Another debt came due. Robert Bond got a new lawyer as promised. The state granted him a new trial for his second murder conviction, but Bond balked at the outcome. Authorities made promises he had relied on to his detriment. Suffolk County denied making any deals with the informant, but Bond insisted representatives had pledged a lesser charge of manslaughter, a decision that could reduce his time behind bars. Bond filed a motion on November 15, 1985. The disgruntled snitch had believed assurances from investigators working on Joan's case, but they had no standing in Bond's matters. George Webster had sent people to see Bond. The people who met with Bond had made pledges the con trusted. Bond's sworn affidavit exposed another crack in the dam. Bond named Tim Burke, Andrew Palombo, Carmen Tammaro, and someone named Bill. Bill probably referred to John Gillen, a correctional officer identified in the January 14, 1983 interview with the Massachusetts State Police. A Rhode Island judge affirmed Bond's story was false. Bond did not get what he wanted in the deal, and by filing a motion in objection, he identified the source of his information, even though it didn't affect anything at that time.

IN THE UNITED STATES DISTRICT COURT

FOR THE DISTRICT OF RHODE ISLAND

UNITED STATES OF AMERICA)   Docket No. CR. 85-010-S
)
       V.   )   Providence, Rhode Island
)   Monday, April 8, 1985
LEONARD J. PARADISO   )   Tuesday, April 9, 1985
                    Thursday, May 9, 1985

VOLUME II

TRANSCRIPT OF TRIAL PROCEEDINGS BEFORE THE

HONORABLE BRUCE M. SELYA, and a jury.

APPEARANCES:

For the United States: MARIE T. BUCKLEY
                   Assistant United States Attorney
                   District of Massachusetts
                   1107 John W. McCormack Post
                   Office & Courthouse
                   Boston, Massachusetts 02109

For the Defendant: OWEN S. WALKER, Esquire
                   Federal Defender Office
                   195 State Street, 4th Floor
                   Boston, Massachusetts 02109

Court Reporter: Louis V. Spertini
                   307 Federal Building
                   Providence, Rhode Island

Volume II Title Page for Leonard Paradiso Bankruptcy Case
CR 85-010-S

1   know, savings account or securities or anything else that

2   is perhaps unearned income.

3   THE COURT: Well, let's see if we can save a little

4   time, Mr. Walker, I suggest that you make that suggestion

5   to some other tribunal, because it's not going to wash

6   here.

7   MR. WALKER: Well, ---

8   THE COURT: All right, that's as blunt as I can put

9   it.

10   MR. WALKER: I think I may have one other point on

11   that, your Honor.

12   (Pause)

13   MR. WALKER: Well, I think I'd better, that's it,

14   your Honor.

15   THE COURT: Let me hear from Miss Buckley, and let

16   me see if I can focus your attention, Miss Buckley. I'm

17   interested in what you have to say as to Count A, although

18   I'm frank to say that my inclination on that count is to

19   hide behind Rule 29(b) and reserve it. I don't need to

20   hear argument on Count E, Count D, excuse me, the last

21   count, because I'm satisfied that there's a jury question

22   here. I do not share Mr. Walker's notion that legal title

23   either to the automobile or to the boat dictates the

24   outcome of those counts. I am very concerned about his

25   arguments that since the evidence in this record is

CR 85-010-S Volume II Pages Bruce Selya Presiding (pg. 1)

1   uncontradicted, that whoever owned the boat and the car,

2   the boat and the truck, Counts C and B, prior to August of

3   1981, that by August of 1981 both of those assets were

4   long gone, and that all that the owner really owned was

5   some type of claim for insurance proceeds, rather than

6   what this indictment charges. I'm very concerned about

7   that, and I'd like to know what you have to say about that.

8   MISS BUCKLEY: Well, your Honor, if I might just

9   make a few preliminary remarks.

10   THE COURT: Surely.

11   MISS BUCKLEY: I think that I'm bothered, too, by

12 the use of terms like "legal title," "equitable interest,"

13 and so on, and I do feel as though we are not here to

14 argue a trust and estate type of case.

15   THE COURT: As I say, it would be all right with

16 me for purposes of this motion, at least, to put that one

17 side, because I don't think that the law in this area is

18 quite as narrow as Mr. Walker says. But if you forget

19 that there's even a title question, if you assume that

20 you have proven beyond a reasonable doubt that in 1980 or

21 thereabouts that Mr. Paradiso owned a twenty-six foot

22 Chris Craft with the appropriate vanity plate, et cetera,

23 all right, what bothers me is that what you've got to

24 prove to make out this indictment is that he owned that

25 boat on the date of the filing of the, either the filing

CR 85-010-S Volume II Pages Bruce Selya Presiding (pg. 2)

194

COMMONWEALTH OF MASSACHUSETTS

SUFFOLK, ss.

SUPERIOR COURT
CRIMINAL NO.
037586

COMMONWEALTH OF MASSACHUSETTS)
)
VS.   )
)
ROBERT BOND   )

MOTION TO ENFORCE PLEA BARGAIN AGREEMENT

Now comes defendant in the above matter and moves this court to enforce the plea bargain agreement entered into between defendant and the government's representatives in the above matter.

In support of this motion, defendant relies on the attached affidavit.

By his attorney:

signature

Martin D. Boudreau
BOUDREAU & BURKE
One Milk Street
Boston, MA 02109
338-6721

Robert Bond Motion and Affidavit (pg. 1)

AFFIDAVIT

1. My name is Robert Bond and I am defendant in the instant matter;

2. I have been told on numerous occasions by the following representatives of the District Attorney's Office that in return for a change of plea to guilty in the instant matter I would receive a recommendation from the government of a sentence of 15 to 20 years:

1) Tim Burke, Assistant District Attorney
2) Andrew Palumbo, Massachusetts State Police Officer
3) Carmine Tammara, Massachusetts State Police Officer
4) Bill (last name unknown), Massachusetts State Police

3. My attorney has informed me that he has, through his discussions with the various representatives of the District Attorney's Office, been told that there is no such deal for a plea bargain agreement and that such plea bargain agreement is not possible;

4. I have specifically relied on the representations of above-mentioned representatives of the District Attorney's Office, to my detriment and the government has failed to fulfill its obligation as it has, through its authorized representatives, agreed.

Sworn under the pains and penalties of perjury.

_____ 11/15/85
Robert Bond

Robert Bond Motion and Affidavit (pg. 2)

Chapter Eighteen
The Keys to the Crime Scene

Lenny Paradiso's legal battles continued. He maintained his innocence for Marie's murder and filed a motion for a new trial. The full weight of the system piled on the beleaguered man, determined to keep him down. The conviction he hoped to reverse was one wobbly leg of the stool holding up the accusations in another case. The tabloids still prosecuted Joan's case with the presumption of guilt, and journalists reminded the public on a regular basis of the alleged murder at sea. Judge Roger Donahue pithily considered Paradiso's motion. He determined everything had been kosher in his own courtroom and denied the motion for a new trial on February 13, 1986.

Other charges on the horizon compelled the inmate not to give up on due process. Paradiso filed again to reconsider the motion for a new trial. The problem was Marie Iannuzzi's murder wasn't the focus of his condemnation, only the path to another end. Like before, the motion died on Donahue's desk. The biased judge rejected the notion that anything was out of order in his courtroom, and tossed out the second request on July 1, 1986. Two days later, Paradiso filed a notice for an appeal.

ୱ

Trooper Palombo snatched control of the Janet McCarthy incident from other enforcers when she came forward in 1983, seeing another chance to hound his target. The revised version of her assault made sensational headlines in 1984. The prospect of another conviction was too tantalizing to resist. Two convictions handed the shellfish peddler decades behind bars already but didn't satisfy the end game. Paradiso found himself in a Suffolk County courtroom again on August 13, 1986.

The trial was a battle between opposing badges, the first responders who documented what happened, and Palombo, who helped refresh Janet's memory. The media followed the case and inflated every update with speculation about Joan.

The police report taken at the time indicated that Janet had hitched a ride from the North End. She got into a large, white, four-door vehicle with a man who had ulterior motives. When she escaped the clutches of the would be predator, she climbed a plain white retaining wall and flagged down a passing motorist. The Good Samaritan drove her to the police station to take down the details of her complaint. Officers noted the victim had a bloody knee, messed up hair, and had been drinking. There were inconsistencies in her story, and she couldn't identify the offender from mugshots.

Seeking vengeance against someone, anyone, Janet pointed to Lenny Paradiso. When she had testified before during the Iannuzzi pretrial hearing, Janet had a slightly different version of her story. As Palombo helped her remember, the assailant had picked her up in a yellow car. Sometimes she described the vehicle as a two-door, but sometimes it had four. After she scaled the wall, the first car to stop was the man she accused, and he laughed at her as he sped away. In court, Janet claimed two men picked her up, and took her to their place to freshen up before going to the station.

Palombo bolstered the revised account. He told the court she had a vivid recollection and had guided him right to the spot where the officer needed her to be. The barrier covered with graffiti was in close proximity to the Weyant's home in Revere. Numbed by the unrelenting persecution, Paradiso stared at the large trooper hell bent on breaking him down. Palombo just smiled. The headline laced the latest guilty verdict with the image of Joan at the bottom of the ocean.

⁂

As the fifth anniversary of Joan's disappearance approached, Leonard Paradiso fought to get a fair hearing and reverse his conviction for the murder of Marie Iannuzzi. Suffolk County mounted an objection to Paradiso's latest appeal and enlisted Tim Burke as a special counsel. Burke had manipulated the grand jury to avoid indicting Marie's boyfriend. Marie's case anchored Burke's strategy to blame his target for Joan's murder. If the court reversed the decision, Burke's quest fell apart. He had no evidence connecting Paradiso to Joan Webster. He had no body. Instead of filing charges to try Paradiso for Joan's murder, he chipped around the edges and tried the suspect in the papers. The weakest links connecting the two cases were the anonymous caller Patty Bono, Robert Bond's false testimony, and Death Row Tony's unsubstantiated conversations.

Burke continued to rehash the unverified or manipulated stories that shocked the public as if they were fact. Keeping information hidden in other case files gave Burke the advantage of controlling the narrative. He proved you could make people believe anything if they didn't have all the facts. At this point, the public believed Paradiso murdered Joan on his boat and discarded her body in Boston Harbor.

Burke's legal assistant interrupted the appeal proceeding. She whispered into Burke's ear that his wife had just suffered a miscarriage. Burke accepted the condolences from his colleagues, but he blocked out the suffering he inflicted on others because of his obsession. The goal was never justice for Marie Iannuzzi, but a predetermined outcome for Joan. The deception tipping the scales of justice rebuffed Paradiso's legal right to an appeal in a murder conviction. The court denied Paradiso's petition.

ɞ

Burke proffered a lame excuse why he didn't file charges in Joan's case. To date, neither Joan nor her body had ever turned up. In truth, the state lacked any real evidence to make the case against Paradiso. Robert Bond was the only hope to take Paradiso to trial. Bond felt the state had screwed him before, and the rat rejected the state's efforts for him to tattle again. According to Bond, they tried several times to persuade him. Palombo even corresponded with the killer, but Bond refused to comply.

"He told me not to change my story," Bond said.

Regardless of the finding, Burke, Palombo, and George Webster renewed a push to keep the boat story alive. The three men hit the airwaves in November 1987, six years after the melodrama had begun. As each man stared into the cameras, the audience could look deep into their penetrating eyes. The trio of Svengalis tempted the public to believe them.

"He's [Paradiso] got her onboard his boat, sexually assaulted her, killed her," Burke insisted. "Then, he took her body out in the Boston Harbor area, sunk her body, and then brought his boat back into the Pier 7 area, cleaned it up, and sunk it two days later."

"If she did go on that boat, she was attacked by Paradiso," Palombo told the news outlet. "She was murdered on that boat, and her body was disposed of from that boat."

"He's almost like a serial killer," George accused. "I think he's completely amoral."

While Burke, Palombo, and George Webster were still selling the boat theory to the public, contrary to Judge Selya's finding, Burke's ineptitude was handled discreetly. The phone rang in Burke's office. His assistant recognized Paul Leary's voice. Burke's former boss wanted a word with his old pupil. He was not happy about what Burke did with the alleged crime scene. Burke had taken the liberty of rewarding Anthony Pascucci for services rendered. The investigator worked for Suffolk County but was a frequent visitor in Burke's office. In return for the miscellaneous errands and beer runs the state employee made for Burke, the lawyer handed him the keys to the crime scene. Judge Selya may have sunk the lawyer's story—the *Malafemmena* was long gone before Joan disappeared, but Burke was still promoting the tale. If Joan's case ever went to trial, the unforced error of giving away the boat would sink it again. Burke gave the boat, his alleged crime scene, to Anthony Pascucci. The revelation of Burke's generosity proved one of two things. Either the lawyer didn't believe his own bull, or he was the stupidest lawyer to ever pass the bar.

In the past, George Webster, had sent people to see Bond, but the recruits failed to get Bond to cooperate with George's cause. According to Bond, George and Eleanor Webster visited the convicted killer themselves in the winter 1987. They knew the story, but they needed Bond to tell it. Bond struggled in the prison system. He made a lot of enemies and got into serious fights. Fellow inmates ratted on the con who bragged about framing an innocent man for crimes he didn't commit. Fearing for their own safety, prisoners took a preemptive strike. They stabbed Bond and sent him to the infirmary. The Department of Corrections shuffled the instigators to other facilities. Bond wrote to Senator Ted Kennedy hoping for some favored treatment. As a result, officials moved him to a less rigid federal penitentiary and his living quarters improved.

FD-36 (Rev. 8-26-82)

FBI

TRANSMIT VIA:
☐ Teletype
☐ Facsimile
☒ AIRTEL

PRECEDENCE:
☐ Immediate
☐ Priority
☐ Routine

CLASSIFICATION:
☐ TOP SECRET
☐ SECRET
☐ CONFIDENTIAL
☐ UNCLAS E F T O
☐ UNCLAS

Date _____ 7/24/85

TO: DIRECTOR, FBI
        (ATTN: FUGITIVE/GENERAL GOVERNMENT CRIMES UNIT,
         INTERPOL LIAISON, CID)

FROM: SAC, BOSTON (62D-5738) (C)

SUBJECT: CHANGED

         LEONARD J. PARADISO - SUBJECT;
         JOAN L. WEBSTER - VICTIM;
         DOMESTIC POLICE COOPERATION - INTERPOL
         (OO: BS)

            Title marked "Changed" to reflect the identification
of LEONARD J. PARADISO as a subject in this case.

            Re Bureau airtel to Newark and Boston, 6/13/85.

            Enclosed for the Bureau is an original and three copies
of an LHM relative to this matter.

            For the information of the Interpol Liaison Unit,
consensus of investigators in Boston is that sufficient information
has been developed indicating that subject PARADISO murdered
victim WEBSTER in 11/81. Based on this conclusion, there appears
to be sufficient justification for the cancellation of the
Interpol "International Blue Notice".

            The Domestic Police Cooperation case relative to this
matter is now closed in Boston.

6 - Bureau (Enc. 4)
1 - Boston
SDB/dw
(4)

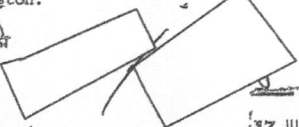

17 JUL 30 1985

Approved: _____   Transmitted _____   Per _____
                            (Number)   (Time)

53 SEP 10 1985

U.S. GOVERNMENT PRINTING OFFICE : 1984 0 - 449-465

Consensus FBI Report to Close FBI Cooperation
in Joan Webster Case

202

In Reply, Please Refer to
File No.

Boston, Massachusetts

July 24, 1985

LEONARD J. PARADISO - SUBJECT;
JOAN L. WEBSTER - VICTIM;
DOMESTIC POLICE COOPERATION - INTERPOL

On November 28, 1981, JOAN L. WEBSTER, a HARVARD UNIVERSITY graduate student, departed Newark, New Jersey, on an EASTERN AIRLINES flight to Boston, Massachusetts. WEBSTER was last seen in the baggage claim area at Boston Logan Airport. WEBSTER's purse was later found in a marsh in Saugus, Massachusetts, and one of her two suitcases was discovered in a locker at the Greyhound Bus Depot in Boston, Massachusetts.

Since November, 1981, investigation conducted by state, local and federal authorities has developed strong evidence that WEBSTER was abducted and murdered by LEONARD J. PARADISO, a convicted murderer. This evidence is not currently considered strong enough to convict PARADISO mainly because WEBSTER's body has never been recovered. Although PARADISO has not been prosecuted for WEBSTER's murder, the consensus of the state, local and federal investigators of this case is that sufficient facts have been established to cancel the Interpol "Blue" notice.

1*

62-119655—49

U.S. Department of Justice Closes the Interpol Blue Notice

Chapter Nineteen
Chebacco Road

Life went on, and Joan's name faded from the headlines. The public assumed the lost soul rested at the bottom of the harbor, and Paradiso had put her there. Meanwhile, Paradiso languished in jail with little hope of redemption. He maintained his innocence, but with the parade of sensational witnesses Burke marched to the stand, few people believed the hapless shellfish peddler. Burke held an advantage. As long as Joan's case remained open, the state guarded the records. Either Bond testified again to pin Joan's murder on Paradiso, or colleagues concealed Burke's tactics. In Burke's mind, it was a win-win.

❧

The house sat on a bluff overlooking Chebacco Lake in Hamilton, Massachusetts. The remote, heavily wooded area was sparsely inhabited. Twenty-five miles north of Logan Airport, it was a popular destination for hikers and bikers and motorcycle gangs. Law enforcement frequently patrolled the area, as it was an isolated location known for criminal activity. Small, unfurling, green buds tipped the branches announcing spring's arrival. The winter thaw often flooded the lower hollows of the copse and softened the ground. At the top of the hill, Karen Wolf pulled on her boots. The veterinarian moseyed out the door to walk her dog and survey the lower basin of her property.

Deep puddles filled the depressions in the rutted, gravel road. Water barely trickled through the drainage pipe that ran under

Karen's steep driveway. Looking for the obstruction blocking the flow, she saw an object clogging the channel. From a distance, the item looked like a punched-in volleyball. As she got closer, she recognized the distinctive suture-like zig zags and pulled back in horror. Karen rushed back up to her house and called the police.

The first officer on the scene confirmed the discovery: Karen Wolf had found a human skull on her property on April 18, 1990. Weather, occasional flooding, and animal activity had loosened the earth to yield her secrets. Police patrol vehicles and unmarked cars soon congested Chebacco Road, a narrow, winding path through the forest. The first cursory search of the terrain yielded nothing more to identify the unfortunate victim. Police tape cordoned off the area, and local law enforcement planned their next steps. Phones rang and anxious families submitted names of the missing hoping for closure in their own ordeals. Authorities downplayed the prospect that the skull belonged to Joan Webster. Even George Webster dismissed the possibility his daughter had surfaced in the remote hamlet. He told reporters all the evidence pointed out to sea.

The recovered cranium offered a few clues. Long, dark hair on the left side of the head narrowed the list of possible victims. Investigators had no dentals to compare. At some point, the upper and lower jaws had dislodged from the skull. A gaping hole obliterated the entire right side of the victim's being, and decomposition had erased the rest. Identification of the skull alone was difficult with the technology of the day.

Hamilton Police Chief Walter Cullen organized a grid search of the area. Day after day, volunteers joined police to comb the area. They found miscellaneous trash, animal bones, a gun wrapped in aluminum foil, and a black boot, but no body. After a week-long search, Hamilton detectives almost gave up. Resigned, Paul Grant, Scott Janes, and Paul Accomando stood under the rustling canopy of the forest. Accomando leaned over and reached into the sediment of a decaying log on April 26, 1990. He grasped a hard clump between his fingers. The three officers stared at the human vertebrae in stunned silence. They had found the grave.

The power company routinely thinned out the woods and left the timber right where they chopped it. Investigators peeled back the layers to uncover the unmarked tomb. Under the first pile of cut logs, the recovery team found a second layer of chopped timber in a more advanced stage of decay. The depression, sometimes flooded with water, was a natural dip that the offender had filled with a body. The stealth undertaker covered his sins with leaves and debris before stacking a layer of cut logs over the grave. Someone went back later and piled on more wood to deepen the dark secret.

The search mission turned into a recovery. Teams excavated the grave a handful of dirt at a time. Medical examiners joined the effort to carefully lift out the bones and transport them to the pathology lab. Off to the side, a curious onlooker watched the exhumation with interest. The unidentified man had traveled to the remote area from Malden or Melrose, a neighborhood much closer to the heart of Boston. Although an intriguing spectacle for any random passerby, officials restricted access to the scene. No one bothered to check if the man just happened across the recovery operation, or if he had a vested interest in the skeleton's resurrection.

The recovered jawbones gave forensic dentist Stanley Schwartz the pieces he needed to identify the poor soul abandoned in the woods. Already familiar with her dental charts, he knew the minute he saw the remains that it was Joan. Positively identified on April 30, 1990, Joan Webster had returned back to the living to help us solve her murder.

What the Hamilton Police found was not what the public was led to believe. An offender had buried Joan in a remote wooded area under two distinct layers of cut logs. She had a two inch by four inch hole in the right side of her head. A gold neck chain and gold ring remained on the skeleton, but these items weren't uniquely identifiable. The bracelet and signet ring were still missing. The culprit had stripped Joan of all clothing. None of it or her belongings turned up anywhere in the vicinity. The assailant had discarded the devalued young woman in a black plastic trash bag that had broken open beneath her.

Most people missed the out-of-state ruling that affirmed Paradiso's boat was long gone before Joan disappeared. They didn't know the state's star witness had repeated a lie under the tutelage of the story's creator, Massachusetts Sergeant Carmen Tammaro. The passage of time dulled memories, but Joan had surfaced a long way from her alleged graveyard in Boston Harbor. These woods, 25 miles north of Logan, was not even remotely close to the harbor or Pier 7. Surely, any reasoning person now understood that Bond was a false witness.

Burke scrambled to save his reputation. He admitted that investigators knew Paradiso's boat had a broken rudder when they brought the sunken vessel to the surface on September 27, 1983. The boat wasn't navigable. Just like David Doyle's excuses, the lawyer's story changed. He still maintained Paradiso murdered Joan on the *Malafemmena*, but twisted Bond's allegations to suit the indisputable new facts. Bond claimed Paradiso took his boat way out and dumped Joan in Boston Harbor. Now, Burke insisted "way out" wasn't clearly defined. Burke twisted Bond's statements to mean Paradiso hoisted the dead body off his boat, drove Joan way out, and buried her more than 30 miles away. Burke had cleverly sealed the foundational Bond documents years ago during the Marie Iannuzzi case; no one had the records to challenge Burke's latest version.

George and Eleanor traveled to Hamilton, Massachusetts. Chief Cullen respectfully showed them the resting place where investigators had uncovered their daughter. The couple sat down in front of the cameras to take questions about their ordeal. They expressed their gratitude for all the efforts to bring Joan home. One chapter had closed, but they resolved to press on until Joan's killer faced justice. The intelligence-trained parents stood firm with Tim Burke, expressing their conviction that Paradiso had murdered Joan. One reporter asked the next logical question: Why did Joan's parents believe Paradiso was guilty? You could have heard a pin drop in the crowded room. Eleanor sternly glared at her husband, who kept his mouth shut.

The pathologist collected the evidence over the next two and a half months. The examiner determined the manner of death was a homicide. The cause of death was blunt force trauma to the head. Although authorities had accused Paradiso of the crime for years, officials had denied his participation in the process or access to the records, as dictated by law. George Webster ratcheted up the heat at Harmony Grove Crematory on July 13, 1990, under the direction of the Murphy Funeral Home in Salem, Massachusetts. The state's public servants eventually bent to George's will. The law allowed the release of remains for cremation only when there was no further examination or judicial inquiry necessary concerning the death. The homicide was unresolved; it was an open case. It was insanity to allow the victim's father to incinerate the best evidence, the victim's remains, but ashes were easier to sweep under the rug.

Saying goodbye to a loved one is never easy. George and Eleanor notified the family of Joan's interment but closed the simple graveside service to anyone else. At such times, most families find solace and comfort from others who share in their grief, but the Websters remained stoic. Nevertheless, there was no church service to celebrate her life and let friends say goodbye. Joan's brother Steve and his wife, Eve, were the only two people standing next to George and Eleanor at the cemetery. Bucky, the choir director from their church, said a few words to offer Joan some final peace. Her sister Anne was a no show. After a few quiet moments of reflection, the committal was over. George approached the large granite stone and momentarily dipped one knee to the ground. The words George had uttered when the nightmare began stuck in Eve's memory on the solemn day.

"She's gone," George said. "We have to move on."

☙

The family gathered for their annual ritual in Nantucket in August 1990. Seeds of doubt crept into the private discussions about Joan in the inner sanctum. Eleanor told Steve's wife it had been too long to know what really happened to Joan. They agreed with authorities that they had the right suspect. Because of scant evidence, they probably couldn't take Paradiso to trial, but at least he was locked up for other crimes. Anne's husband had similar doubts; Joan's remains were buried on land, miles from the alleged crime.

"Why do you still think Paradiso did it?" he asked.

"His girlfriend had Joan's ring," Eleanor replied.

The two in-laws didn't hear the same answer, but tiptoed over the eggshells to not unsettle parents who had just buried their youngest child. Claiming Paradiso's girlfriend had some of Joan's jewelry was similar to Tim Burke's false assertion to the FBI. He insisted Charlene Bullerwell handed Paradiso a photo of herself wearing a bracelet identical to Joan's one-of-a-kind charm bracelet. If anyone associated with their suspect had anything of Joan's, the prosecution had a slam dunk case. Now they had the body, eliminating Burke's rationale to dodge trying to prosecute Paradiso before. Regardless of Eleanor's ridiculous declaration, any endeavor to charge Paradiso for Joan's murder abruptly stopped after she surfaced.

Location of Joan Webster Gravesite
on Chebacco Road in Hamilton, MA

Right Side of Joan Webster Skull

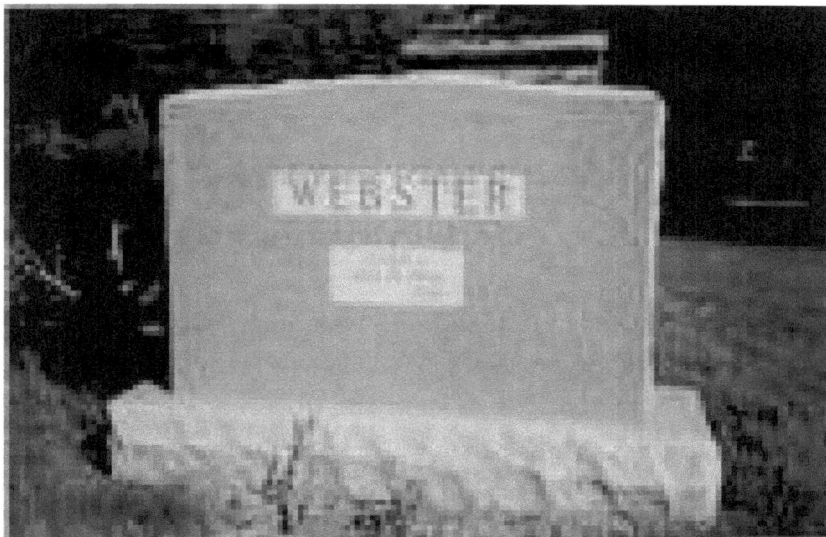

Joan Webster Headstone in Bloomfield, NJ

Chapter Twenty
Three Infested Departments

After Joan's remains were found, the Hamilton Police renewed the hunt for her killer, and her speculated fate was revived in the papers. Paradiso's heart raced. He thought the discovery vindicated him for the years of the state's persecution. Locating the skeleton added another baffling element to the mystery. Joan vanished leaving Logan Airport. Her purse and wallet turned up a few days later in the Saugus marshes, about seven miles north of the airport on the southbound side of the road. Two months after she disappeared, a Greyhound employee discovered her suitcase at the bus station west of the airport. Now, more than eight years later, the missing grad student had surfaced in a remote woodland 25 miles north of where she landed. A raging fire the night of her disappearance detoured a direct path from the airport to the grave.

Investigators met daily. They debated all kinds of scenarios, but the known facts simply did not fit together in any logical sense. There were divergent opinions. Some officers rejected the theory that Leonard Paradiso murdered Joan Webster. Trooper Palombo insisted he did. A new team reviewed the past statements of Robert Bond without the benefit of the letter and interview transcript Burke had sealed during the Iannuzzi pretrial hearing. The location of Joan's remains was a glaring discrepancy.

The Hamilton Police Chief, Walter Cullen, digested the known facts. A seasoned officer, he knew Chebacco Road. The secluded setting known for criminal activity complicated the state's promoted boat theory. Cullen concluded the offender likely knew the locale; it wasn't an easy place to find. At night, the area was pitch black except for headlights driving back into the abyss. In his educated opinion, Cullen suspected that Joan knew her assailant. He considered whether the grave site was the scene of the murder. If it wasn't, a dead body was hard for one person to move. The chief's deliberations matched known facts still buried in locked files. The eyewitness had described a bearded man with Joan at Logan. The unidentified man maneuvered Joan to a blue car. Joan willingly changed vehicles at the man's instruction suggesting she knew him. The driver of the second car pulled away from the curb at Logan with Joan and the bearded man. Another person participated in Joan's disappearance.

Chebacco Road was a considerable distance from Logan and even further from Pier 7. The chief remembered a psychic had investigators searching very close to the spot where they finally found Joan. Cullen acknowledged that Palombo knew the area. At the time Joan disappeared, Palombo lived nearby. State and local police in the vicinity were familiar with the criminal activity and suicides in the desolate spot. It was irrational to suggest that the shellfish peddler, with an eighth grade education, pulled off a diabolical crime that baffled battalions of enforcers. Palombo knew none of the evidence he gathered placed Paradiso in the Hamilton forest, but he persisted with his increasingly illogical views.

The Hamilton Police labored for the next year to figure out what happened to Joan. They crossed a couple of peripheral suspects off the list, but not before putting them through the rigors. Joan didn't know anyone in Hamilton, and neither did her parents. The location of the grave raised more questions than it answered. Nothing the new detective team understood connected the known points of Joan's murder. The renewed surge for answers stalled again.

"We need someone to come forward with information," Cullen implored. "We're at a dead end."

ೲ

The methods and practices of the Suffolk County District Attorney earned his office convictions. Fighting crime and seeking justice were the responsibilities delegated to the public servants. During the summer 1991, defense attorneys uncovered misconduct during a murder trial. Suffolk County had maintained secret and duplicate files. The case of Kenneth Spinkston exposed folders known as the "Kiernan Files." John Kiernan was the head of the homicide division in Suffolk County. His locked cabinets contained exculpatory evidence influencing the outcome of cases handled in Assistant District Attorney Tim Burke's office. The revelation of malfeasance impacted cases from 1980-1988, the tenure of Kiernan's position. Burke's relentless pursuit of Paradiso fell in the heart of Suffolk County's transgressions.

By this time, the public knew Robert Bond's allegations were false. Joan was not in Boston Harbor. His deceit in Joan's case raised questions about his credibility in Marie Iannuzzi's litigation. The convicted felon was a known liar who angled for favorable treatment by cooperating with the state against Paradiso. The conviction Burke gained for Marie's murder was a prosecution that logically needed review. By the time Suffolk County's dirty tricks came to light, the Massachusetts State Police had transferred Joan's records to the third District Attorney to handle Joan's probe. Essex County became the new custodian when Joan surfaced in their jurisdiction. The action severed the two crimes after years of tying them together. The fracture further eroded a path to Joan's justice. As long as no one asked about the validity of Marie's case, the verdict prevailed. Suffolk County no longer handled the entangled investigation of Joan Webster. Joan was not their problem anymore, so they didn't bother to reconsider if Burke had mismanaged her case.

When the Hamilton detectives reached a dead end, Essex County retrieved the boxes of materials from the local police department. The memory of a vibrant young woman collected dust in the archives of the state's defenders of justice. Each custodian took their turn guarding the files from prying eyes. The obligation to find answers fell through the cracks in the dysfunctional system. Keeping the secrets overruled any queries into the matter. Panic set in whenever someone mentioned Joan Webster's name. Only amateur sleuths kept the murder in the public domain with one outlandish claim after the next. Fantastic tales, devoid of facts, widened the gap between sensation and what really happened. Officials, content to let people ruminate, shirked their responsibility. Joan's case became the third rail of injustice, a maelstrom no one wanted to touch.

∽

An anonymous pen pal mailed a series of three letters to Paradiso. The author went to a lot of trouble to disguise his identity. The mysterious correspondent typed the message first, photocopied the text, and then postmarked the unsigned notes in Boston. The method avoided any handwriting or fingerprint samples that might identify the source. The writer admitted he knew Lenny Paradiso was innocent; he knew how Joan Webster died, and he knew why. The covert messenger asserted that he knew the whole thing was a set up. Paradiso had no idea if the author was a crackpot or someone involved with the crime who suffered pangs of remorse. He confided in Ray Morgan, a private investigator, one of the few people who kept the faith with the scorned man. This anonymous information added yet another bizarre twist to the riddle.

∽

The next shoe dropped in 1997 when investigators handed down indictments surrounding the Boston FBI's mishandling of the mob. Mob boss Whitey Bulger had terrified Boston citizens during the era of Joan's investigation. Bulger allegedly ratted out Mafia figures to the FBI. In return, his handler tipped him off when state authorities threatened his operation. Corruption infected Boston's system of justice on every level. Dedicated public servants suspected many of the leaks originated with the Massachusetts State Police. Carmen Tammaro already showed the propensity for leaking information when he told Paradiso about the Feds' plans to go after the Mafia.

Suffolk County and the Boston office of the FBI both worked on Joan's case, and the Massachusetts State Police controlled the direction of the investigation. Tim Burke had a hand in Bulger's affairs. He wrote warrants to bug Bulger at the Lancaster Street Garage. According to Burke, that was when he first met Palombo. In a covert operation, Burke described a long-haired state trooper driving a van into Bulger's garage. Burke's assistant was the female companion who enticed Bulger to let them park inside overnight. Another trooper hid under furniture in the van. The concealed state trooper snuck out after dark to plant the listening device. The plot failed because someone alerted Bulger. Three infested departments—Suffolk County, the Boston office of the FBI, and the Massachusetts State Police—all peddled an impossible projection of Joan's murder.

"Everything is falling apart," Palombo confided to Paradiso's estranged daughter.

Palombo approached the young woman again in 1997. Her memory flashed back to the uncomfortable ride Palombo gave her from the airport in 1982. Palombo suggested Paradiso murdered women that reminded him of her. He swore to put her father away for a very long time. She cut off the officer before he unloaded whatever was weighing on his conscience.

❧

Joan's name faded from the headlines again. Weeks turned into months that turned into years without definitive answers. Family and friends walked on eggshells as each holiday season approached. George and Eleanor traveled to the Midwest to celebrate Christmas with his son's family in 1997. Anne and her children joined the gathering. George rebuked his daughter-in-law's wishes to exclude Anne's guest from the Christmas Day celebration. Anne was married but separated. George decided Anne's new boyfriend had a place at the Christmas table. Eve suggested he be invited for brunch the next day instead, but George objected. George was not used to the word no, and his disrespect for her boundaries ruffled feathers during the visit. Eve bit her lip as Anne's new boyfriend sauntered up the sidewalk on Christmas Day and rang the doorbell.

Once back in New Jersey, word of Paradiso's condition reached George and Eleanor. Leonard Paradiso was reportedly on his deathbed. Joan's father didn't expect a confession with Paradiso's last breath. George had the eyewitness report and composite secretly filed away. The man seen with Joan at Logan Airport was a much smaller man than the man her parents accused of murder. The *Malafemmena* was sunk months before Joan disappeared. Even on his deathbed, Paradiso could not be expected to confess to an impossible crime just because George Webster accused him of it, but George dispensed his judgment on December 29, 1997, to render the final declaration of guilt.

"We still believe he killed our daughter," George said. "Knowing the type of individual he is, and how he has lied all the way through, I cannot believe he would turn around."

Chapter Twenty-One
Dear God

The cryptic correspondence Paradiso had received in the mail steeled his resolve. His condition improved, and he escaped the clutches of the grim reaper. Another piece of the puzzle fell into place, with the anonymous letters. The discovery of Joan's brittle bones confirmed the grisly death she suffered, but a deceptive conduit foretold the outcome long before her body was found. Pinning the murder on Paradiso satisfied the question of motive in people's minds. According to the creators of that tale, Paradiso was a sexual predator, a serial killer, and Joan was a chance victim in the wrong place at the wrong time. Describing Joan's murder as a random act was palatable to the public, but the author of the letters said he knew why. Motive for Joan's murder was simply hard to fathom, but the unidentified source alluded to premeditation. Joan had been targeted.

☙

After leaving the fireworks display in Lynn, Massachusetts, Palombo waited for the light to turn green. The undercover cop gradually accelerated his motorcycle up the hill and around the curve. The roads were familiar, and his speed was not fast. His life ended as he rounded the bend when his motorcycle hit an oil slick and skidded into the guardrail. Doctors pronounced Andrew Palombo dead on July 4, 1998. His silenced lips went to the grave, but he left a long trail to follow.

❧

Twenty years had passed without answers. Half the country away, Steve Webster's family struggled through the tumultuous teenage years with their daughters. Joan's brother rarely talked about the tragedy of his murdered sister with anyone, and most often, he tried to change the subject when it was broached. Steve mirrored his father's position that Joan was gone, they had to move on. The acorn didn't fall far from the tree; Steve was just like his dad. Anne described her brother as a chauvinist, but in truth he was insecure and didn't think for himself. His immaturity stirred the pot in favor of fun instead of supporting good values and healthy boundaries for the next generation.

One day, Eve opened the desk drawer looking for keys. In the back of the drawer she found three folded pages. "Dear God" the letter began. Joan's sister-in-law carefully folded the letter and put the gut wrenching prayer in her pocket. She fell to the cold, hard tile on the bathroom floor and tried to throw up. Dry heaves only intensified the anguish. Nothing purged the terrifying words, the horrifying accusation, written on the pages. God had given Eve a task, but she wasn't sure what it meant or where it would lead.

The letter alleged a dark family secret. If true, a member of the Webster family had committed a heinous felony, and there were other victims. The accusation wasn't precise. Jumping to the wrong conclusion would be detrimental to everyone involved. Joan's blood kin banded together against an invasion of privacy, privacy as defined by the Websters. Eve was the only non-blood relative in the immediate family when Joan disappeared. Now, she threatened the family's image by seeking help outside their four walls.

The family vehemently denied the allegations of sexual abuse, but instead of resolving concerns, the Websters deployed their proven strategy of projection and alienation. History repeated. Just like the wild stories circulated about Paradiso, Eve became the family's new target of destructive gossip. Razing the good name and gentle heart of one of their own was critical to preserve the Websters' public persona.

At the time, Eve didn't know Anne's ex-husband had raised similar concerns a few years before. Anne's behavior created the suspicion that Anne may have been molested. But, in true Webster fashion, she refused to discuss the concerns with her husband. Their relationship soured as Anne's husband struggled with isolation within the family. Ultimately, the union ended in divorce.

The author of the letter to God appeared in court. Under oath, the witness falsely accused Eve of altering the letter. Eve was not the type to be quiet, and the family knew it. The Websters disapproved of a whistleblower in their midst. There was no question who penned the allegations. Copies sat in multiple files including family counselors and the local police, contemporaneous evidence reported at the time. Corroborating evidence supported real worries. The alleged offender, identified in the letter to God, told the vulnerable accuser that the incident was her imagination. The gaslighting technique instilled doubt.

Sexual abuse wasn't a specific offense, and needed to be clarified to properly support any victims. The alleged victim who penned the letter to God made an entry in her journal and projected her anger onto a vulnerable target, Eve. Four letters spelled out the dark secret in the Webster family, rape. The violation of a child is controlling behavior. Was the family shielding Joan's brother, Eve's husband? Was there a pattern of controlling behavior passed down from George? Either way, at the time of Joan's murder, Eve was an expectant mother. She *needed* to know about a potential risk to her children. Joan had realized that.

The allegations were impossible to prove or disprove, but the family showed a much different face than the sympathetic loved ones seeking justice for Joan. The conflict ended the 25-year marriage of Joan's brother Steve to his wife Eve. The campaign of head games intensified when George and Eleanor learned their now former daughter-in-law had started asking questions about Joan. Steve was the first to insist Joan's murder had nothing to do with the incriminating letter. The persistence to sever the two circumstances only convinced the beleaguered Eve that there was something in Joan's records to help her find answers.

The more Joan's next of kin, George and Eleanor, vilified the mother of their grandchildren and labeled her delusional, the more she dug into Joan's records. They were the ones insisting that Paradiso murdered Joan on a boat that was already 35 feet under water when she landed at Logan. They were the ones that had locked the eyewitness description and composite in their files. The discrepancies contained in Joan's records were staggering compared to what the family professed. The fact remained: Joan was dead. The fear was whether other innocent victims were endangered.

As the Websters closed ranks to malign Eve, George and Eleanor packed their bags. They headed north to the Commonwealth of Massachusetts. Once Joan's body had surfaced, a trial to prosecute Paradiso for Joan's murder was impossible. Frightening allegations had leaked out of the inner sanctum and threatened the mirage. Shrewd George and Eleanor turned to the lawyer who had manifested their case. Tim Burke opened the door of his vacation retreat in the summer of 2005 and welcomed Joan's parents into his den. They wanted to know everything about their daughter's alleged killer, and Burke willingly obliged. He took advantage of the twenty-fifth anniversary of Joan's fateful flight to announce his book. His tome sought to close the door on the story of the grad student's murder. The venture seemed ill-advised, a former prosecutor publishing unproven accusations in a still open, unresolved homicide. Burke's hubris erased any apprehension, and the Websters were satisfied. The lawyer was sure no one could get to the fragmented and concealed records.

The former prosecutor had an ace up his sleeve. The Massachusetts State Police had shifted Joan's records to Essex County in 1990, except for the box Burke had removed. John Dawley was the First Assistant District Attorney in Essex County at that time. The responsibility for Joan's case fell squarely on his shoulders. When Dawley passed the bar in 1982, his first job was in Suffolk County with Burke. The most notorious and publicized investigation in Dawley's new office was Burke's relentless pursuit of Leonard Paradiso and the fate of Joan Webster. John Dawley knew Tim Burke; they were colleagues under the same tutelage.

Dawley intersected with Suffolk County again as a defense lawyer in private practice. Charles Stuart and his pregnant wife, Carol, were driving home from a birthing class in 1989. Authorities found the couple in their car with gunshot wounds. Sadly, Carol and her unborn baby died, but Charles survived the ordeal. He told the police a black man had carjacked their vehicle and robbed them. The assailant allegedly shot them before fleeing the scene. There was no gun at the location, and Carol's jewelry was missing. Investigators in Suffolk County scoured the neighborhood for clues. They arrested a vulnerable black man and accused him of murder. Charles even pointed out the suspect in a line-up. Suffolk County might have administered their brand of justice, but a witness came forward. Charles' brother, Matt, told authorities that Charles had murdered his wife. Matt was an accomplice. He had taken the gun and jewelry from the scene and disposed of them in the river. Charles sat down behind closed doors with his attorney for two hours. Charles left the meeting with Dawley and committed suicide. Even though Charles was dead, Dawley refused to relieve Carol's family with any admissions the killer made.

Dawley returned to public service, joining the Essex County District Attorney's Office shortly after Jonathan Blodgett was elected as District Attorney in 2002. As First Assistant District Attorney, Dawley was the number two man in charge, becoming the custodian of Joan Webster's case. Transparency was not his definition of ethics. He was the single arbiter standing between a former prosecutor, Tim Burke, with privileged access to files, and Joan's justice.

Burke took one last shot at soliciting a confession from Paradiso. Guards transferred Robert Bond to the Lemuel Shattuck Hospital on February 7, 2008, hoping to situate Bond by Paradiso's bedside. The shellfish peddler was suffering from stage four cancer. Bond balked at the attempted plot to get a deathbed confession. To Burke's dismay, the ploy failed, and Paradiso never confessed to the crime that was impossible for him to have committed in the first place.

Burke published his book in February 2008 to another blitz of media fanfare. George and Eleanor publicly supported Burke's book and had contributed to it. The author dedicated his text to Joan's parents to ease the pain of their loss. The story closely followed the Burke's version of the crime, but had some noticeable rewrites when inconvenient facts contradicted the discourse. Regardless, Burke's published version conflicted with the actual records. His book was now evidence in an open murder case under the jurisdiction of his old friend in Essex County. The paradox was that the parents of a brutally murdered daughter, pleading for justice, had sanctioned a book that distorted or blatantly lied about the facts. Handing a family a name, someone, anyone to blame was not justice at all.

Memories fade, but the vision of Paradiso murdering Joan on his boat remained deeply ingrained in the public's perception. For those who lived through this on a personal level, and suffered real consequences, Burke's published account was more than a slap in the face. Burke's conduct aided and abetted Joan's killer while the man he accused lay on his deathbed. Leonard Paradiso listened to the mockery of other inmates calling Joan's name down the hall. Finally, he took his last breath and escaped Burke's torture. Paradiso died on

February 27, 2008 from bladder cancer. His predator even slanted the man's cause of death and falsely claimed Paradiso died from testicular cancer. Paradiso wasn't a saint, and he had many failings to atone for. However, the overwhelming evidence in verified records supported a wrongful conviction for Marie Iannuzzi's murder. No real evidence connected Paradiso to Joan Webster. He didn't need forgiveness for crimes he didn't commit.

Tim Burke's book had unexpectedly opened a can of worms for the Websters. The family wanted the story to be the final word on the subject. They retreated behind a wall of privacy, but privacy doesn't extend to covering up murder. *Secrecy* was a more accurate term for the family's behavior.

Meanwhile, the Websters bristled at the questions raised by the source documents in Joan's case, and Burke's published version of events. The postman rang once and tucked a letter in the mailbox. The postmark from South Jersey on August 23, 2008 was just north of George and Eleanor's retirement community. The neat cursive writing on the envelope suggested a friendly greeting inside, but the outward appearance was deceptive. Candy's boyfriend Lenny Paradiso had also received anonymous letters, and now she was on the mailing list. The author lauded the wonderful Tim Burke after reading his book, while typed words ridiculed and devalued the woman who told the court the boat was gone months before Joan disappeared. The covert correspondent wished Candy damnation in hell as an accomplice for Paradiso's alleged evil. The intimidating letter was an unvarnished warning not to talk.

The questions kept coming. The next special delivery arrived half the country away on January 9, 2009. The stamped envelope wasn't postmarked, but hand delivered to Eve. The typist copied the same tactic used against Paradiso to solicit an admission. The Websters painted Eve as a delusional woman who suffered from mental disorders. Catching the family lying about Joan's investigation and the suspected dark secret called for drastic measures. The anonymous correspondent deployed a gaslighting technique, a psychological head game to cause a person to doubt their own sanity. This time the courier was in the Midwest where Joan's brother Steve lived.

Eve hired a private investigator to help dig into Joan's case. He received a thick packet from the FBI answering a Freedom of Information Act request. Steve answered his phone. The caller asked Steve about an extortion incident. The media never reported the dramatic 1982 episode, but Eve vividly remembered the occurrence. Steve feigned forgetfulness, furthering the illusion his ex-wife was out of her mind. The caller held the report in his hand and listened to Steve lie about events surrounding the murder of his sister.

"Honest to God, I don't remember anything like that," Steve said. "Honest to God."

Just like David Doyle, Joan's brother conveniently forgot information when it furthered his objective to squelch a threat to the family's image. Delusions were not incidents corroborated in FBI files, and the Websters never suggested Eve was illiterate or stupid.

Thirteen emails flooded Eve's inbox in July 2010. They all conveyed the same message as the hand delivered anonymous letter. The creator had filled out forms distributing Eve's name to mental health organizations including a government list. The secretive author, hidden behind a keyboard, deceptively filled in the blanks as if Eve had submitted them herself. This malicious head game went a step further, labeling Eve as paranoid. Eve was hovering over the target, and the antagonists were firing back. The crafty typist left a trail; she lacked the skills of her intelligence-trained parents. One of the forms displayed the originating IP address. Tracing the number ended at a company computer in Phoenix, Arizona. Syntellect was Anne Webster's employer in Phoenix. Eve's former sister-in-law had participated in the family's assault on her character.

The private investigator and attorney Eve hired in Boston facilitated the recovery of source documents and interviewed players in the long-running murder mystery. On May 6, 2008, they stepped into the caged world of Robert Bond at the Shirley MCI facility in Massachusetts. The burley convicted killer eyed them warily and was reticent to talk. Bond feared George Webster or Tim Burke had sent them to see him. The investigator described Bond as decidedly unintelligent and extremely suspicious.

"I wasn't born yesterday," Bond huffed. "You're working for money. You were sent by the guy in New Jersey."

On October 8, 2009, Eve went with the private investigator to face Bond herself. Nothing in her Midwestern Christian upbringing prepared her for that moment, facing an unrepentant killer in the bowels of a prison. She shivered as the convicted felon ambled toward the small cubicle, a room set apart from the open space where inmates congregated with their visitors. The interview shed some light. Bond said he corresponded with Palombo up until Joan's remains surfaced, and the officer instructed Bond not to change his story. Bond defiantly insisted he didn't owe the Websters anything.

"I could tell you something to make your ears smoke," Bond said, referring to the letters he exchanged with the undercover enforcer, Andrew Palombo.

Tim Burke was shameless. Doctors tested Bond for prostate cancer three times in January of 2008. The Suffolk County District Attorney's Office was in cahoots with Lemuel Shattuck Hospital, and technicians had wired Paradiso's room. Paradiso suffered from stage four bladder cancer. When guards took Bond back to the hospital on February 7, 2008, the plan was to have Bond visit Paradiso and elicit a confession. Bond didn't want to go in and avoided Burke's attempt to record a deathbed confession from Paradiso. Instead, he went back to the prison.

In late 2012, Eve reached out to George and Eleanor and requested a meeting to address the discrepancies in source documents. George fired back at 10:13 p.m. on Christmas night 2012. No one dared to challenge George Webster except Eve, the mother of his grandchildren, the woman the family lied to—and possibly Joan. Both women were abruptly ousted from the family albums. The leader of the pack stepped out of the shadows himself to pass his judgment. The reply, laced with profanity, echoed the same tirade of the Websters' gaslighting techniques.

"You have no f------- idea. You are delusional," George adamantly insisted. "You are sick, go away. Die."

Tears rolled down Eve's cheeks seeing the true colors of a family she had loved and trusted. She realized she wasn't the only victim betrayed by that family. Joan had been too. This devaluation steeled her resolve to uncover the truth about what happened to her sister-in-law while others remained vulnerable to the hidden, darker side of the Websters, including her children. George's Christmas wish scarred every happy family memory she tried to hold.

"Die," George Webster lowered.

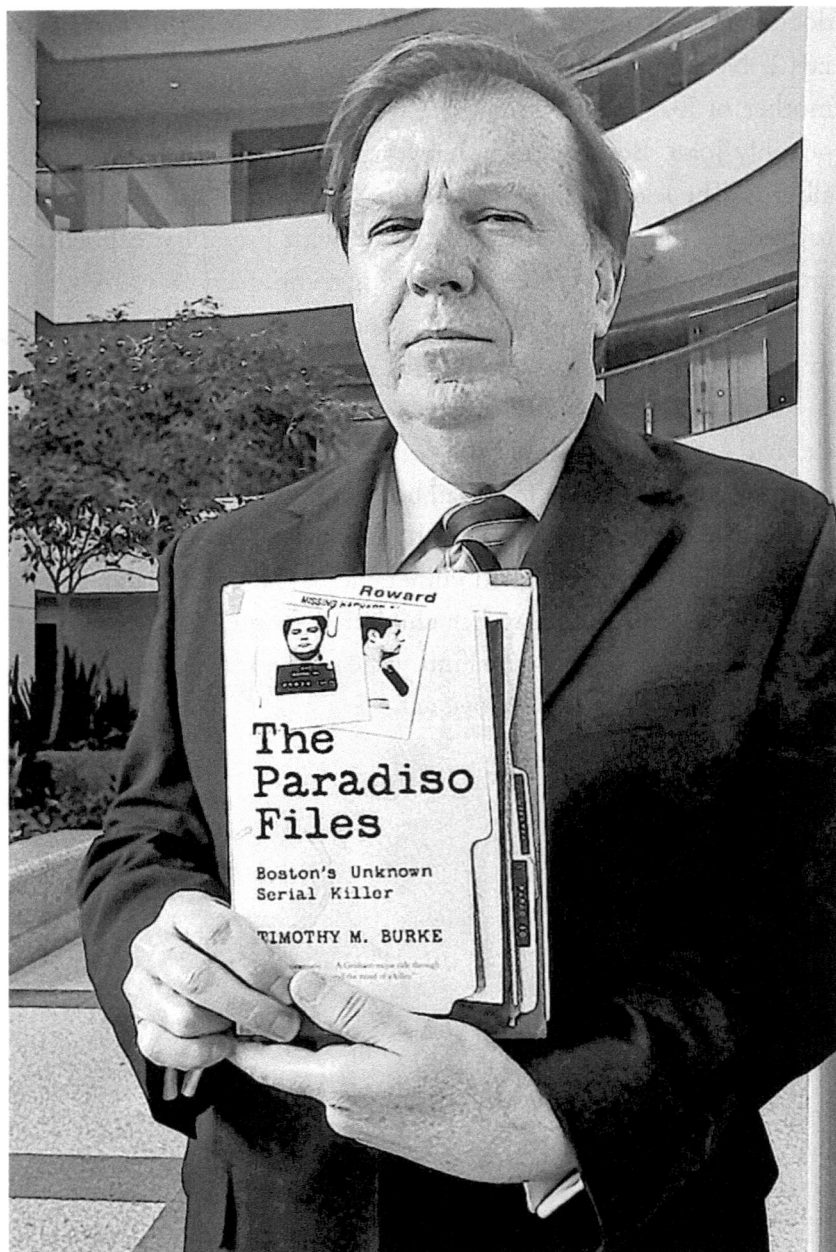

Former Suffolk County Prosecutor Tim Burke
Photo Credit *Boston Herald*

Re: Bonds

From: investigative.com>

To: "eve carson" <eve_carson@yahoo.com>

Cc: @mac.com>

Dear Eve:

Regret to report that our attempted interview of Robert Bond was a complete exercise in futility.

Thanks to my connections at MCI Shirley, we were able to take all of the relevant documents, The Paradiso Files, and a tape recorder inside to meet with Mr. Bond. However, we were advised by the guards that they hoped we knew that Bond would not talk to us and that he was "A grumpy old man".

Unfortunately, as the guards predicted, Mr. Bond was completely uncooperative, and repeatedly suggested that ▇▇▇ and I had been hired by George Webster or Tim Burke. He repeatedly asked if we thought he was "born yesterday," accused us of "working for money" and "working for the guy in New Jersey."

Although my style of conducting an interview is decidedly different then ▇▇▇, neither of our approaches would present us with any cooperation.

Mr. Bond is decidedly unintelligent and extremely suspicious. Despite our best efforts (and years of experience), neither ▇▇▇ nor I was able to gain his trust in any way. Although we showed him the e-mail and his affidavit about the deal Burke reneged on, he had nothing to gain, and therefore would not talk.

So despite our best efforts, we only learned two things of substance:

(1) Mr. Bond is definitely too unintelligent to have remembered and written down all the details contained in his statements and Grand Jury testimony (i.e., the boat registration numbers); and

(2) When asked if George Webster had ever come to see him, Mr. Bond answered in the negative, adding, however, that Webster had "sent people" to talk to him. Although we questioned him repeatedly about the identity of those persons and how he knew they were sent by Webster, Mr. Bond refused to answer. Also note that he kept insisting that that "we were sent by the guy in New Jersey", in reference to George Webster.

There is a slight chance (about 5%) that Mr. Bond may respond to written communication, and to that end, ▇▇▇ suggested and he will write him a letter explaining our position in an attempt to gain his cooperation.

Needless to say, I found the entire experience extremely frustrating – as stated, Mr. Bond is extremely unintelligent and suspicious, and all efforts to gain his confidence met with negative results.

As to his lack of mental capacity, even if Mr. Bond could recall (for example) the name Conley & Daggart, he would certainly not be able to spell it!

Naturally, I had hoped to be reporting a much more positive encounter with Mr. Bond, but remain hopeful (to some degree) that ▇▇▇ letter will at least open the door to the possibility of another attempted interview.

If not there are other avenues available to us to seek some of the answers we were seeking from Bond's. For instance, the others mentioned who had dealings with him in prison and possibly current inmates that he associates with in Shirley.

I will, of course, continue to keep you updated as to the progress of the investigation.

▇▇▇   .

PI Report of Interview with Robert Bond

THE COMMONWEALTH OF MASSACHUSETTS
OFFICE OF THE
DISTRICT ATTORNEY FOR THE ESSEX DISTRICT
SALEM   NEWBURYPORT   LAWRENCE

JONATHAN W. BLODGETT
District Attorney

Ten Federal Street
Salem, Massachusetts 01970

TELEPHONE
VOICE   (978)745-6610
FAX   (978)741-4971
TTY   (978)741-3163

October 24, 2008

▮▮▮▮ and ▮▮▮▮
Investigative Services
▮▮▮▮▮▮▮▮

Dear Sirs,

I write in response to your September 30, 2008 request, made pursuant to the Massachusetts Public Records Law, G.L. c. 66, § 10, for "any and all records regarding the investigation of the Joan Webster murder in Massachusetts in 1981." As we discussed on the phone, I appreciate your understanding as to the delay in responding.

As you are aware, Ms. Webster's homicide remains an unsolved and open case. Further, please be advised that this Office has recently renewed its investigation into this matter. Accordingly, much of the information in the investigative file is not subject to public release under the so-called "investigatory" exemption to the Public Records Law, G. L. c. 4, § 7 cl. 26 (f). In addition, absent a release from the next of kin, much of the information also qualifies for the so-called "privacy" exemption to the Public Records Law, G. L. c. 4, § 7 cl. 26(a).

That said, please find enclosed the following responsive documents, the contents of which have for the most part been released previously:

1.   Harvard Police Department Missing Person Report, December 2, 1981.
2.   Hamilton Police Department Report re: Recovery of Human Remains, April 4, 1990.

As you know, the remains were later identified as those of Ms. Webster; the names of other missing persons considered as possible matches have been redacted under the above-mentioned exemptions.

As we discussed on the phone, the applicable fees for this request have been waived. You may appeal this decision to the Supervisor of Public Records. Thank you for your inquiry.

Sincerely,

David F. O'Sullivan
Assistant District Attorney

DFO:fhs
Encl.

Joan Webster Case Remains Open in Essex County

Subject:	Re: my phone call
From:	grgwb345@aol.com (grgwb345@aol.com)
To:	███████@yahoo.com;
Date:	Tuesday, December 25, 2012 10:13 PM

You are sick
You need help
You ████████████████████████ You go to court claiming defamation. What the f--- is
this about?
You have no f--- idea
You threaten
You are sick go away
Die.

George Webster Email to Eve Carson

Chapter Twenty-Two
The Evidence

The persistence in pinning Joan's murder on Paradiso defied common sense. Any evidence to connect him to the crime was nonexistent. Analyzing the evidence Burke and Palombo gathered was the first step to identifying the purveyors of injustice. Morsels of truth filtered through but escaped the scrutiny needed to identify the true killer.

A clam digger had found Joan's wallet on December 2, 1981, and police found her purse in the same location later that day. Plotting the location on a map indicated the culprit had tossed Joan's belongings from a car headed south towards the airport. The offender took the cash but left her identification and other personal belongings. The FBI carefully catalogued the contents, but keys were noticeably missing from their inventory. Joan had planned to return to her dorm, and she needed keys to get back into her room.

Two months after Joan disappeared, her suitcase turned up at the Park Square Greyhound Bus Station in Boston. That point on the map was west of the airport. Nothing appeared to be missing from her luggage. Authorities never recovered Joan's carry-on tote bag or its contents. Her one-of-a-kind gold charm bracelet was among the missing items, either carried in her purse or in the leather tote.

When Palombo executed a search warrant at Candy Weyant's home under the cover of the Marie Iannuzzi case on April 25, 1983, he snatched a coffee table book on Mayan civilization from Paradiso's bookshelf. Palombo portrayed the volume as a textbook belonging to Joan. *Maya (Monuments of Civilization)* by Pierre Ivanoff was a large hardcover book released multiple times by different publishers. The edition in Candy's home where Lenny Paradiso lived at the time was published by Grosset and Dunlap, and the volume was out of print in 1975, six years before Joan landed at Logan. Paradiso's prints were on Paradiso's book, but Joan never touched the pages. The volume Paradiso acquired, a Reader's Digest offering, wasn't a textbook. The book didn't belong to Joan. Strike one.

Later that year, Special Agent Steve Broce raided the safety deposit box jointly owned by Paradiso and his girlfriend. He seized a red silk jewelry pouch. Burke told the Feds he showed black and white photos of the pouch to Joan's roommate, and this mystery person identified the sheath as Joan's. Joan lived alone at Perkins Hall. Burke supposedly showed this unnamed witness a photo that concealed the size and color of the jewelry bag. Palombo went a step further and claimed he added the purse to an assortment of similar items, and this unidentified witness picked it right out. The red silk bag was part of a three-piece set. Candy gave the pouch to Lenny to sheath his prized shark's tooth. She still had the box and two matching pieces. Strike two.

The crane carefully lifted Paradiso's boat out of the water. The public knew right away Joan was not onboard. The FBI scoured the boat for clues. Burke kept the findings close to his vest, but eventually the results leaked. FBI lab technicians found absolutely nothing on or around the *Malafemmena* that tied Paradiso and Joan together. The umpire ruled Burke's tip a foul ball, but just how foul was yet to be seen.

Investigators identified a woman from a photograph in Paradiso's albums. A confidential source told the Feds that Paradiso had lavished Charlene Bullerwell with jewelry stolen from his victims. He claimed the woman knew where Paradiso allegedly dumped Joan's body. Burke embellished the story, adding that the photo pictured Bullerwell in a bracelet identical to Joan's missing one-of-a-kind gold charm bracelet. All Paradiso ever gave her was a gold-dipped seahorse without a loop. He took it back and never gave it to her again. After two agents pressured the witness, she testified Paradiso was a hitman for the mob, he chopped up bodies, weighted them with cinder blocks, and dumped them into the ocean. Joan's killer had buried Joan on land more than 30 miles from the alleged scene of Burke's fiction. Strike three.

Usually, it is three strikes and you're out, but Burke kept on swinging. Diver Nick Saggese jumped in the water at Pier 7 at the precise spot that Burke directed. Saggese surfaced with a realistic looking .357 magnum replica that assigned divers had suspiciously missed. Burke insisted Paradiso had used the gun to force Joan on his boat. Burke provided no proof of ownership, and he neglected to send the fake gun to the FBI lab with the rest of the refuse dredged out of the harbor.

Burke harassed Paradiso's girlfriend on the stand during the Marie Iannuzzi pretrial hearing about the navigational equipment recovered from her attic. The prosecutor tried desperately to weave Joan into that case. His "gotcha" moment was a complete swing and a whiff. Officers recovered Danforth equipment. The *Malafemmena* was fitted for Ray Jefferson instruments, and the two different makes were not interchangeable.

Burke had a pinch hitter in the federal courts. The little leaguer got on base with an invisible error. Judge Bruce Selya affirmed the *Malafemmena* was long gone when Paradiso filed for bankruptcy on August 26, 1981, months before Joan disappeared. Burke's case fell apart without his crime scene, but the hometown tabloids favored their boy and reported the sentence without any finding of facts. Burke seemed to be out of his league. He handed the keys to the Chris Craft to a gopher who made beer runs out of his new office. So much for the relevance of Paradiso's boat, which no longer existed when Joan disappeared on November 28, 1981.

Burke filed a new motion with the court. He wanted to slice and dice Paradiso's finger to fish out a metal splinter. Palombo supplemented the request, and both men swore to the court that they found several glass shards on Paradiso's boat. The allegation was a complete fabrication verified in the FBI files. The only item Burke suggested was glass turned out to be debris unsuitable for testing. Burke admitted his own failure to produce real evidence. He pleaded with the judge that the splinter may be the *only* evidence connecting Paradiso to Joan's murder. Paradiso suffered a broken finger from heavy-handed enforcers trying to X-ray the digit, but the splinter was gone.

Burke and Palombo kept throwing things up against the wall to see what would stick. In their minds, repeating the envisioned crime often enough somehow made it true. They had nothing, but tried to force pieces to fit. Managers benched poor performance in a legitimate quest, but George Webster kept Burke and Palombo in the lineup. The objective seemed to be on track for the desired outcome. Either the team was an incompetent pair of Keystone Cops or diabolical pretenders executing a finely tuned plan. The reasonable conclusion was a premeditated plot to frame Lenny Paradiso for Joan Webster's murder.

The Marie Iannuzzi case crumbled under scrutiny. The manipulated outcome in the case served as the predicate to accuse Paradiso of murdering Joan. When the dubious verdict in Marie's case was exposed, nothing remained to tie the two cases together. The conviction Burke gained was nothing more than a fabricated smokescreen to shield Joan's real killer.

જ

Every crime has a solution, but finding the answers in Joan's case wasn't easy. Authorities either overlooked clues or deliberately concealed them, because the real clues pointed in a different direction. The eyewitness lead, locked away in files, answered that question. The Massachusetts State Police and the Websters both had that information in December 1981, and they chose not to share it with anyone outside their inner circle.

When the Hamilton Police recovered Joan's skeleton, they noticed the offender had stripped her clothing. Police had the description of what Joan wore the night she disappeared. The clothing was identifiable, but her attire was missing and never found. Two pieces of common jewelry remained on the bones, a gold neck chain and a gold ring with a semi-precious stone. Law enforcement already knew her distinctive gold charm bracelet wasn't among retrieved belongings. Joan probably removed the bracelet when she traveled. The assailant likely snatched the amulets from her purse or tote bag.

Joan always wore another ring, a gold signet ring with her initials. The identifiable band signified exclusive membership in the Webster clan. George and his offspring all wore them all the time. Like George's private phone number, if the police didn't know about the gold circle, they couldn't know it was missing. A pattern emerged of personal and distinguishable items being stripped from the victim that obscured her identity. The culprit devalued Joan by removing recognizable jewelry, her keys, and even her clothes, as if to say she's gone, move on.

Tim Burke perused Joan's effects in the police evidence room looking for clues. One piece of evidence stared him right in the face. Joan had carefully packed pictures from a Nantucket vacation in her suitcase. Burke observed the photos tucked in Joan's pair of gray shoes. He claimed Robert Bond described the contents of Joan's luggage, but he didn't. Bond only remembered the state police had Joan's luggage after talking to Carmen Tammaro. Suggesting Paradiso told Bond that Joan stuck her prints in the shoes to keep them from bending was ridiculous. That level of detail in any confession was absurd. But Burke's slip was a bigger problem. Joan had carried her gray shoes in the leather tote bag, the satchel police never recovered. The FBI catalogued everything in the Lark suitcase, and there were no shoes or footwear of any kind. Burke placed an item from the missing carry-on in police evidence, meaning law enforcement put them there. Burke connected someone with access to police evidence to Joan or the offender after she landed at Logan.

Another subtle hint slipped through the cracks. When Anthony Belmonte found Joan's wallet in the Saugus marshes on December 2, 1981, he called the number on a business card. Instead of the logical step to call the owner of the lost clutch or the police, Belmonte called an out-of-state number. He'd found a handwritten note on George Webster's business card that said, "If found, call this number." The honest clam digger tipped George off first. Joan lived in Cambridge, Massachusetts, in a single room at Perkins Hall. Her parents lived in Glen Ridge, New Jersey. The card with George's instruction to call Daddy was a highly unusual note for an adult, an independent 25-year-old woman, to stick in her purse. But no one bothered to find out how, why, or even when the card was put there. George had taken the lead in Joan's inquiry.

During the Massachusetts State Police interview on January 14, 1983, and in Bond's written letter, received after the interview, the state's star witness described the cause of Joan's death with correct detail. That was information known only to the killer or someone complicit with the crime. The cause of death deviated from the modus operandi authorities suggested in other accusations they piled on Paradiso. Bond claimed Paradiso had confessed the details to him. Then Bond added another morsel.

According to Bond, Lenny Paradiso had said, "They [the police] said she was seen getting into a cab at the airport."

The authorities and the Websters kept that secret detail locked in their files. The eyewitness account in Fenton Moore's statement described a much smaller man than Leonard Paradiso. Joan's killer, no matter who it was, wouldn't know about the Town Taxi cabbie's observations. Public reports indicated that Joan, last seen at the luggage carousel, vanished without a trace. Bond promised Tammaro and Palombo that he could get Paradiso to say anything. Tammaro planted the seed of the boat allegation on August 1, 1982. If their target repeated the absurd accusation, knowing his boat was 35 feet under water, the officers twisted any comment into a confession.

If Paradiso ever said anything about Joan getting into a cab, he heard it from the messengers sent by George Webster. Tim Burke sealed the foundational documents during the Marie Iannuzzi pretrial on March 13, 1984, hiding what Bond told the police and hiding the source. The snitch offered a multiple choice for Joan's cause of death during the interview led by Tammaro. Palombo and Tammaro "chose" the correct cause of death with correct details more than seven years before Joan surfaced.

Maya: Monuments of Civilization by Pierre Ivanoff

Box and Remaining Two Pieces of Jewelry Set Owned
by Candace Weyant

Joan Webster Wearing Her Gold Charm Bracelet

Chapter Twenty-Three
The Modus Operandi

Peering into the depraved mind of an executioner was risky. Common sense warned that the predator would avoid detection at all costs. If anyone turned over the right rock, they would suffer the wrath of an amoral soul. How the offender went about his business brought us one step closer to unmasking the identity of Joan's killer. A murderer not engaged in his enterprise looks like anyone else, and a clever despot stayed ahead of the curve.

The physical description Fenton Moore gave the Saugus Police was the starting point. Neil Meehan documented the eyewitness account and constructed a composite, but insiders concealed the lead. The culprit stayed a step ahead of justice. The man seen with Joan at Logan Airport on November 28, 1981 was a middle-aged, white male. The man had dark, wavy hair, wore wire-rimmed glasses, and had a beard. He was under six feet tall and weighed approximately 160 pounds. Without a doubt, Leonard Paradiso was not the perpetrator. Stature and race were hard to cloak, but other characteristics left room for possible disguises.

Joan traveled alone and engaged a Town Taxi cab outside the Eastern Terminal in Boston. Her planned destination was Cambridge, back to school. After Moore loaded his fare's suitcase into his trunk, Joan informed the cabbie someone was with her. The introduction indicated she knew the man who caught up with her in the cab line. He knew when Joan would be there. The bearded man carried a noticeably heavy suitcase and argued with the driver overloading the bag. The assailant turned to Joan and said "we" don't want to take this cab, further indicating the two travelers knew each other. Moore removed the luggage from his trunk, and Joan and the bearded man switched cars. She undoubtedly trusted the man with her. The offender's temperament was demanding, but he probably feigned some of the indignation to maneuver Joan to the blue car in the cab line. At the moment the blue car pulled away from the curb, Joan vanished.

The mysterious man's attire distinguished him from a run-of-the-mill perp randomly prowling for victims. His dark overcoat was a standard wardrobe basic for a professional man and not something usually worn by cabbies or students.

The driver of the blue car added a second offender to the abduction, because no one came forward when Joan's plight hit the news. Identifying another party to the crime opened a new element to Joan's disappearance. The second vehicle was ready and waiting in the cab line, and the driver knew the protocols to blend in with the other taxis. The second driver also knew when to be there. Changing cars sealed Joan's fate. The precision of the exchange clearly pointed to premeditation. Joan was the target.

The profile narrowed the field of suspects. The bearded man knew Joan and knew the change in her travel plans. He operated discreetly and avoided detection with help from insiders. The white male was older than Joan and was of average build, but he also had to have had an unidentified partner in crime. The suspect controlled the outcome with meticulous planning. In hindsight, the bearded man's intention was clear: isolate his victim with as little attention as possible.

The abductors started off with an advantage. No one checked on Joan's safe arrival. Most students returned Sunday after the Thanksgiving break, not Saturday, so no one immediately noticed her absence. After a full day of missed classes, a worried friend called her mother on Tuesday morning. The first three days for a missing person are critical. The disruption of the holiday gave the killer three days to cover his tracks.

The conscious design of the murder derailed any legitimate investigation. The fatal blow to the head took enormous force. One of the two villains had tremendous physical strength. The killer bludgeoned the right side of Joan's skull, one of the hardest bones in the human body. Death was certain. Blood gushed from the large, gaping hole in her head. The pair of exterminators had shrewdly inflicted a death sentence with blunt force. Guns and knives leave traceable clues, but random objects do not. A thick branch, a bat, or a tire iron were easily accessed and just as easily disposed of without drawing attention.

The evil designer of the plan schemed down to the smallest detail. Clothing helped identify victims, so the killer stripped all of Joan's garments away. Investigators never found the clothing Joan wore that night on her flight back to Boston. The gold chain and gold ring found on her bones were common, ordinary trimmings many women wore. However, one of the attackers knew to slip the easily identifiable signet ring off Joan's delicate finger. The distinctive, gold charm bracelet and a band with the victim's initials disappeared. Removing signature items diminished the odds of knowing who she was and degraded a beautiful life to nothing. The deliberate removal of identifiable items wasn't random, but carefully considered to hide the killers' sins.

In the dead of night, one or both thugs drove to an isolated spot deep in the woods. The fire in Lynn, Massachusetts raged between the airport and the secluded destination. At least one of the culprits knew the area well and bypassed the roadblocks set in their path. The killers then placed Joan's lifeless body in a black plastic trash bag and discarded the young woman in a shallow basin under some trees. Darkness concealed the unceremonious burial as a stealth assassin or assassins heaped on dirt, leaves, and cut logs to conceal the grave.

The aggressors took no chances. Belongings disbursed over a broad area complicated a search for the missing grad student. The purse and wallet ended up in a known dumping ground on the southbound side of the road headed toward the airport. The odds of the clam digger finding and returning the red leather shoulder bag found in the sprawling marsh were slim, but the fortunate find was the first lead. The suitcase stashed in the bus station locker bought more time for the shrewd criminal to escape detection. Stowed items sat in the locker for 30 days before employees opened the vault. No one noticed the tag when they opened the locker, so the unclaimed bag sat in a caged storeroom for another 30 days before a handler noticed Joan's name on it.

The bearded man and the driver of the blue car efficiently disposed of Joan's other belongings. No one ever found the clothes she wore. The gold signet ring and unique gold charm bracelet evaporated into thin air. Authorities never recovered the leather tote bag or its contents, except for one item that Tim Burke identified in police evidence. Joan carried her gray shoes in her carry-on tote. Only the police placed items in their evidence room. Burke's disclosure about the gray shoes implicated a member of law enforcement. Whomever placed the gray shoes in police evidence either encountered Joan after she landed at Logan or the killer or both.

A second layer of logs placed over Joan's secret grave added another clue to the mystery. Someone knew where she was and returned to bury her more deeply. Pieces of the puzzle arrived over an extended period of time. The years gradually filled in the gaps and revealed an orchestrated enterprise to shield the bad actors. The evidence shifted Joan's murder from a random act to a premeditated hit, and the inner circle covered up the truth about the crime. Then Joan reappeared to give the grieving some answers.

Chapter Twenty-Four
The Messengers

The bearded man and his driver had an advantage, the media factor. The tabloids repeated the Paradiso boat story over and over again, until the public presumed the crazy speculation was true. The sources cleverly omitted relevant facts, like that the boat, the alleged crime scene, was 35 feet underwater when Joan landed at Logan. The promoters knew the power of the press to influence perceptions. In a criminal investigation, the concept of a guilty person trying to pin the crime on somebody else was nothing new. However, this offender knew how to sell the story and had the access to do it.

The killers had a different skill set than a shellfish peddler with an eighth grade education. Two offenders snatched Joan from the airport. The man Joan knew with the heavy suitcase was the one with the motive to silence his victim. The bearded man maneuvered her to the second car for her final, fateful ride. The driver knew where to go. The modus operandi narrowed the field of suspects to a small number of people with that level of expertise. George Webster sent people to see the jailhouse snitch, Robert Bond, and confabulate a story. His messengers were the people to scrutinize first.

Investigators delegated the responsibility to resolve offenses had learned the methods criminals use to avoid detection. "I am familiar with many procedures criminals use in attempts to avoid detection," Andrew Palombo swore to the court. When they used the skills for crime resolution and public safety, the outcome served justice. However, several bad apples infected Boston's dysfunctional system during Joan's investigation.

The lead officer for Joan's investigation knew the schemes offenders plotted. The thought of a cop's involvement was horrifying, but Palombo's actions during the search for Joan's killer raised a serious red flag. He hid exculpatory evidence. The eyewitness lead from the cabbie was locked in the Massachusetts State Police files. Andrew Palombo ignored evidence that Paradiso's boat sank in July 1981, months before Joan disappeared, and continued to promote an impossible story. Palombo and his partner, Tim Burke, filed false documents with the courts, and reported bogus information to the FBI. Andrew Palombo, an undercover cop, was one of the messengers George Webster enlisted to work with Robert Bond. Trooper Andrew Palombo corresponded with Bond and told him not to change his story. Palombo knew the correct cause of Joan's death with correct detail more than seven years before her remains confirmed it. When the officer worked with Bond in January 1983, how Joan died was known only to the killer or someone complicit in the crime. The enforcer in charge had to be a suspect.

Even though Palombo frequently sported a beard, he was far too large to be the bearded man with Joan at the airport. At six foot four and 230 pounds, Palombo was an intimidating presence. The former defensive lineman knocked out the opposition with tremendous force. He tied his long hair into a ponytail and concealed his intent behind his dark shades. On the streets, Palombo mingled with the unsavory; he understood the criminal mind. At the end of his day, the hulking figure turned into the driveway at 247 Lynn Street in Peabody, Massachusetts. Life was difficult on a cop's salary. Raising four little girls in a small, modest house was limiting for a man with expensive hobbies. Fast cars, motorcycles, and sailing were his passions.

Criminals operate on familiar turf, and Palombo undoubtedly knew the Boston area like the back of his hand. The verified locations in Joan's murder closely tied to the officer's regular routine. The

Department of Public Safety assigned Palombo to the F Barracks at Logan Airport. He worked at the very place where Joan disappeared. The driver of the blue car in the cab line needed to know airport protocols and have credentials to get into the line. Palombo's undercover appearance allowed him to blend in with the masses, but showing his badge gave him immediate access.

The main thoroughfare between Palombo's crime fighting at the airport and his home address was Route 107, Lynn Marsh Road. The four-lane split roadway went straight into Lynn, Massachusetts, but blockades detoured traffic on November 28, 1981 because of the Great Lynn Fire. Palombo's turnoff avoided the barricades veering left on Broadway Street before entering Lynn. In reverse, his path went right by the southbound Saugus marsh location, where the clam digger would find Joan's purse and wallet.

The dumping ground was familiar to Palombo. When he took over the lead on Marie Iannuzzi's murder case in February 1981, boaters found Marie's body further north on Route 107 behind a shuttered business on the northbound side of Lynn Marsh Road. These points checked off the first two settings of Joan's baffling murder.

The stealthy killer had placed Joan's suitcase in the Park Square Greyhound Bus Station locker by 9:30 a.m. on Sunday, November 29, 1981. The Glen Ridge, New Jersey police documented undercover police activity at the bus station. A covert cop gave a stranded traveler a ride on January 9, 1982. The small roster of clandestine enforcers all watched for illicit drug activity at identified ports of entry like the bus station. Palombo offered a taxi service on December 12, 1982, when he followed Paradiso's estranged daughter at Logan Airport and gave her a ride.

Joan's grave was remote, and the driver of the blue car had to know that hidden spot. Palombo's house in Peabody was a couple of blocks from the onramp to Route 128, the Yankee Division

Highway. Exit 16 to Chebacco Road was only a few minutes east. Hamilton Police Chief Walter Cullen confirmed Palombo knew the area. The site, known by law enforcement for criminal activity, was also popular for motorcycle gangs, the seedy sorts Palombo rode with on the streets. The gravesite was almost in his backyard.

The broad disbursement of Joan's belongings and the location where remains surfaced baffled earnest investigators. Nothing seemed to connect the dots. An assailant with investigative skills knew how to complicate the search, and Palombo swore he knew the methods to avoid detection. The four critical points— Logan Airport, Lynn Marsh Road, the Park Square Greyhound Bus Station, and Chebacco Road—all logically converged in Andrew Palombo's wheelhouse.

Sergeant Carmen Tammaro coordinated efforts during the Joan Webster investigation. He kept a pulse on the activity and worked closely with Joan's father. He was another tall man, well over six feet, but had a more tailored and groomed appearance. Tammaro, as the ranking state trooper, delegated assignments from the F Barracks at Logan Airport. Tammaro was not the bearded man who maneuvered Joan to a second car. Sergeant Carmen Tammaro was, however, one of the messengers sent by the George Webster to meet with Bond.

Tammaro grew up in the Italian neighborhood in the North End of Boston. Wise guys and Mafia figures were familiar faces on the streets, and their mayhem was notorious. As a youth, the rowdies nicknamed him "Buster," and he witnessed the criminal elements all around him. During high school, Tammaro attended a floating party in the harbor when jealousy rocked the boat. Bruised egos settled scores with clenched knuckles in the North End. The testosterone onboard turned the harbor cruise into an untethered brawl. Paddy wagons waited at the pier to coral the unruly revelers, and police arrested Carmen Tammaro as part of the pack. In the North End, even a small slight metastasized into a full blown, malignant vendetta. Buster's brush with the law planted a seed; a man with a badge controlled the outcome.

Tammaro knew Leonard Paradiso growing up. The rivals parked their pushcarts on opposite corners during the summer feasts of the patron saints. Paradiso sold his clams and Tammaro peddled vegetables in the crowded streets. Over time, they took different forks in the road. Paradiso played hooky and dropped out of school. Tammaro joined law enforcement and was now the man with a badge. The advantage went to the Massachusetts State Trooper when their paths crossed again.

Sergeant Tammaro mentored his subordinate Andrew Palombo. The two men worked together at the F Barracks at Logan. In times of trouble, Palombo's superior demonstrated he had his underling's back. Tammaro became an integral player during Joan's investigation, and he knew just who to go after to settle any feigned score. Palombo knew Paradiso too. When he took the lead on the Marie Iannuzzi cold case in February 1981, the two men plotted to kill two birds with one Paradiso.

Buster's childhood friend Patty Bono placed the anonymous call to the Saugus Police on January 20, 1982, and implicated Paradiso for the murder of Marie Iannuzzi and for Joan Webster's disappearance. Everyone in the North End knew Paradiso was questioned about Marie's murder. Bono offered no evidence of either crime. When the whole picture came together, Tammaro's friend dropping the dime was no coincidence. The tip gave Tammaro and Palombo the contrived justification they needed to pursue their target for Joan's murder in early 1982.

Sergeant Tammaro attended George Webster's assembly in late February 1982. Paradiso was the focus, but the collective enforcers had no evidence connecting their patsy to the victim. The group paired Tammaro's subordinate, Andrew Palombo, with Tim Burke. The duo hid behind the smokescreen of the Marie Iannuzzi case, but Marie's justice wasn't the objective. The team cast the villain for Joan's murder early in the investigation, but kept Paradiso's name under wraps for a full year.

Palombo arrested Paradiso on July 6, 1982 for the murder of Marie Iannuzzi. This was months *before* the officers produced a witness to condemn him. Tammaro strolled into Paradiso's cell at the Charles Street Jail on August 1, 1982. Casually dressed, Tammaro played the "good cop" role, there to help his old rival. Paradiso just listened as Tammaro planted the seed.

"I hear you took Webster out on your boat and killed her," Tammaro claimed. "Then, you threw her overboard."

The nature of the crime depended on the culprit that Tammaro put in the crosshairs. He knew Paradiso had boats over the years, but he screwed up on one critical point. Tammaro never bothered to find out if Paradiso had a vessel when Joan disappeared. Police training 101 instructed officers to follow the facts, but since the facts didn't matter, it was on with the show.

Tammaro picked a villain, then cleverly set the scene, confident Paradiso would repeat the impossible allegation. Now the cagey man needed a mouthpiece to sell the story. A burly killer entered stage left. The Department of Corrections transferred Robert Bond to the Charles Street Jail on December 8, 1982, awaiting trial for the murder of Mary Foreman. Invisible forces pulled strings, and guards positioned the state's rat close to the cheese. The trap was set.

"There's nothing that I can't get out of him," Bond boasted.

The author of the boat allegations coached Bond to repeat its creator's story. The taped interview, led by Tammaro, produced Paradiso's alleged confession of two murders. The snitch struggled with details, and the dimwit suggested the cops choose Joan's cause of death. In January 1983, only the offender or an accomplice knew Joan was dead and how it happened. When the final story played out, Bond was well-rehearsed. The snitch embellished the tale of the two murders with additional details he learned from the cops. By December 29, 1982, authorities caged Bond miles away from Paradiso. Tammaro, Palombo, and Burke were Bond's only source of new information after the taped interview. From Bond's multiple choice, Tammaro selected the correct cause of Joan's death with correct details more than seven years before her bones proved it.

Tim Burke took control from the prosecutor's table. The rookie litigator had stepped into the picture at the Websters' high-powered meeting in late February 1982. Paired with Palombo, he seated a grand jury for Marie Iannuzzi's murder with no more evidence than they had had in August 1979. He targeted Paradiso, but presented witnesses that implicated Marie's boyfriend. This prosecutorial trick, naming Paradiso as the suspect, assured Burke dodged an indictment against David Doyle in the first grand jury. Indicting Doyle would have severed the only connection to Paradiso for Joan's murder; namely, the anonymous call from Tammaro's childhood friend. Burke proceeded to lie and claim the first grand jury was a John Doe investigation. Trooper Carl Sjoberg revealed the real mandate to pursue Paradiso on March 11, 1982, six days after the first grand jury for Marie Iannuzzi.

"Paradiso may be a suspect in a new case in the Boston area," the trooper told Lenny's parole officer.

Burke put the cart before the horse. He switched the grand jury to a John Doe investigation, and then put witnesses on the stand to connect his target to certain locations. With out-of-order and tampered parole notes, Burke manufactured consciousness of guilt, falsely claiming Paradiso rushed to his parole officer before anyone identified the victim. Six months before the team tutored a snitch, Burke had his patsy behind bars.

The Suffolk County prosecutor had difficulty reading his calendar. Burke said he received an unsolicited letter from Robert Bond on January 5, 1983. Burke allegedly arranged an interview with the Massachusetts State Police based on the letter. Bond actually mailed the letter on January 10, 1983, *after* Bond met with Carmen Tammaro. Burke received the solicited letter *after* the taped interview on January 14, 1983. The headlines broadcast the "break" in Joan's case not knowing Paradiso was already the state's suspect, a marked man for more than a year.

The whole story the state promoted started with a lie. Burke and Palombo both filed false documents with the court under the pains and penalties of perjury, but Burke cleverly hid the foundational documents for Joan's case during the Marie Iannuzzi pretrial hearing. Pressure from higher-ups kept the lawyer on a malevolent track. Exculpatory evidence from the eyewitness cabbie and the doubtful existence of the boat remained locked in the police and Webster family files. False witnesses took the stand. During the Marie Iannuzzi trial, Burke put on a shameful display of distorting the facts. He picked scabs with Marie's uncle Benjamin Puzzo to misrepresent the age of Doyle's scratches. He bolstered the credibility of felons and painted Doyle as a wrongly accused victim. Somehow, the jury bought into all four of Doyle's and his mother's explanations for the scratches and pitied the boyfriend who took flight to New Jersey.

Convicting Paradiso for Marie's murder was the nail Burke needed to hang Joan's murder on his target. There was no evidence connecting Joan to Paradiso, but Burke relied on sensational speculation. The guilty verdict against Paradiso for Marie's murder on July 22, 1984 was symbolic for Joan's death. However, neither Marie nor Joan received justice with that declaration. Burke swelled his accusations against Paradiso for Joan's murder. The public consumed the lawyer's inane contention that his own diver found a gun under the mooring that assigned divers missed. Burke trumpeted that Paradiso used the gun to force Joan onto his boat. The facts buried in an out-of-state court revealed Burke's deceit. The informant Burke secretly credited with finding the gun told the

Feds his diver found a Mercedes. No reasonable person mistook a handheld firearm for a two ton car.

Judge Bruce Selya dashed Burke's obsessed notion of murder at sea. The boat was long gone when Paradiso filed for bankruptcy in August 1981, months before Joan disappeared. The unrefuted evidence established an inconvenient fact that Carmen Tammaro's envisioned crime was impossible. Regardless, Burke and Palombo kept selling the story to the media in November 1987. They were committed.

"He got her on his boat," Burke told WBZ channel 4. "He sexually assaulted her, killed her, striking her in the head with a blunt object. He then took her out in the Boston Harbor area, and sank her body. Then, he brought his boat back into the Pier 7 area, cleaned it up, and then sunk it two days later."

"If she did go on the boat, she was attacked by Paradiso," Palombo told the outlet. "She was murdered on that boat, and her body was disposed of from that boat."

Tim Burke anchored his allegations against Paradiso on the testimony of two convicted felons. He claimed Paradiso confessed the details of his sins to two conmen, Robert Bond and Ralph Anthony Pisa. In Marie's case, the prosecutor made a connection between the suspect and the victim. They both had attended the same wedding. Candy gave the victim a ride from a house party to a bar in East Boston, and then returned to the party. When Candy and Lenny left to go home, they found Marie's belongings in Candy's car and returned them. That was as far as the actual evidence went until two rats, Bond and Pisa, embellished the story. The good deed of returning Marie's stuff and then holding a door made Paradiso a murder suspect.

In Joan's case, Burke had no evidence to link the two people together except the untrustworthy words of the two tattlers, Bond and Pisa, looking for favorable treatment. Robert Bond said the guy from New Jersey, George Webster, sent people to see him. When promises fell short of expectations, he ratted out the messengers—Tim Burke, Andrew Palombo, and Carmen Tammaro. Burke was one of the people sent by George Webster. Ralph Anthony Pisa testified about the assurances he made to George Webster. Death Row Tony found himself on a fast track to walk out of prison.

Joan's remains surfaced on April 18, 1990, in Hamilton, Massachusetts. Burke's whole story fell apart publicly. He backpedaled about the boat, conceding that he knew the boat was not seaworthy when they raised the vessel on September 27, 1983. The *Malafemmena* had a broken rudder. It was too late to change the story, but Burke massaged Bond's recitation to fit. Now, "way out" at sea meant Paradiso took the body off the boat and drove more than 30 miles to bury her on Chebacco Road. Burke's hubris had no bounds. After meeting with George and Eleanor Webster in 2005, Tim Burke penned a tome to close the case on Joan Webster. He alleged Paradiso murdered Joan Webster on the *Malafemmena*, a boat that was 35 feet underwater when Joan disappeared.

Andrew Palombo, Carmen Tammaro, and Tim Burke drove a false explanation for Joan's murder. None of them knew Joan, or had a personal motive to harm her. Motive for each of these men to obstruct her justice wasn't clear, but the intent was obvious. They were the messengers for George Webster, and Webster supported Burke's phony book billed as true crime. Burke, Palombo, and Tammaro's complicity aided and abetted the man with the motive, the bearded man seen with Joan at Logan Airport on November 28, 1981. The text also helped uncover what the true crimes really were. Tim Burke's book became evidence in an open, unresolved homicide in Essex County, Massachusetts.

Chapter Twenty-Five
Simple, Safe, and Secret

No one seemed to notice the mammoth elephant in the room. Surely, the three messengers, Tim Burke, Andrew Palombo, and Carmen Tammaro, didn't think they fooled the intelligence-trained parents about what happened to their daughter. After Joan's remains surfaced, George refused to answer why he still believed Paradiso was the killer. Recovered source documents revealed Joan's parents had the eyewitness lead on December 21, 1981. The stature of the man the cabbie saw with Joan at Logan was a much smaller man than Paradiso. George corresponded with the Department of Justice handling the bankruptcy case involving Paradiso's boat. The court findings debunked the boat narrative, but Joan's father still insisted Paradiso killed her on the phantom ship. Paradiso sank his boat months before Joan landed at Logan. George directed people to meet with Robert Bond, and the team came up with an implausible scenario. Nevertheless, authorities used kid gloves with the Websters, a Kennedy-like treatment that gave them a pass.

Probing into the mindset of George and Eleanor, secretive agents trained by the CIA, was a daunting challenge. No one in Massachusetts' dysfunctional system challenged the people closest to the victim with the tough questions. Control was the centerpiece of intelligence training. During George and Eleanor's tenure with the agency, mind control was the umbrella project, crossing boundaries into illegal and immoral practices. Methods ranged from drugs and radiation to torture and rape. Sometimes subjects volunteered, but other times operatives slipped an unwitting victim a mickey or used family members as test subjects. The unbridled culture of the department was often amoral during the mind control era.

George's history revealed some illuminating morsels and gave a more complete picture. As the Director of the Defense Group with ITT, George Webster was no stranger to managing perceptions. During the 1960s and 1970s, George's telecommunications division at ITT partnered with his former employer in a covert operation to topple the duly elected government in Chile. With his background in the agency, and his position working with the Department of Defense, George was an asset in the thick of the action. It is hard to say who George really worked for. Regardless, the corporate directive disseminated through ITT instructed the spreading of propaganda or disinformation through the media. George understood the effective use of news outlets to slant opinions. Joan's parents made themselves readily available to the press during the entirety of the Joan Webster ordeal.

"The Websters know how to sell their story," one reporter observed.

George had the prerequisite qualities described by the cabbie. He was of average build, a similar stature to the man seen with Joan at the airport. George was under six feet, and his poor posture made him appear even shorter. In a public setting, he used hair tonic to tame his dark, wavy main. The middle-aged white male wore wire-rimmed glasses with rounded edges. The dark overcoat Fenton Moore described was the standard uniform George wore for business, travel, and attending social gatherings. The garment was an all-purpose cloak.

Obviously, George knew Joan, and he knew where and when she was going to be at Logan Airport. Exchanging words with the cabbie over a heavy suitcase was probably a ruse to get Joan into the second car but accurately reflected his demanding personality. George ruled the family with a strict patriarchal fist. He conditioned his children to never question. The man with Joan uttered words she trusted and obeyed.

"I don't think *we* want this cab," the man directed.

George Webster traveled over the Thanksgiving weekend, an uncharacteristic itinerary for the ITT executive. The savvy culprit knew that a holiday weekend provided a window of opportunity before anyone noticed Joan was missing. Three critical days allowed the offender to avoid detection. No one checked George's whereabouts on the night of November 28, 1981.

Joan was an independent grad student living in Massachusetts. Her parents lived in New Jersey, five hours away. When Anthony Belmonte found Joan's wallet, he followed the handwritten directive on George's business card and called George Webster's office. No adult woman living on her own wanted someone to call Daddy in another state if she lost her purse. The business card with the handwritten note seemed out of place but, apparently, nobody noticed. Tipping off George first kept him ahead of the investigation and provided another example of his controlling nature.

The only variance from the eyewitness description was the beard. George was clean shaven. Some characteristics were hard to disguise like the offender's race and build. It was not unheard of for the CIA to use disguises in a cover operation. The tactic was used by ITT during George's tenure with the company.

During Watergate and ITT's clandestine affairs in Chile, a former CIA operative borrowed disguises from the agency for his secret missions. E. Howard Hunt was one of the Watergate plumbers, convicted for the notorious political break-ins. Hunt also donned his disguise to persuade ITT lobbyist Dita Beard to change her story and keep ITT out of legal hot water. Her leaked memo exposed ITT's influence over Richard Nixon's Department of Justice during an antitrust investigation. The entangled D.C. scandals, unraveled during the Church Senate Hearings, put ITT under a Congressional microscope. Past practice made the concept of a former intelligence operator wearing a disguise more tenable. When a criminal was not engaged in his enterprise, he looked like anyone else. But, when engaged in wrongdoing, a beard concealed recognizable traits.

CIA documents exposed deep, dark secrets, molding the intelligence mindset. A 1953 CIA training manual, uncovered through the Freedom of Information Act in 1997, showed the unseemly side of an unbridled government agency. George and Eleanor both worked for the CIA in 1953, and they remained faithful to their oath of secrecy. Regardless of their involvement, the pages of the manual read like the master plan of Joan's murder. "A Study of Assassination" gave the intelligence agency a license to kill. Deploying tactics against enemies of the state garnered some support, but the instructions included elements found in Joan Webster's murder, a private U.S. citizen.

The definition described the planned killing of a person. Instructions were never to be committed to writing, and the guide implored that only an absolute minimum number of persons be involved. No report recorded the planned operation to avoid tracing the origin of a plot, but stealth operators relied on news sources to cover the outcome. Murder was not morally justifiable. However, if the victim had damaging knowledge, an actor could justify self-preservation as a motive. Committing a deliberate murder was not for the squeamish burdened by conscience. In other words, the dirty deed required an emotionally detached assailant.

"She's gone," George stoically told the family on Christmas 1981, without shedding a tear. "We have to move on."

The method of the murder depended on the status of the subject. Joan landed at Logan unmindful of the danger she faced. Witnesses described Joan's upbeat demeanor that night. The unguarded quarry trusted the man who caught up with her in the cab line. If Joan had the slightest suspicion or discomfort, the shift to the deadly blue car would have failed. The instruction manual categorized subjects as simple, chase, or guarded. Joan was unaware of the danger, and the job was *simple*.

No compromise existed for the assailant. Either the killer died along with the victim, and the operation was termed lost, or the killer escaped. Avoiding detection placed Joan's murder in the category of *safe*, safe for the perpetrator. Although speculation targeted Leonard Paradiso, no evidence connected him to the crime. Joan's case remained unresolved with no charges. The executioner got away with murder; the man with Joan at Logan and the driver of the blue car were *safe*.

The instruction manual had three classifications for the victim. If the murder required publicity to be effective, a warning, the hit was terroristic. A subject widely known to be a target fell into the open category. In some circumstances, the specified target needed concealment. In other words, the clandestine operator shrouded the fact that the victim was the intended quarry. The classification for murder with a hidden agenda was *secret*.

Source documents for Joan's investigation exposed secrets. George Webster had locked the eyewitness lead and composite in his filing cabinet. The lead was a *secret*. George Webster sent people to see jailhouse snitch Robert Bond and received assurances from Death Row Tony Pisa. The felonious pair of conmen provided false and unverified testimony against Paradiso. George corresponded with the Department of Justice, influencing the bankruptcy case involving the alleged crime scene. The boat was long gone before Joan flew back to Boston early from the Thanksgiving weekend. The fact the boat did not exist when Joan disappeared was a *secret*. George's business card with the handwritten note kept him one step ahead of the investigation. Publicly, the Websters supported a fallacious book about the brutal murder of their daughter. The

Websters were the ones with the secrets, otherwise they would have looked for the real killer. Any family secrets Joan knew went to the grave with her, but given the chance, she might have forewarned her pregnant sister-in-law of looming danger. Did the lamb leave the fold prepared to spill damning secrets?

The classification for Joan's murder was, in CIA lingo, *simple*, *safe*, and *secret*.

The kill training manual went on to describe methods. A transient perpetrator minimized exposure in the area and allowed safe evacuation with minimal contact. Travel over the holiday weekend added a window of time and facilitated that requirement. An effective, tactical plan was mental without any written evidence of the plot. Death needed to be certain. The simplest local tools were often the most efficient, easy to procure and easy to dispose of. Weapons like guns, knives, and even ropes left traceable evidence. Anything hard, heavy, and handy sufficed and had the added advantage of apparent innocence. The unidentified weapon delivered the type of blunt force trauma to Joan's skull that the manual recommended.

Using a blunt object required anatomical knowledge. The CIA manual trained operatives to strike the temple, the area just below and behind the ear, and the lower rear portion of the skull. Whatever device the killer used to murder Joan, the perpetrator knew right where to hit her. Death was instantaneous and certain. Blood drained quickly from the large hole in the right side of her head. A whiskey bottle in a cramped boat cabin, where you couldn't even raise your arms, was a ludicrous explanation, but the Websters maintained that's what happened.

Two of George's messengers revealed the correct cause of death with accurate detail through a story repeated by Robert Bond in January 1983. The strategy to add an element of truth to an otherwise false allegation, more than seven years before her skull surfaced, added a measure of protection for her offenders. Claiming Paradiso had revealed the cause of death, a large hole in the right side of Joan's head and a lot of blood, deflected doubters' questions. But Carmen Tammaro crafted the boat story that Bond regurgitated, and the snitch embellished the story with new details that the police supplied when Paradiso was out of Bond's reach.

Of the four people promoting the Paradiso boat theory—Tim Burke, Andrew Palombo, Carmen Tammaro, and George Webster— George was the only one who knew the victim. No one else had any personal motive to silence Joan or guard family secrets. George was the only one who knew about Joan's identifiable items like the gold charm bracelet and gold signet ring. George determined Paradiso murdered his daughter; he made up his mind as if he was the final authority. In any murder investigation, the notion of a killer trying to blame someone else for the deed isn't unusual. Finally, the pieces of Joan's baffling murder fit.

Four people maintained Leonard Paradiso murdered Joan Webster on the *Malafemmena* on November 28, 1981. All four had exculpatory evidence in their possession that supported Paradiso's innocence of the crime. The most trusted people held the secrets and assured a near perfect crime.

Four people knew with certainty where and when Joan arrived at Logan. George, Eleanor, Anne, and Joan Webster knew about the changed travel plans. No phone records supported George's explanation that Joan spoke to a classmate Saturday morning, or that she returned back to school early to work on a project. George never disclosed his private phone line, and the calls he made on it were never checked.

Two people abducted Joan from the airport, the man Joan knew who maneuvered her to a blue car, and the driver who knew his way around.

Knowledge of the four identifiable locations in Joan's case matched up with familiar settings in Trooper Andrew Palombo's normal routine. His superior officer Sergeant Carmen Tammaro had his back and crafted a story. They were two of the messengers George Webster sent to meet Robert Bond. Enlisting a malleable prosecutor clinched the desired outcome, blaming a scapegoat for Joan's murder. All four men relentlessly pursued Paradiso knowing he was not the man described in the eyewitness report. They framed a vulnerable but innocent man. Simply put, this nightmare was a cover up.

Two men, Andrew Palombo and Carmen Tammaro, knew how Joan died and added correct details to the description they funneled through an untrustworthy jailhouse informant. The revelation came more than seven years before Joan's remains confirmed the facts. The cause of death and precise details was information only known to the killer or someone complicit in the crime.

Only one person arranged for Joan to be in the precise time and place that led to her death, and he lied about why she was there. Joan's own father, George Webster, betrayed his lamb.

"Oh, Men of Dark and Dismal Fate."

God bless you and keep you Joan; you are loved and dearly missed. Rest in peace.

Young George Webster

George Webster

Joan Lucinda Webster August 19, 1956 - November 28, 1981

Index of Important Names

Webster Family & Friends

George Webster – Father of murder victim Joan Webster

Eleanor (Terry) Webster – Mother of murder victim Joan Webster

Thomas Hardaway – First husband of Eleanor Webster

John Selsam – Adoptive father of Eleanor Webster

(George) Steven (Steve) Webster – Brother of murder victim Joan Webster

Eve Carson (Webster) – Married to Steve Webster and Joan Webster's sister-in-law

Anne Webster – Sister of murder victim Joan Webster

Joan Webster – 1981 murder victim

Wittpenns – Webster family friends

Joys – Webster family friends

David Duncan – Classmate of Joan Webster

Keith – Friend of Joan Webster

Judy – George Webster's secretary at ITT

New Jersey Officials

Officer Thomas Guthrie – Glen Ridge, New Jersey, Police

Detective Tom Dugan – Glen Ridge, New Jersey, Police

Detective Ken Swain – Glen Ridge, New Jersey, Police

Detective Richard Corcoran – Glen Ridge, New Jersey, Police

Jack McEwan – George Webster's liaison, Head of ITT Security

Special Agent Frank Barletto – Newark FBI Office

Massachusetts Murder Victims

Barbara Mitchell – 1971 murder victim

George Deane – 1973 murder victim

Marie Iannuzzi – 1979 murder victim

Mary Foreman – 1981 murder victim

Joan Webster – 1981 murder victim

Carol Stuart – 1989 murder victim

Iannuzzi Family & Friends

Marie Iannuzzi – 1979 murder victim

David Doyle – Live-in boyfriend and suspect of murder victim Marie Iannuzzi

Kathy Leonti – Sister of murder victim Marie Iannuzzi

Tony Leonti – Married to Kathy Leonti and brother-in-law of Marie Iannuzzi

Benjamin Puzzo – Uncle of murder victim Marie Iannuzzi

Jean Day – Stepsister of Marie Iannuzzi

Rosemarie Doyle – David Doyle's mother

Vincent Milano – David Doyle's uncle and Rosemarie Doyle's brother

Jimmy Milano – David Doyle's cousin

Freddie Milano – David Doyle's cousin

Rosemary Sullivan – David Doyle's cousin

Christine DeLisi – Friend of murder victim Marie Iannuzzi

Ann Marie Kenney – Friend of murder victim Marie Iannuzzi

Eddie Fisher – Marie Iannuzzi's paramour

David Dellaria – Friend of David Doyle

Michael DeLisi – Friend of David Doyle

Suspect & Friends

Leonard Paradiso – State's prime suspect for the murder of Marie Iannuzzi and Joan Webster

Candy Weyant – Leonard Paradiso's girlfriend

Elaine Covino – Friend of Leonard Paradiso

George Murphy – Leonard Paradiso's boss

Local Massachusetts Authorities

Detective Joe Marshall – Revere, Massachusetts, Police

Sergeant Neil Meehan – Saugus, Massachusetts, Police

Inspector Arthur Cook – Saugus, Massachusetts, Police

Inspector Howard Long – Saugus Massachusetts, Police

Chief Donald Peters – Saugus, Massachusetts, Police

Detective Charles Gleason – Boston, Massachusetts, Police

Officer Nick Saggese – Scuba team diver for Boston, Massachusetts, Police

Sergeant Robert Hudson – Boston, Massachusetts, Police

Lieutenant Larry Murphy – Harvard Campus Police

Chief Walter Cullen – Hamilton, Massachusetts, Police

Detective Paul Grant – Hamilton, Massachusetts, Police

Officer Paul Accomando – Hamilton, Massachusetts, Police

Officer Scott Janes – Hamilton, Massachusetts, Police

Massachusetts State Authorities

Sergeant Carmen Tammaro – Massachusetts State Police

Trooper Andrew Palombo – Massachusetts State Police

Trooper Jack O'Rourke – Massachusetts State Police

Trooper Carl Sjoberg – Massachusetts State Police

District Attorney Newman Flanagan – Suffolk County, Massachusetts

First Assistant District Attorney Paul Leary – Suffolk County, Massachusetts

Assistant District Attorney Tim Burke – Suffolk County, Massachusetts

Assistant District Attorney John Kiernan – Head of Homicide, Suffolk County, Massachusetts

Anthony Pascucci – Investigator for Suffolk County, Massachusetts

Judge Roger Donahue – Suffolk County Superior Court Judge

Judge James McGuire – Suffolk County Superior Court Judge

John Gillen – Suffolk Superior Court Officer

Assistant District Attorney Carol Ball – Middlesex County, Massachusetts

Assistant District Attorney Tom Reilly – Middlesex County, Massachusetts

Assistant District Attorney Laurence Hardoon – Middlesex County, Massachusetts

Assistant District Attorney James Sahakian – Middlesex County, Massachusetts

Judge Harry Elam – Middlesex Superior Court Judge

District Attorney Jonathon Blodgett – Essex County, Massachusetts

First Assistant Attorney John Dawley – Essex County, Massachusetts

Parole Officer Victor Anchukaitis – Leonard Paradiso's Parole Officer

Parole Officer Jim O'Neil – Leonard Paradiso's Parole Officer

Inspector David Williams – Marine Examiner

Doctor Donald Dixon – Medical Examiner

Doctor Stanley Schwartz – Forensic Dentist

Mark Grant – Department of Safety Crime Lab Chemist

Doctor George Katsas – Medical Examiner

Federal Authorities

William H Webster – Director of the FBI, Washington DC

Special Agent Steve Broce – Boston office of the FBI

US Attorney Robert Swann Mueller III – Department of Justice, Massachusetts Office

Judge Robert Keeton – Federal District Court of Massachusetts

Judge Bruce Selya – Federal District Court of Rhode Island

US Assistant District Attorney Marie Buckley – Department of Justice, Massachusetts Office

Senator Ted Kennedy – Massachusetts Senator

Leonard Paradiso Defense Team Members

Attorney Judd Carhart – Defense Attorney

Attorney Walter Prince – Defense Attorney

Attorney Steve Rappaport – State Court appointed Defense Attorney

Dennis Slawsby – Defense Team Private Investigator

Ray Morgan – Defense Team Private Investigator

Attorney Owen Walker – Federal Court appointed Defense Attorney

Witnesses

Fenton Moore – Town Taxi cab driver at Logan Airport

Anthony Belmonte – Clam digger that discovered Joan Webster's wallet

Lynda Walsh – Stranded traveler at the Park Square Greyhound Bus Station

Harvey Martel – Known felon, attempted Webster extortion

Patty Bono – Friend of Sergeant Carmen Tammaro implicated Leonard Paradiso in January 1982

Willie Fopiano – Author of *The Godson*, North End wise guy, Patty Bono's alleged defender

Robert Bond – Two-time convicted murderer, the state's star witness, guilty in Barbara Mitchell and Mary Foreman murders

Ralph Anthony Pisa ("Death Row Tony") – Convicted murderer of security guard George Deane, and sentenced to death row

Francis Dion – Witness during the Ralph Anthony Pisa murder trial

Constance Porter – Assault victim hitchhiking in 1973, Leonard
  Paradiso convicted in 1974

Janet McCarthy – Assault victim hitchhiking in the North End of
  Boston, Leonard Paradiso convicted in 1986

Charlene Bullerwell – Occasional date of Leonard Paradiso

Jimmy Cardinale – Bartender at Cardinales Nest Bar contradicts state's
  timeline in Maria Iannuzzi murder

Patty Cardinale – Owner of Cardinale's Nest Bar contradicts state's
  timeline in Marie Iannuzzi murder

Patty Capozzo – Waitress at Cardinales Nest Bar

Carol Seracuse – Patron at the Cardinales Nest Bar contradicts state's
  timeline in Marie Iannuzzi murder

Dennis Albano – Friend of witness Christine DeLisi

Louis Tontodonato – Friend of witness Jean Day

John O'Connell – Developer of Pier 7 in 1980, convicted of perjury in
  HUD fraud investigation

Karen Wolf – Resident that discovered Joan Webster's skull on Chebacco
  Road in Hamilton, Massachusetts

Historical or Notable Figures

Gareth Penn – Author of *Times 17* alleging Joan Webster murder was part of the Zodiac killer's spree

Angiulos – Mafia family in the North End of Boston, Massachusetts

James "Whitey" Bulger – Notorious Mob Boss in Boston, Massachusetts, and figure that exposed FBI corruption in the Boston office

President Richard Nixon – 37th President of the United States, was in office during the coup in Chile on September 11, 1973, and resigned over the simultaneous Watergate scandal

E. Howard Hunt – Former CIA operator, one of the Watergate Plumbers, and involved in influencing a witness in an ITT scandal

Dita Beard – ITT lobbyist pressured by E. Howard Hunt

Kenneth Spinkston – Murder suspect tried by Suffolk County, Massachusetts, and exposed corruption in the District Attorney's Office

Charles Stuart – Husband of murder victim Carol Stuart, later exposed to be the offender and committed suicide

Matt Stuart – Charles Stuart's brother, accomplice in Carol Stuart's murder, and came forward

John Webster – Refers to the 1850 John Webster murder case in Massachusetts, and now sets the standard for "reasonable doubt" in jury deliberations

Timeline

August 11, 1979	Leonard Paradiso, Candy Weyant, Marie Iannuzzi, and David Doyle attended the wedding of Michael Milano in Saugus, Massachusetts.
August 12, 1979	Marie Iannuzzi was murdered and discarded on the banks of the Pine River in Essex County.
August 13, 1979	Anthony Iannuzzi, Tony Leonti, and David Doyle identified Marie Iannuzzi's body.
August 17, 1979	David Doyle arrested in New Jersey stealing luggage at Newark Airport.
February 1981	Trooper Andrew Palombo was assigned as lead officer on the Iannuzzi unresolved case.
June 15, 1981	Robert Bond was paroled for Barbara Mitchell's murder.
July 26, 1981	Candy Weyant filed an insurance claim for the *Malafemmena*, a 26-foot Chris Craft, with Liberty Mutual Insurance.
August 26, 1981	Leonard Paradiso filed for bankruptcy.
September 29, 1981	Liberty Mutual Insurance paid the claim for the boat and navigational equipment to Candy Weyant.

November 23, 1981	Joan Webster presented her 11-week auditorium project at the Harvard Graduate School of Design.
November 27, 1981	George, Eleanor, Anne, and Joan Webster attended *The Pirates of Penzance* on Broadway.
November 28, 1981	The Great Lynn Fire started in a shoe factory in Lynn, Massachusetts, at 2:35 a.m.
November 28, 1981	George, Eleanor, and Anne Webster drove Joan to Newark Airport.
November 28, 1981	Joan Webster disappeared from Logan Airport in Boston, Massachusetts.
November 30, 1981	Leonard Paradiso appeared in court to have his bankruptcy discharged.
November 30, 1981	Leonard Paradiso had his left index finger X-rayed at Lynn Hospital.
December 1, 1981	A concerned classmate, David Duncan, called Eleanor Webster.
December 1, 1981	George Webster returned from an out-of-town trip.
December 2, 1981	Anthony Belmonte discovered Joan's wallet in the marshes on the southbound side of Route 107, the Lynn Marsh Road.
December 4-7, 1981	Authorities conducted interviews at Logan Airport.
December 9, 1981	Websters received an extortion call from an exchange in Nutley, New Jersey.

December, 18, 1981	Websters received an extortion call demanding $20,000 in small bills. The rendezvous was at the European Bank in New York City.
December 21, 1981	Detective Richard Corcoran hand delivered the eyewitness lead from Town Taxi cabbie Fenton Moore to Eleanor Webster.
December 25, 1981	Media outlets aired a prerecorded appeal for information from George and Eleanor Webster.
January 9, 1982	An undercover police officer gave a ride to a stranded passenger, Lynda Walsh, from the Park Square Greyhound Bus Station in Boston, Massachusetts.
January 18, 1982	The Websters offered a $10,000 reward.
January 19 or 20, 1982	The Saugus Police received an anonymous call. The woman alleged Leonard Paradiso murdered Marie Iannuzzi and was responsible for Joan Webster's disappearance.
January 29, 1982	Joan Webster's Lark suitcase was discovered at the Park Square Greyhound Bus Station.
February 1982	George Webster held a meeting with involved agencies at Harvard. Trooper Andrew Palombo and Assistant District Attorney Tim Burke were paired to go after Leonard Paradiso for the murder of Marie Iannuzzi.

February 27, 1982	*The Boston Globe* published an article about Tim Burke investigating a triple homicide.
March 5, 1982	Tim Burke seated a grand jury, *Commonwealth v. Leonard Paradiso*, cause number 038655, for the murder of Marie Iannuzzi, in Suffolk County.
March 11, 1982	Trooper Carl Sjoberg notified Leonard Paradiso's Parole Officer Jim O'Neil that the subject was a suspect in a new Boston crime.
April 5, 1982	Tim Burke renamed cause number 038655, for the murder of Marie Iannuzzi, a *John Doe Investigation*, and called witnesses in another grand jury hearing.
April 23, 1982	Tim Burke seated witnesses in the John Doe grand jury hearing.
June 28, 1982	The grand jury handed down a true bill against Leonard Paradiso for the murder of Marie Iannuzzi.
July 6, 1982	Trooper Palombo arrested Leonard Paradiso for the murder of Marie Iannuzzi.
Summer 1982	Jean Day, Marie Iannuzzi's stepsister, was assaulted and went into hiding.
August 1, 1982	Sergeant Carmen Tammaro met with Leonard Paradiso at the Charles Street Jail and accused him of murdering Joan Webster.
October 12, 1982	George and Eleanor Webster increased the reward, to $25,000 for information and $50,000 for a conviction of the offender.

October 14, 1982	The Websters received an extortion call.
October 15, 1982	George Webster met with extortion caller Harvey Martel in Concord, New Hampshire.
October 25, 1982	The Websters received an extortion call claiming Joan was in Maine.
November 5, 1982	Leonard Paradiso's fingerprints were submitted to the FBI for comparison in the Joan Webster case.
November 24, 1982	Authorities received negative results for Leonard Paradiso's fingerprints in the Joan Webster case.
November 30, 1982	ITT Head of Security, Jack McEwan, scheduled a meeting in New Jersey with a Webster investigator for December eighth or ninth, 1982.
December 8, 1982	Robert Bond was transferred to the Charles Street Jail awaiting trial for Mary Foreman's murder. Guards moved Bond from cell number 68 to cell number 31, in close proximity to Leonard Paradiso.
December 12, 1982	Undercover officer, Trooper Andrew Palombo, followed two women at Logan Airport and then gave them a ride.
December 13, 1982	Robert Bond found guilty of Mary Foreman's murder.
December 29, 1982	Robert Bond transferred to a prison facility in Concord, Massachusetts.
January 10, 1983	Robert Bond sentenced to life at Walpole.

January 10, 1983	Robert Bond met with Sergeant Carmen Tammaro at the Suffolk County courthouse.
January 10, 1983	Robert Bond mailed a letter from Concord addressed to his wife. An inner envelope addressed to Tim Burke contained a two-part letter and made allegations against Leonard Paradiso in the murders of Marie Iannuzzi and Joan Webster.
January 14, 1983	Robert Bond was interviewed by Sergeant Carmen Tammaro, Trooper Andrew Palombo, Corporal Jack O'Rourke, Sergeant Robert Hudson, and Court Officer John Gillen.
After January 14, 1983	Tim Burke received the mailed letter from Robert Bond.
January 27, 1983	News outlets reported a "break" in Joan Webster's case.
Late January 1983	Janet McCarthy came forward.
Late January 1983	Ralph Anthony Pisa came forward.
Early February 1983	Patty Bono came forward.
February 17, 1983	Robert Bond testified at Marie Iannuzzi grand jury for rape charges, cause number 043033.
March 3, 1983	An Interpol Blue Notice for a missing person was issued for Joan Webster.
March 28, 1983	Tim Burke traveled to FBI Headquarters in Quantico for a Joan Webster meeting.

April 25, 1983	Trooper Andrew Palombo executed a Marie Iannuzzi search warrant at the Weyant home.
April 28, 1983	Ralph Anthony Pisa took a new polygraph, changing his involvement in the 1969 George Deane murder.
May 3, 1983	Tim Burke contacted the FBI regarding Leonard Paradiso's bankruptcy.
June 1, 1983	Leonard Paradiso declined the Commonwealth's plea deal for a lesser charge in the Marie Iannuzzi case.
June 6, 1983	The grand jury handed down a true bill for rape in the Marie Iannuzzi case, cause number 043033.
June 13, 1983	Ralph Anthony Pisa submitted an eighth motion for a new trial.
July 12, 1983	Tim Burke seated a John Doe grand jury for the murder of Joan Webster.
July 27, 1983	Candy Weyant was called before a John Doe grand jury for Joan Webster.
July 28, 1983	Special Agent Steve Broce executed a search warrant on the jointly held safety deposit box of Leonard Paradiso and Candy Weyant at the Haymarket Co-Operative Bank.
August 12, 1983	Special Agent Steve Broce received an FBI 302 report from the John O'Connell interview.

September 8, 1983	Candy Weyant was sentenced to three months in Framingham for contempt during the Joan Webster grand jury.
September 27, 1983	Dive teams raised Paradiso's submerged boat, the *Malafemmena*, at Pier 7 in Boston, Massachusetts.
September 27, 1983	Trooper Palombo filed a search warrant for the *Malafemmena* with the court.
September 29, 1983	A confidential source contacted the FBI with the name Charlene.
September 30, 1983	A confidential source contacted the FBI again claiming Charlene knew the location of Joan Webster's body.
October-November 1983	Assigned divers continued the search at Pier 7.
October 4, 1983	Special Agent Steve Broce and a second man interviewed Charlene Bullerwell.
October 20, 1983	Tim Burke took his own diver, Nick Saggese, to Pier 7. The diver recovered a fake .357 magnum.
January 23, 1984	The court appointed Stephen Rappaport to represent Leonard Paradiso.
February 9 & 16, 1984	Federal John Doe grand jury convened in a bankruptcy case.
Late February 1984	Ralph Anthony Pisa was transferred to a prerelease facility.
March 5-12, 1984	Judge Roger Donahue presided over the Marie Iannuzzi pretrial hearing.

March 9, 1984	Leonard Paradiso and Candy Weyant were indicted for bankruptcy and mail fraud.
March 13, 1984	Tim Burke pleaded for the release of Ralph Anthony Pisa before Judge Harry Elam in a Middlesex County court.
March 13, 1984	Judge Roger Donahue sealed Robert Bond's written statement and police interview transcript in the Marie Iannuzzi pretrial.
March 28, 1984	Leonard Paradiso and Candy Weyant were arraigned in federal court for bankruptcy and mail fraud.
July 9, 1984	The Marie Iannuzzi murder trial began, Judge Roger Donahue presiding.
July 22, 1984	The jury found Leonard Paradiso guilty of murder in the second degree and assault with intent to rape.
July 25, 1984	Judge Roger Donahue imposed the sentence.
November 28, 1984	Insurance fraud charges were filed against Leonard Paradiso regarding his boat, the *Malafemmena*.
January 3, 1985	Ralph Anthony Pisa changed his plea for the 1969 murder of George Deane and was sentenced to time served.
January 21, 1985	Federal Judge Robert Keeton changed the venue for Leonard Paradiso's bankruptcy fraud case.
February 13, 1985	Judge James McGuire ordered an X-ray on Leonard Paradiso's left index finger.

February 18, 1985	Leonard Paradiso was acquitted of insurance fraud charges involving his boat, the *Malafemmena*.
April 4-9, 1985	The federal bankruptcy case was held in the Federal District Court of Rhode Island, Judge Bruce Selya presiding.
April 5, 1985	Leonard Paradiso was treated for a six week old broken finger.
April 9, 1985	A jury found Leonard Paradiso guilty on three of four counts in the federal bankruptcy case.
May 10, 1985	Judge Bruce Selya imposed the sentence for the bankruptcy case.
May 28, 1985	A garden dedication for Joan Webster was held at Harvard's Gund Hall in Cambridge, Massachusetts.
July 24, 1985	Boston investigators reached a consensus that they had developed sufficient evidence to conclude that Leonard Paradiso murdered Joan Webster.
November 5, 1985	Leonard Paradiso filed a motion for a new trial in the Marie Iannuzzi case.
November 15, 1985	Robert Bond filed a motion during the retrial for Mary Foreman's murder naming the individuals making promises he relied on.
November 23, 1985	Robert Bond convicted in the retrial for Mary Foreman's murder.

February 13, 1986	Judge Roger Donahue denied the motion for a retrial in the Marie Iannuzzi case without a hearing.
June 11, 1986	Leonard Paradiso filed a motion to reconsider his motion for a new trial in the Marie Iannuzzi case.
July 1, 1986	Judge Roger Donahue denied the motion to reconsider a new trial for the Marie Iannuzzi case without a hearing.
July 3, 1986	Leonard Paradiso filed a notice of appeal for the Marie Iannuzzi case.
August 13, 1986	The Janet McCarthy case against Leonard Paradiso began.
August 14, 1986	The jury found Leonard Paradiso guilty of assault with intent to rape Janet McCarthy.
April 18, 1990	Karen Wolf found a human skull on her property on Chebacco Road in Hamilton, Massachusetts.
April 26, 1990	Hamilton Police found the full grave of the victim on Chebacco Road.
April 30, 1990	The victim on Chebacco Road was identified as Joan Webster through dental records.
July 13, 1990	Joan Webster's remains were cremated in Salem, Massachusetts.
July 15, 1991	The Suffolk County District Attorney's Office was exposed for secret and duplicate files.

1997	Corruption in the Boston office of the FBI was exposed over the handling of mob boss Whitey Bulger.
July 4, 1998	Trooper Andrew Palombo dies in a motorcycle accident in Lynn, Massachusetts.
June 2001	Joan Webster's sister-in-law, Eve Carson, discovered an incriminating letter.
November 28, 2006	Tim Burke announced his upcoming book about Leonard Paradiso, supported by George and Eleanor Webster.
February 7, 2008	Robert Bond was taken to Lemuel Shattuck Hospital in a failed attempt to obtain a confession from Leonard Paradiso.
February 18, 2008	*The Paradiso Files, Boston's Unknown Serial Killer* by Tim Burke published.
February 27, 2008	Leonard Paradiso died from bladder cancer at the Lemuel Shattuck Hospital.
May 6, 2008	Private investigator and attorney met with Robert Bond at Shirley MCI in Massachusetts.
May 20, 2008	Private investigator and attorney met with former Hamilton Police Chief Walter Cullen.
Late August 2008	Candy Weyant received an anonymous, harassing letter.
January 22, 2009	Eve Carson received an anonymous, harassing letter.

October 8, 2009	Eve Carson and a private investigator met with Robert Bond at Shirley MCI in Massachusetts.
May 20, 2010	Eve Carson and a private investigator met with Assistant District Attorney John Dawley and three representatives from the Massachusetts State Police in Essex County.
June 15, 2010	Eleanor Webster passed away from metastasized breast cancer.
July 12 & 17, 2010	Anonymous harassing emails sent to Eve Carson from a company computer at Syntellect in Phoenix, Arizona, Anne Webster's employer.
January 18, 2012	Robert Bond denied parole by unanimous vote.
December 25, 2012	Eve Carson received harassing email from George Webster.
May 1, 2017	Eve Carson met with ADA John Dawley in Essex County.
May 9, 2017	The Parole Board conducted a hearing for Robert Bond.
March 21, 2018	George Webster passed away at White Horse Village in Newtown, Pennsylvania.

Author's Notes

Andrew Palombo died in a motorcycle accident on July 4, 1998. Leonard Paradiso died from bladder cancer on February 27, 2008. Eleanor Webster died from metastasized breast cancer on June 15, 2010. George met his Maker on March 21, 2018. The Websters' obituaries memorialized their stints with the CIA. Robert Bond died on June 23, 2019. Whether the surviving participants, Tim Burke or Carmen Tammaro, know where the driver took Joan before discarding her in Hamilton, Massachusetts, or who inflicted the fatal blow, remains a secret.

❧

I met with the custodian in Essex County on May 20, 2010, and again on May 1, 2017. John Dawley affirmed he knew Tim Burke, but didn't want to focus on him. Dawley stated that I should not probe deeply into Joan's case, and family secrets would only come out if I disclosed them. He refused to publicly discredit the false narrative published by his colleague. Efforts to work with proper authorities in the Boston system and the Department of Justice are ongoing, but to date, the system has failed in the administration of justice for Joan Webster.

❧

Former prosecutor Tim Burke's own words are the title of Chapter Thirteen, "It's show time" was a callous cry from this officer of the court. He demonstrated his lack of humility and humanity with his presentation. God sits in judgment, not me, but there is a lot to answer for. His actions during the investigation and beyond had unforeseen consequences that hurt real people, innocent victims, and devalued Joan.

℘

A private investigator and attorney in Boston facilitated the recovery of documents. Freedom of Information Act responses produced other records. Source documents include police reports, court records, FBI files, Department of Correction records, sworn statements, interviews, and verified personal correspondence and notes. My personal knowledge of Joan's case was an advantage to know where to look for relevant information.

℘

Making connections with people who wanted the truth was simply the hand of God. Those individuals deserve my heartfelt thanks and gratitude for the contributions they made. Out of an abundance of caution and consideration, they are not named here. They know who they are. The history found in source documents exposed the malevolent treatment inflicted on anyone challenging the state's premise, destructive malice I've experienced myself. Know that your input was invaluable for understanding what really happened to Joan.

℘

Thank you to the many dedicated members of law enforcement who earnestly searched for the truthful answers. Each small piece of information helped me unwind a tangled web and brought me a step closer to a resolution. Joan would be grateful as well.

જ

God blessed me with loving parents, now at home with the Lord. My sister and brother never wavered in their support of me as I struggled through each shocking discovery in the records. They never lost faith in me; they know my foundation. When the pieces finally started to come together, they saw the documents for themselves to validate my concerns. My extended family knows my character and my dogged determination. They all understood and supported my urgency to find the truthful answers. The greatest gift God granted me are my two daughters. My unconditional love for them will never falter, and they are safe in my heart.

જ

Supplemental information and documents can be viewed at justiceforjoanwebster.com.

About the Author

Eve Carson was born and raised in Danville, Illinois. She is the middle child with an older sister and younger brother. The close-knit family faced life's hurdles together, a source of strength through the many obstacles families face.

Eve graduated from Purdue University with a degree in Industrial Management and Economics. She worked for General Motors and IBM in her early career. She married Joan's brother Steve on January 5, 1980, and was the only non-blood relative in the immediate family when Joan disappeared. She has two daughters, who sadly never knew their Aunt Joan.

Eve has published multiple articles and given numerous interviews. Articles about the Joan Webster murder have appeared in *Crime Magazine*, *The Journal of Forensic Research*, *The Precious Hearts Foundation Magazine*, *The Journal of Forensic and Crime Investigation*, *Medium*, and *Unsolved Magazine*. In addition,

Eve presented aspects of Joan's case to the International Forensic Research Conference twice, the Stu Taylor program, and on *The Whistleblower* television series.

Today, Eve resides in the Midwest and perseveres for justice. She continues her writing and works as a consultant in an unrelated field.

www.ingramcontent.com/pod-product-compliance
Lightning Source LLC
Chambersburg PA
CBHW062118020426
42335CB00013B/1017